D1809065

Comparative Cultural Studies and the New *Weltliteratur*

Comparative Cultural Studies
Steven Tötösy de Zepetnek, Series Editor

The Purdue University Press monograph series of Books in Comparative Cultural Studies publishes single-authored and thematic collected volumes of new scholarship. Manuscripts are invited for publication in the series in fields of the study of culture, literature, the arts, media studies, communication studies, the history of ideas, etc., and related disciplines of the humanities and social sciences to the series editor via e-mail at <clcweb@purdue.edu>. Comparative cultural studies is a contextual approach in the study of culture in a global and intercultural context and work with a plurality of methods and approaches; the theoretical and methodological framework of comparative cultural studies is built on tenets borrowed from the disciplines of cultural studies and comparative literature and from a range of thought including literary and culture theory, (radical) constructivism, communication theories, and systems theories; in comparative cultural studies focus is on theory and method as well as application. For a detailed description of the aims and scope of the series including the style guide of the series link to <http://docs.lib.purdue.edu/clcweblibrary/seriespurdueccs>. Manuscripts submitted to the series are peer reviewed followed by the usual standards of editing, copy editing, marketing, and distribution. The series is affiliated with *CLCWeb: Comparative Literature and Culture* (ISSN 1481-4374), the peer-reviewed, full-text, and open-access quarterly published by Purdue University Press at <http://docs.lib.purdue.edu/clcweb>.

Volumes in the Purdue series of Books in Comparative Cultural Studies include <http://www.thepress.purdue.edu/series/comparative-cultural-studies>

Elke Sturm-Trigonakis, *Comparative Cultural Studies and the New* Weltliteratur
Lauren Rule Maxwell, *Romantic Revisions in Novels from the Americas*
Liisa Steinby, *Kundera and Modernity*
Text and Image in Modern European Culture, Ed. Natasha Grigorian, Thomas Baldwin, and Margaret Rigaud-Drayton
Sheng-mei Ma, *Asian Diaspora and East-West Modernity*
Irene Marques, *Transnational Discourses on Class, Gender, and Cultural Identity*
Comparative Hungarian Cultural Studies, Ed. Steven Tötösy de Zepetnek and Louise O. Vasvári
Hui Zou, *A Jesuit Garden in Beijing and Early Modern Chinese Culture*
Yi Zheng, *From Burke and Wordsworth to the Modern Sublime in Chinese Literature*
Agata Anna Lisiak, *Urban Cultures in (Post)Colonial Central Europe*
Representing Humanity in an Age of Terror, Ed. Sophia A. McClennen and Henry James Morello
Michael Goddard, *Gombrowicz, Polish Modernism, and the Subversion of Form*
Shakespeare in Hollywood, Asia, and Cyberspace, Ed. Alexander C.Y. Huang and Charles S. Ross
Gustav Shpet's Contribution to Philosophy and Cultural Theory, Ed. Galin Tihanov
Comparative Central European Holocaust Studies, Ed. Louise O. Vasvári and Steven Tötösy de Zepetnek
Marko Juvan, *History and Poetics of Intertextuality*
Thomas O. Beebee, *Nation and Region in Modern American and European Fiction*
Paolo Bartoloni, *On the Cultures of Exile, Translation, and Writing*
Justyna Sempruch, *Fantasies of Gender and the Witch in Feminist Theory and Literature*
Kimberly Chabot Davis, *Postmodern Texts and Emotional Audiences*
Philippe Codde, *The Jewish American Novel*
Deborah Streifford Reisinger, *Crime and Media in Contemporary France*
Imre Kertész and Holocaust Literature, Ed. Louise O. Vasvári and Steven Tötösy de Zepetnek

Comparative Cultural Studies and the New *Weltliteratur*

Elke Sturm-Trigonakis

Translated from the German by
Athanasia Margoni and Maria Kaisar

Purdue University Press
West Lafayette, Indiana

Copyright 2013 by Purdue University. All rights reserved.

Printed in the United States of America.

Library of Congress Cataloging-in-Publication Data
Cataloging-in-Publication data on file at the Library of Congress.

Cover image: The painting *Constellations* (acrylic on canvas 50x50 cm) is by Pavlos Vassiliadis (Thessaloniki), 2005. Copyright release by Pavlos Vassiliadis to Purdue University Press.

To Kostis

Contents

Acknowledgments

A book in the humanities is always the result of the scholar's solitary work of reading and writing—of the "loneliness of the long-distance runner"—in cultural and literary scholarship. My first and most important thank you is to my spouse, Konstantinos Trigonakis, who accompanied me with his emotional, intellectual, and—last but not least—financial support. Scholarship in the humanities also springs from many conversations and brainstorming and I thank my colleagues at Aristotle University Katerina Zachou and Alexandra Rassidakis, for the inspiring discussions about the concept of New *Weltliteratur*; Athina Sioupi, for her advice for the linguistic parts of the book; Georges Freris, who opened the wide horizon of the Francophonie to me; and Eleni Georgopoulou, for her critical reading of the German version of the book during a hot Greek summer. I also thank Karin Boklund-Lagopoulou and Yiorgos Kalogeras, as well as his spouse, the linguist Linda Manney, for their helpful suggestions: they were among the first to suggest an English translation of the book and always had an open ear to my questions concerning not only the subject of the book but also the academic environment beyond Europe. The project of the translation and publication of my book in English would have not been realized without the invitation and encouragement of Steven Tötösy de Zepetnek—editor of the Purdue University Press monograph series of Books in Comparative Cultural Studies—to whom I express my gratitude for his enthusiasm, his support, and his editing of my book, including suggestions of new material in several languages.

    Comparative Cultural Studies and the New Weltliteratur is a substantially revised and updated version of my *Global playing in der Literatur. Ein Versuch über die Neue Weltliteratur* (Würzburg: Königshausen & Neumann, 2007) and I thank the publisher for the copyright release of the book. Athanasia Margoni and Maria Kaisar performed an excellent translation and working with them was a pleasure. Further, the Adamas Foundation had the kindness to finance part of the translation of *Global playing in der Literatur* and I am grateful for this recognition of my work. Last but not least, I am indebted to Pavlos Vassiliadis (Thessaloniki) for the permission of his 2005 painting *Asterismoi* (*Constellations*) for the front cover image of my book.

Introduction

The title of the book is *Comparative Cultural Studies and the New* Weltliteratur in order to refer to the two main axes of my argumentation: the theoretical framework of comparative cultural studies—with its emphasis on interdisciplinarity, the contextual approach, and evidence-based methodology—and Goethe's idea of *Weltliteratur* understood in today's situation of globalization.

Since the 1960s and increasingly since the 1980s there has been a continuous boom of "transnational" fiction which can hardly be classified under the rubric of "national literature" as it breaks the mold of the national in terms of language and content. Azade Seyhan describes "transnational literature as a genre of writing that operates outside the national canon, addresses issues facing deterritorialized cultures, and speaks for . . . 'paranational' communities and alliances" (10). Seyhan exemplifies the discourse about transnational literature using texts from US-American Chicana literature and German-language texts by Turkish-German writers, and by doing so she studies literatures "outside the nation" (as is the title of her study). One possibility is to locate such texts outside of nation and another is to locate them under the heading "minority literature" or "intercultural literature" within a national literature. In order to escape this dilemma, I prefer the more neutral term "hybrid literature," even if hybridity is a term that has lost its sharpness owing to its almost inflationary use. I agree with the view of Thomas Meyer that "all cultures . . . are hybrid at heart" and that the "homogeneity [of] fictions, where they should draw their consecration from, [are] always late political fabrications, which remove the supposedly doubtful from the hybrid original process through an act of decisive nostrification and transform its products into a secure, undivided ownership of the members, one that no one can raise claims on" (34; unless indicated otherwise, all translations are by Athanasia Margoni and Maria Kaisar; note: quotations from primary texts are more often than not from the original in English translation). On this basis, Néstor García Canclini defines hybridization as a sociocultural process in which originally separate structures or practices are combined into new structures and practices through conflation, and he emphasizes that even the source structures themselves are always the result of hybridization processes (see also Bronfen and Marius; Burke). The term "hybrid literature" is employed similarly for texts which—unlike hybridity

1

as defined by M. M. Bakhtin—are a mixing of languages produced in various social spheres and that are composed in two or more languages which, in turn, do not have to be "pure" standard languages, but may appear, for example, as a sociolect, a dialect, or Créole. In addition, the process of mixing extends to cultural practices in the broadest sense and they implement the hybridization processes which arose over the course of globalization.

Ulrich Beck made precise distinctions between globalism, globalization, and globality. For Beck the concepts describe the primacy of economy over politics, the key innovation of a "second modernity" in comparison with the precursors of modernity and postmodernity (see, e.g., his *The Cosmopolitan Vision* and *What is Globalization?*; see also Reichardt). Globality, on the other hand, designates every unrevisable condition of second modernity characterized by the absence of closed spaces and the existence of a global society on many levels from politics to economics and from technology to culture. Globality can also be understood as the processual element over the course of which the formerly sovereign nation-states are overtaken by transnational agents in various fields and whereby "transnational social ties and spaces" are created and "third cultures—a little bit of this, a little bit of that" are produced: "globalization is carried out in several dimensions: communicative-technical, environmental, economic, labor organizational, cultural, civic, religious. Therefore, 'world society' means difference, plurality" (Drechsel, Schmidt, Gölz 133). Anthony Giddens describes this change simply as "revolutionary" and stresses its impact not only in economy but also in politics, technology, and culture (10): the first "global cosmopolitan society" in the history of humanity emerged from globalization, "whose contours we can as yet only dimly see"; yet, according to Giddens, "it is shaking up our existing ways of life, no matter where we happen to be," and it is characterized by chaos as it is still carried out in "an anarchic, haphazard fashion, carried along by a mixture of influences" (31). Thus, in most cases here when we speak of globalization, we do it so as to accommodate the incompleteness and the inherent dynamics of the processes underway. It is beyond dispute that this change affects all activities of life and leaves its marks on literary production as well.

In 2000, Manfred Schmeling, Monika Schmitz-Emans, and Kerst Walstra made an attempt to describe "literature in the age of globalization" (*Literatur im Zeitalter der Globalisierung*). In the volume, Horst Steinmetz challenges the writing of the history of literature, and, despite the dissemination of the literary studies since the 1970s, he postulates that "globalization has to mean an altered or altering state of the world, which alters or has already altered the literature as well, which therefore makes a different, a new writing of the history of literature appear necessary or, in any event, desirable" (191). Only from this perspective, as Steinmetz claims, could the dichotomies caused by globalization—such as internationalism versus nationalism, heterogeneity, and cultural coherence, or interdependence versus hegemony—be overcome and the altered role of literature be accommodated (190). Consequently, Steinmetz also rejects the traditional comparative concept of "literary internationalism" as a "reciprocal literary influence" that is still taking place and to a greater extent than ever before, but under the conditions of globalization it brings forth "qualitatively different results in comparison to the traditional literary internationalism" and "can be described as a sort of prehistory of the globalized literature" (191). Instead, Steinmetz argues that new categories should be created "which are useful for the inventorying and historical classification of the literatures of the period of globalization" (200). I begin exactly at this point as it provides hybrid texts with a literary category I designate as "new world literature" (NWL).

In my opinion, there is the need to overcome the marginalizing categorization of "minority literature," "(im)migration literature," "commonwealth literature," and so on, as counterparts of alterity, or—at best—subsets of a linguistically homogeneous national literature produced in a defined geographical area and disseminated institutionally. This type of classification is accompanied by approaches which are rooted, still, in individual philologies even if the effort for interculturally and cultural studies-oriented literary studies has certainly borne fruit to the contrary in the last two decades. In comparative literature there has been and still is more often than not an orientation toward national philology with bilateral, at the maximum trilateral, attempts, for instance, in the style of the influence of French literature on postwar German literature or Poland in the work of Günter Grass. Although such scholarship is meritorious, it suffers from the fact that the point of reference remains national literature as a standard or the concept of the nation-state as monocultural, so that theory and methodology fail when an author exhibits more than one national culture and a text in more than one standard language. Of course, I mean not to say that scholarship has not produced a wider view, for example, with regard to multicultural and multilingual literary texts: much work is available—particularly in English-language scholarship—in fields such as postcolonial studies and cultural studies. Yet my assessment of US-American, Gallo-Roman, or intercultural German studies brings about a feeling of dissatisfaction, for we find ourselves confronted with hundreds of individual parts of a puzzle, down to the relation of a minority literature to a national. For example, "Blackness" is analyzed in a text by Toni Morrison, but it is not correlated with the "Indianness" in works by Louise Erdrich and Juan Felipe Herrera and much less with the "Blackness" of a French-language author from the Caribbean such as Maryse Condé. The inter- and multicultural and multilingual complexity of such texts is not taken into account, because they are measured against a monocultural and monolingual system. Such literary texts are differentiated, specified, and divided, and what is missing is the comparative synthesis on both the levels of the text and the metalevel.

In German-language scholarship, the 1999 collected volume *Interpretation 2000: Positionen und Kontroversen* (De Berg and Prangel) is characteristic of the attempt to relocate and redefine interpretation as the main practice of literary studies. In the introduction Elrud Ibsch draws up a frame of reference for the objectives of interpretation consisting of five points: the keyword "interpretation as recommendation" subsumes "interpretive acts . . . which seek to draw attention to a literary text" either by reapproaching older texts under contemporary discourse contexts such as deconstruction, feminism, or postcolonialism, or by providing an "access to the canon" to recent texts so that they ultimately constitute "part of the poetology of a certain age" (20–22). Closely associated with this objective is the "interpretation as a literature-history categorisation principle," where a "historical communication-situation" prototype is selected, which by virtue of its "characteristic markedness and richness of features is characteristic of a genre or flow" (Ibsch 22). As in New Historicism, the reciprocity between literature as a highly complex system and social developments is brought once again on stage through the back entrance and a paradigm shift toward foreignness and culture is established, one which is by no means confined to the entourage of "intercultural German studies," although the term "interculturality" booms even there "as a theory and constitution of a cultural intermediate position" (Wierlacher 168; see also Nell). Also, Schmeling rejects any "monolithically oriented national philology" which under the conditions of globalism is not able to interpretatively deal with the "internationality and interculturality of literature" ("Interpretation" 201–02). According to Ottmar Ette's diagnosis, cultures, economies, and nations have set themselves in motion and the study of literature has been left behind, especially in German-language scholarship. Thus, I suggest that conventional national philologies became overwhelmed by the task and it is only comparative cultural studies that can put to the test and redefine "concepts and ideas about national cultures and their homogeneity, the transmission of traditions, or about the 'original' character of ethnic groups" (Görling 7).

An ambitious project this appears. Who meets the stringent requirements—inter alia the knowledge of several contemporary and classical languages as suggested in traditional comparative literature (see, e.g., Bernheimer)? How can research findings regarding "minority literatures" from several individual philologies be collected, reviewed, and condensed? It is in this context that I formulate a line of thought and attempt a modest beginning by interrelating in typological comparison primary texts from so-called intercultural or ethnic minority literatures (see Tötösy de Zepetnek, "Migration"). Thus, these texts are wrested from the literary discourse of each national literature and are recontextualized in the frame of reference of my proposed NWL. By literary discourse I denote, following among others, Xoán González-Millán, an "operative category that not only includes the institutions and communities that produce, distribute and consume an object recognised by society as 'literature,' but also observes the evaluation instruments used in these processes and the (oral or written) texts, which they influence" (4) as my point of departure.

Given the overused notion of "world literature," the question may arise as to whether recourse to Goethe is necessary and helpful, especially for such a recent phenomenon as literature under conditions of globalization. The answer should be affirmative, for many contemporary texts reflect a similar zeitgeist: the fictional heroes in the texts I analyze live, as in Goethe's time, in the knowledge that they are witnessing radical changes in the fields of economy, technology, and communication accompanied by an equally profound transformation of the perception of time and space (see Mommsen, *"Orient und Okzident"*). A further point is that Goethe launched his *Weltliteratur* against the concept of the national literature promoted by the Romantics. This also shows his attachment to the cosmopolitanism of the Enlightenment, that is, a "relic" from a previous period, and we realize how ground-breaking Goethe's idea was and that it pointed to the future and offers connections, for instance, with Beck's claim for a "cosmopolitan vision" against the national perspective. The term "new world literature" is therefore an expression of a two-dimensionality: it denotes the recourse to already existing configurations of thought and at the same time their adaptation and utilization in new contexts. Thus it rests upon the awareness of tradition and change: the attribute "new" refers to the historicity of the construction, more specifically to phenomena of contemporary globalization. It is widely understood that the current globalization is only one out of three (i.e., Peter Sloterdijk) or five consecutive ones (i.e., Erhard Schüttpelz). What has changed over the passage of time is only the forms of manifestation, but not the essence of the process of mutual influence and penetration. In this spirit, Karen Margaret Simonsen and Jakob Stougaard-Nielsen emphasize that

> a renewed engagement with the "old" concept of world literature, in a markedly changed, multi-directional and networked global age, is one way in which literary and cultural studies may contribute to a fruitful understanding of how the globalisation of literary expression, production and reception has taken place in the past, how it is shaping our world today and what directions it may take in the future. We need to keep in mind that globalisation is not something that *happens* to literature. On the contrary, literature is one of the driving forces behind globalisation, interacting as it does with other cultural expressions, policies, technologies and communication networks across national borders and oceans. (10)

The "new" exists not only in its embedding in the current historical context, but also in the way of dealing with the objective of research: literary texts are considered as a subset of a discourse of cultural practices, which on the one hand are influenced by the phenomena of globalization such as global marketing strategies or media presence, but on the other hand generate globalization precisely through their hybridity. Consequently, my selection criteria for the corpus of texts rests on two parameters or features that are codified as such in their essence, but whose respective shape and functionalization vary from text to text: a structural presupposition for accepting a text in the NWL is multilingualism, which I discuss in its different forms in chapters 4 and 5. My other presupposition pertains to the level of action and consists in the literary processing of any kind of discourse of globalization in the narrative or poetic contexts, as I discuss in chapters 6 and 7. These parameters are based on the empirical observation of a variety of texts on the one hand and to the findings of the sociology of globalization processes that is oriented toward systems theory on the other. At this point it should be emphasized that this corpus of texts is naturally thought of as principally open and prompts for expansion, precisely in the areas which I avoid owing to lack of expertise, since I confine myself to texts in languages I am familiar with. Only when substantiated studies (e.g., by experienced bilingual researchers) were available have I taken the corresponding texts into consideration, for example, those by Emine Sevgi Özdamar. Her Turkish language structure that underlies the German language would certainly have been unverifiable by me; however, the number of analyses on this subject allowed me to accept the works by Özdamar in the corpus I selected. In my opinion, working with translations is less than optimal, yet in some cases I have taken this risk as well. Since a single detailed analysis of the works is in no case intended here, I have chosen this method being aware of its shortcomings, in the hope to do justice to the texts despite all their structural and thematic characteristics.

In German-language literary histories and encyclopedias (i.e., where the legitimization of the canon occurs), Özdamar appears rarely. Further, in the work of Sargut Şölçün, she is described as someone who has a "natural Oriental narrative talent" but this does not constitute a literary category and thus her writing remains marginalized as exotic. The alienation of the "German language with fragments from the Turkish" (Şölçün 152) is far from a meaningful linguistic description of interlingualism and interference. The fact that an author who has a command of several languages by no means obligatorily applies this command in every text as a stylistic device is overlooked. Salman Rushdie, for example, is represented here with two works—which can be attributed to NWL as hybrid literature—but has also written others, such as *Grimus* (1975), that in my view thematize neither transnationalism nor localism as typical phenomena of globalization and are polyphonic at most in the classical sense of Bakhtin, but are not multilingual. Confusions and impurities of this type arise because hitherto binding classificatory parameters are missing, which could then—in a subsequent step—lead to an aesthetic evaluation of a standard that no longer represents a national literature.

The canon debate is also important in this context because hybrid literature evades the established national literary canons. In German scholarship, for example, many texts of hybrid literature are either not recorded at all in literary histories or are recorded under a heading such as *Migrantenliteratur,* and histories of other European literatures are similar in this (see, e.g., Blioumi; Amirsedghi and Bleicher). This type of literature finds its entrance into scholarship usually as "the other," but the documentary character of the texts stands in the foreground, not their literariness. A separate text category such as NWL offers here the advantage of aligning the asymmetric relation among the categories approximately in the same way that "world music" or "ethnic" is placed just next to the shelves with German, Greek, and Italian pop music, and no one reproaches their performers with lack of respect for the performers of US-American or French mainstream music: each has its audience and no one would ever transfer to Orient pop the measures of value applicable to jazz. And given the rising of global (im)migration, an end of hybrid cultural practices is far from expected. Therefore a further increase in the production of texts of NWL is predictable.

I place special emphasis on theory and methodology as postulated by Steven Tötösy de Zepetnek in his framework of comparative cultural studies (see, e.g.,

"From Comparative," "The New Humanities"; see also Tötösy de Zepetnek and Vas-vári). His approach provides a useful framework and avoids the lack of contextual-ization and supra-national pluralism. In this context I discuss at length the concept of "world literature," which, of course, begins with Goethe and leads up to the present. Over the course of the globalization debate we frequently take recourse to this magic word, yet in alternating contexts, thus making the differentiation from tags such as "literature of globalization" or "world fiction" seem necessary, as I discuss in chap-ter 2. The performance of the traditional national philologies of German-, English-, French-, Spanish-, and Portuguese-speaking countries with respect to their dealing with the respective "minority literatures" is another focus of chapter 2, where prob-lems and shortcomings but also recent developments in the direction of comparative and interdisciplinary scholarship are discussed. In the course of it, it becomes clear that the call to look over the fence of the proper discipline is heard everywhere in re-cent years and therein rests the connection to findings in sociology and especially in systems theory, which has also overcome the classic container paradigm. Therefore, the fiction of a nationally defined object of investigation has moved on to pastures new and transnational. Consequently, systems theory is one of the theoretical bases for the configuration of NWL with which which hybrid texts—which seem anarchic in comparison to well-defined national literatures—can be analyzed, and this the fo-cus of chapter 3. The key differences of NWL are multilingualism on the expression plane on the one hand and phenomena of globalization and regionalism on the con-tent plane on the other. This operation equates different texts from different cultural contexts in order to make them comparable: "The equating procedure is part of every category performance, which brings something into a category that was not already beforehand part of this category. . . . We cannot avoid this equating procedure, but we have to make clear the genesis of categories and thus their internal contingence" (Waldenfels 127).

Following my theoretical postulates, in chapter 4 I present a short survey of the history of multilingualism and in chapter 5 I focus on the forms and functions of multilingualism, metamultilingualism, and transtextuality. In chapters 6 and 7 I in-vestigate the oscillation of the texts between transnational and regional or local as a characteristic of the discourse of globalization discourse, concentrating on nomadic biographies, literature and the city, transnational spaces, and different time layers. And finally, in the conclusion I reexamine the main ideas of the book.

Chapter One

Goethe's *Weltliteratur* and the Career of an Idea

Dieter Lamping states that "*Weltliteratur* is one of the great ideas of the nineteenth century and one of the few which have survived the epoch of its genesis . . . Owing to this idea we do not perceive literature as something exclusively national, as a mere sum of single literatures, which evolve according to laws of their own, completely independent from each other, even in confrontation to each other" (9). Lamping argues that the idea of *Weltliteratur* is long lived and still sells on the cultural market, on the one hand, but now needs an actualization and a more precise definition under globalized conditions on the other hand, as it is experiencing controversial interpretations. Although the term itself was circulating before Goethe (see Lange 25–26 on its use by August Wilhelm Schlegel; see also Schmitt), it became popular through Goethe's period of cosmopolitanism. Since then, world literature as a theme has been a literary evergreen and perhaps because of this it produces a certain weariness. It has, however, been experiencing a new boom in recent years as its applicability proves opportune because of the impact of globalization (for a list of single-authored books and edited volumes on world literature including Goethe, see Tötösy de Zepetnek, "Multingual"). Since Goethe's idea has already received much attention, in the following I refer to the extensive literature on this subject only to the extent that it contributes to clarify the performance of "world literature" with regard to the discourse of globalization. Consequently, the focus of my remarks is on the question of the direction in which this idea can be thought of today in the course of global differentiation and homogenization and the new contents with which it should be updated.

In order to describe the objective of Goethe's idea of *Weltliteratur* appropriately, we must first give a classification of the term in the context of its creation and release. It turns out that Goethe himself used this designation only in five passages, three of which appear in the journal edited by him, *Über Kunst und Alterthum in den Rhein- und Maingegenden* (1816–1832), in the issues covering the years 1827 and 1828. The other two are found in an essay planned for an issue in 1830, the ideas of which have been mentioned in Goethe's introduction to Carlyle's biography by Schiller, as well as in an edition of the *Wanderjahre* dated 1829 (see Bohnen-kamp 189). The other entries, unpublished during Goethe's lifetime—thirteen in his work and two in Johann Peter Eckermann's conversations—are directly or indirectly connected with articles in the journal *Über Kunst und Alterthum*. The importance is that *Über Kunst und Alterthum* was the platform for an international—for that time—exchange about literature. Despite the limited number of 750 copies printed, *Über Kunst und Alterthum* met with a positive response in Britain, France, and Italy (see Bohnenkamp) and it provided Goethe with the opportunity to acquaint the Ger-man public with works in foreign languages and at the same moment to point out that German literature enjoyed a lively reception in other European countries. *Über Kunst und Alterthum* was for Goethe the means to propagate the thoughts of a mature writer and scholar and to pass on the cosmopolitanism of the eighteenth century to the nineteenth, despite the growing nationally conscious attitude of European na-tions: his idea of *Weltliteratur* constituted work in progress. A definition with quanti-tative or qualitative characteristics, as in the majority of the relevant literature lexica, was not Goethe's task; his notion was a process of "international communication and reciprocal reception" because "every literature, if not refreshed by foreign participa-tion, is in the end bored in its own self" (Bohnenkamp 203). In Goethe's sense this occurs particularly via translations, consequently, *Über Kunst und Altertum* dedi-cated considerable space to the topic of translation and translation criticism, for only through knowledge of other cultural conditions would the ennui in domestic litera-ture be combated effectively. Thus, Goethe never tired of thanking the translators.

In Goethe's view, the merit of the translator is not just that he or she is inter-polated into a hitherto inaccessible, alien culture, but rather that this transfer also creates a counter movement of approach to the other culture by exciting "an irresist-ible attraction for the original" that the translation creates (*Werke* 12: 499). In today's terminology, the translator performs a significant cultural practice, as Goethe con-ceived the concept of translating as extremely wide, by equating the translator, with reference to the Bible and the Qur'an, with a "prophet of his people . . . who practices one of the most important and honorable actions in world communication" (12: 353). While translation was only a second choice for Goethe compared to the original, still, in his pragmatic way he seemed to give unconditional preference to a "veiled beauty" in comparison to a nonbeauty. However, Goethe's didactic concern did not exhaust itself in the perception of the foreign. On the contrary, as a result of it the one is appreciated by means of taking the detour to the other (12: 503). Therefore, in Goethe's view, the mastery of the German native tongue suffices for the majority of the population. In a large part this expresses Goethe's aristocratic attitude, but for him this attitude is less associated with privileges than with duties and first and foremost with the obligation to have the power of judgment regarding the proper environment in accordance with the motto that one "who does not know foreign lan-guages, does not know anything of his or her own" (*Werke* 12: 508). Goethe certainly would have read with pleasure the German poetry of José F. A. Oliver with its bold neologisms and interference from the Spanish and other languages. However, while these views were eccentric for the Romantics, they influenced the German cultural environment of his time. Thus he planned for a school book of poetry from the whole world, the *Plan eines lyrischen Volksbuches*, which he presented upon request by the Bavarian government in 1808, but which the government did not find suitable.

With his positive evaluation of cultural exchange, Goethe set a counterpoint to national literature, primarily through his frequently cited statement of 31 January 1827, which gave distinct utterance to his cultural relativism with the primacy of ancient Greek (qtd. in Eckermann 174). Still, it would be too simplistic to set the cosmopolitanism of Goethe against the unity of national literature and national policy, the way this was established between 1808 and 1815. Although Goethe had campaigned already in 1816 against the language purists, "in the relation of German national literature to world literature he was not interested in German and non-German" (Mayer 15). For example, if we compare his numerous comments on the English and the French, their countries, their cultural characteristics, and literatures with those on the Germans, it is quickly verified, first, that he frequently presented these two nations—with a didactic intention—as superior to the Germans (see Boerner 186), and second, that the majority of these observations refer to the national literatures of the named people and less so to the nations in their totality or their economic or political conditions. In the background of Goethe's interest in "national particularities" lay his effort for exchange and communication between respective national literatures, whereas the universal element in every literature, the "universally human," was important to him because this is exactly where he saw the idea of *Weltliteratur* manifested (see Boerner 186–87). Undoubtedly, there is something old-fashioned in his approach in his era of growing nationalism, and it seems to anchor the old Goethe—backward-looking—in the cosmopolitanism of the Enlightenment (see Seeba 203). It is well known that he was no supporter of the Romantic elevation of the national element and that he rejected the exclusive search for identity in all things German. The question, however, is whether we should shelve his concept of *Weltliteratur* as an exclusive product of the Enlightenment or whether its incompleteness and indefiniteness can inspire us to think further.

In his *Goethes Begriff der Weltliteratur*, Hans Joachim Schrimpf seems to vote in favor of the first option, as he thinks that Goethe's "understanding of world literature, which [was] formulated in old age, cannot be considered only as the result of a long life experience, but [ ] should also be interpreted historically as an expression and awareness of a late period" (50). Goethe wrote in 1831 a short essay, entitled "Epochen geselliger Bildung," in which he designed a four-stage model of the development of social and literary periods (*Goethes Werke* 1: 361–62). The fourth level, the highest, the "expression of every advanced civilization in the stage of a late period," represented for him the "universal epoch" (Schrimpf 50). While the first "idyllic" stage he attributed to narrowly limited popular culture dominated by terms such as "home piety, patriotism, home industry, and national literature," the "universal" stage he defined by characteristics such as "world piety, world politics, [and] world culture," followed by the last stage, *Weltliteratur*. How little he thought of all stages that stood below the universal is evident in his repeated attacks against the "pious religiosity, patriotism, spirit worship, constant transcendence, irrationalism, and the inclination towards the chaotic and elemental" (Schrimpf 22), which he regarded as hazardous components of the Romantic movement. In Schrimpf's opinion, Goethe's position is an "expression of a historical concern" (27) whose right to exist will be confirmed in a terrible way in the twentieth century by the excesses of totalitarian regimes. Schrimpf's 1968 study, along with the still indispensable—owing to its richness in material—1946 study by Fritz Strich, *Goethe und die Weltliteratur*, are ascribed by Manfred Koch to the first phase of the postwar analysis of the term, which accentuates in particular the aspects of international understanding and internationalization. In this respect, we must observe a differentiation: Strich uses the traditional "national stereotypes" uncritically and notes that "Europe [arises as] a real haunted castle of national spirits" (7), while Schrimpf sees "the national clearly disappear into an enlightened internationalism with the help of world literature" (9). Strich sees in Goethe the "most important ancestor of the comparative examination of literature" (93) and finds that Goethe's *Weltliteratur* is "the literature that mediates among nations, that makes them familiar with each other, the spiritual space where people meet and exchange their intellectual goods" (Strich 322).

The fact is that the frequency of comparative references is striking in Goethe's conversation with Eckermann and the conversations give us the impression of Goethe as a continuous comparatist. Here is an example: within a period of only a few weeks, from November 1824 until the spring of 1825, we find many such entries characteristic of Goethe's thinking. On 24 November 1824 he spoke of the preference for the formal in French literature in comparison to the superiority of subjects in German literature and evaluated the increased activity of translation from German to French as positive (Eckermann 96) and therefore they could benefit from German literature. On 3 December 1824 he dealt with Goldsmith, Fielding, and Shakespeare as reference points for all German novels and tragedies and estimated that English literature had taken the place of the classics for the younger generation of writers who were no longer familiar with the languages of antiquity (99). In the next paragraph he dealt with Dante (99) and the conversations of that day ended with comments on the flood disaster in St. Petersburg. On 10 January 1825 he was informed by an English visitor of the great interest of contemporary England in learning the German language and he emphasized that he himself had been occupied with the English language for fifty years (102); and on 18 January 1825 we find his thoughts about intertextual references, which he assessed as positive (107). What sounds like plagiarism by today's standards is, in the case of Goethe, a bow to the superior art of his fellow writers.

The above examples demonstrate the extent of Goethe's horizon and portray him both as a cosmopolitan in the sense of the Enlightenment and as a modern man who takes advantage of all the possibilities of information, brings the world to Weimar, and from Weimar influences the world. Within the scope of the technical possibilities of the time, Goethe already lived in a "network society" (Castells), dominated by a consciousness of similar worldwide processes in a technical as well as cultural respect, which was limited in terms of being "global" for it was more or less identical with the term "European," but nonetheless already existing. In this sense, Goethe's concept of *Weltliteratur* is a synthesis of the experience of the past and a project of the future:

> how often Goethe compared the intellectual exchange of goods between nations with the material exchange, the trade, the world market, where the peoples brought their goods for exchange; this was not only a comparison, instead Goethe traced with really great attention how the trade among the nations, after the Napoleonic Wars, assisted by the ever accelerating pace of modern transportation, express mail, and steamships, developed itself into a world market, how the communication of the citizens of the world was advancing with unprecedented easiness. He spoke of a "velocity" century, of the "rotation" that was being brought about by such a speed of trans-port, of rolling time in this sense, and saw a developing world literature as an intellectual world trade between nations as a necessary and inevitable consequence of this rolling time, which brought the nations closer together and resulted in an indissoluble braiding and interlacing of their interests. (Strich 44)

If we replaced in the above quotation "world" with "global" and "steamships" and "express mail" with "airplanes" and "the internet," we would suddenly stand before a description of the present, in which people have the feeling that they are witnessing a general acceleration, a cancellation of spatial distances, and techno-logical innovations of unknown dimensions accompanied by a globally expanding communication and trade network. At the same time, this parallelization exemplifies a marked difference in the later theoretical configurations in that Strich speaks un-critically of a "communication euphoria" characteristic of the postwar period. Today, the world stands in sceptical distance from the innovations which take place in com-merce, finance, and technology and is divided among vehement globalization op-ponents and proponents. In any event, Strich is certainly correct when he attributes to Goethe the awareness of living in a rapidly changing era, in the era of growing "world densification" (51). The knowledge of a new zeitgeist speaks through Goethe, a zeitgeist in which the radically new is to be discovered in scientific and technical progress. And Koch detects epochal similarities when he writes, "With all differ-ences in the degree of the real expansion and compression of worldwide commu-nication, we deal with a structurally *single* comprehensive process: such being the case, the issues raised in 1800 by wise observers have remained authoritative until today. No participant in the current globalisation debate can assert that the thoughts of authors such as Montesquieu, Smith, Kant, and also Goethe have become entirely obsolete" (14). In this respect, a point of connection for my project of NWL is found in the fact that the phenomena of Goethe's age of "velocification" as he perceived them can be described as essentially cognate with the phenomena of the present.

Goethe's *Wilhelm Meisters Lehrjahre* was published after several years of work in 1796 (the first mention of the project is dated 1777). In this novel Goethe undertakes a survey of the relation of an artistic self and its environment (see *Werke*

7: 683–85). He presents thoughts put into the mouth of Jarno that would well be described today by business buzzwords like "diversification of product range" or "risk management." In the subsequent novel, *Wilhelm Meisters Wanderjahre oder die Entsagenden* (first full publication in 1829), Goethe examines in Lenardo's diary cotton production along the Cotton Road, from Macedonia and Cyprus over Trieste to the Alps, where cotton is refined by spinners and then exported. In the course of this he draws a comparison with the quality of the cotton from East and West India, particularly with that of Cayenne (*Werke* 8: 339). Dark clouds gather over the traditional production and dealer network that is depicted, and the young entrepreneur finds himself facing a dilemma: he must either mechanize production and thus engulf entire valleys in unemployment and misery, or seek personal salvation through emigration to the US. What Goethe represents here is the gradual transition from manufacturing production to mechanical industrial labor, the negative consequences of this structural change being unemployment and the pauperization of entire regions. He also imagines multinational conglomerates with worldwide production and a trade network in which entrepreneurial risk is distributed across different locations and whose parts can counterbalance out one another financially. Thus Goethe anticipates in fiction what Karl Marx and Friedrich Engels shortly after write about the bourgeoisie in the *Manifesto of the Communist Party*.

Goethe, the philologist and writer, was anything but unworldly. On the contrary, he dealt throughout his life with economics which had then just come into fashion. And there is no doubt that he was good in financial matters: during his tenure as head of the Weimar financial administration "he took action for the drawing up and, where possible, also for the observance of a state budget" (Lauer 42). As for himself, he was conscious of his literary market value, mainly in the second half of his life (Lauer 53). Enrik Lauer examines in *Literarischer Monetarismus*—on the basis of Niklas Luhmann's systems theoretical approach—Goethe's "homology of spirit and money." Lauer, who pays attention to the often disregarded financial aspects of literary production, finds Goethe to be innovative. Goethe, the *homo oeconomicus*, also had a sharp eye for the technical progress around him, which brought along improved transportation and communication possibilities and ensured a general cultural opening. The fact that traveling within Germany became gradually easier and less troublesome in Goethe's era encouraged him to deliberate on how the project of a united Germany would encompass regional particularities (see Goethe in Eckermann 533). According to Goethe, the unification of Germany was first and foremost a practical matter, which would be resolved almost automatically by the increasing improvement of roads. Although Goethe's reflections exhibit an almost prophetic character, it was not until the establishment of the German *Zollverein* (Customs Union) in 1834 and the final foundation of the German Reich in 1871 that unification was realized in the form of *kleindeutsche Lösung* (i.e., without Austria-Hungary). At the same time that Goethe favored the unity of a large part of the population he emphasized the advantages of the German *Kleinstaaterei* (proliferation of small states) (see Eckermann 553).

Goethe praised on numerous occasions the cultural progressiveness of the French and the English and contrasted them with German provinciality, but he was not blind to the opportunities inherent in German diversity, especially since—with the Parisian *Globe* or the English *Edinburgh Review* delivered at his doorstep—his possibilities for information were a direct consequence of the improved traffic conditions in Germany. Goethe's *Weltliteratur* emerged from changes in the present as a project for the future and for this reason it is in contrast to the concept of Christoph Martin Wieland's world literature and that Schmeling awards with "full credit for the formation of words" (Schmeling, "1st Weltliteratur" 162). While Wieland's concept refers to the past, specifically to literature in the context of Horace, *Weltliteratur* in Goethe is read as a configuration conceived of in its making. This is made possible by the fact that Goethe conceived of a concept of literature that allows for entrenchment in more than one tradition. The relativization of his own position in the spirit of comparativism takes place in Goethe's work on a synchronic as well as on a diachronic axis; we surely have to agree with Schmeling when he writes that "under the intellectual giants of this period in Germany—Wieland, Herder, Schiller, the Schlegels, and others— Goethe probably had acknowledged most clearly the social function of the cosmopolitan literary scene which expressed itself in the rapid proliferation of international periodicals and in the cross-border exchange of letters and translations" (Schmeling, "1st Weltliteratur" 162). Literature is primarily a cross-border communication, which is closely linked to specific technical capabilities. Goethe thus distances himself from his younger fellow writers, who pay homage to the idea of originality, and defends the ideal of an author who "is rather a collector, editor, and arranger of texts and text fragments than a creative genius" (Koch 247). At the same time he exercises a conscious "world literature politics" by bringing the concept to the European intellectual market: "Germany's most famous author [designed] a model for interpreting literary modernisation that may influence the development of literature and the relationship of literatures among themselves . . . Certain provincialisms are now no longer acceptable; the further use of overcome techniques without knowledge of the changes produced by a country in the field of narration, or by another in the field of drama and so on, provokes justified criticism" (Koch 249). In Koch's opinion, Goethe's theoretical configuration involves a manifest normative character, a view I agree with: probably no other writer before Goethe represented to such an extent a public authority on literary matters. Further, he was an avid reader of new literary publications from England and France as well as of various periodicals, and thus he was certainly one of the best-informed literary critics and readers of his time. From this prominent position, which he was absolutely conscious of, Goethe took it upon himself to criticize his contemporaries on their provincial attitude (see Eckermann 174). What Goethe indicated on several occasions in fictional texts, letters, or conversations with regard to industrialization later grew in Marx and Engels into an analysis of the economy and culture that applies to both fields even today, at least if we interpret, as Beck does, the term "cosmopolitically" in connection with a "global sense, a sense of boundarylessness" and permit in the "cosmopolitan outlook . . . an everyday, historically alert, reflexive awareness of ambivalences in a milieu of blurring differentiations and cultural contradictions" (*The Cosmopolitan* 3).

In his study, *Karl Marx and World Literature*, S. S. Prawer criticizes Goethe's statements as "standardised and undifferentiated" (423) and contrasts them with Marx's ideas on literature that are embedded "in a wide economic, social, [and] historical context" and would always be configured "in relation to other authors, other compositions, in many languages" (423). However, a few lines later Prawer concedes that Goethe had a more universal approach in comparison to Marx, for whom world literature was "essentially the literature of Western Europe" (424). I think that this comparison in favor of Marx will not stand up to closer scrutiny. Certainly, Goethe's rather randomly expressed ideas on world literature are not to be characterized as "standardised," because if they were indeed so, then generations of Goethe scholars would not have processed again and again their limitations and definitions. The accusation of lack of differentiation is also not true, since the idea of *Weltliteratur* owes its origins precisely to Goethe's perceptive analysis of the changes in the economic and social fields; therefore, *Weltliteratur* can be understood on the one hand as a result of the new technical and communication options and on the other hand as developing them further and advancing them through the international information exchange. Marx and Engels illustrate the interdependence of "material" and "intellectual production" that causes the dissemination and appreciation of the various national literatures into becoming common property: a crucial difference to Goethe's views does not seem discernible to me.

As for the historical context, we can surely not deny Goethe or Marx their entrenchment in this. To think in national terms was natural both for Goethe and Marx, for both had their roots in the then contemporary knowledge of philology, linguistics, and philosophy. Marx not only had a solid knowledge of ancient writers, but he was familiar with Shakespeare, Voltaire, and Rousseau and admired the works of Schiller, Goethe, and Hölderlin (see Prawer 1–2). It was precisely these newly established fields that were working throughout Europe for the emerging nationalisms, by upgrading the languages of the people, even the hitherto lesser ones like Czech or Norwegian, and by creating an awareness of the equal status of languages among one another. So when Goethe was discussing "Indian and Chinese poetry" or "Serbian songs" (*Werke* 12: 502), he was not standing outside the intellectual life of his time, but was moving in the same comparative milieu as the beginnings of comparative linguistics, although he was one of the few who could see beyond Europe. The subtle difference lies in the way of understanding the foreign. Goethe's method of approximation does not exhaust itself in traditional "hermeneutics of identity" as an "understanding of the Self in the Others"; instead he practiced a "hermeneutics of alterity" by favoring the "understanding of the Foreign in the Other" (Böhler 236) and putting principles into practice, for example, in the *West-Eastern Divan* (on Goethe's relation with Islam see von Mommsen, *Goethe*).

While many of his fellow German national thinking contemporaries regarded every Other predominantly as a category for the identification and, at worst, the glo-

rification of the self, Goethe allowed for the foreignness of the foreign and supported
the blending in his work, *Maximen und Reflexionen* (*Werke* 12: 502). This sounds
like an *éloge de la créolité* (see Bernabé, Chamoiseau, Confiant) *avant la lettre*; on
the one hand it refers back to related comparative thinkers such as Michel de Montaigne and the school of thought of the Enlightenment, but on the other hand it anticipates the rational flow that could hardly hold its ground in the nineteenth century,
but in the twentieth prevailed against the irrationalism of Ernst Jünger or Gottfried
Benn, in the presence of the Mann brothers. In a summary of Goethe's statements on
Weltliteratur the following parameters are relevant:

1) world literature is a category superordinate to national literatures, but
not to be interpreted as a hierarchy in a qualitative sense.
2) world literature does not stand for anything finished; rather, it is a
process where communication between different national literatures occurs.
3) world literature is to be thought of linked to new technical and economic achievements (i.e., in Goethe's time).
4) world literature includes a utopian moment, which according to
Goethe will be realized "in the near future."

It would be misguided, today, to speak of a concept of world literature as
a theoretical or methodological model—even descriptive characteristics cannot be
awarded in good conscience to the term. In this respect, Goethe has bequeathed us
nothing more, but also nothing less, than the provocation with which every age after
him has been confronted. The many efforts and attempts in the last two decades to
narrow down the term demonstrate that the study of literature, at least of Western
provenance, has hardly gone past world literature and that this has gained again on
actuality as a theoretical configuration, particularly in recent times, through the processes of globalization.

With regard to literary history and Goethe's notion, in 1972 an anthology appeared under the title *Weltliteratur und Volksliteratur* (Schaefer) that, in view of the
"formulaic" solidification and the "dubiousness through rhetorical repetition" of the
term "world literature," attempted to "question the central insights of . . . an exemplary figure like Goethe on their current function value" (Lange 15). The re-exami-
nation is carried out primarily through delimitation to other literary categories such
as folk literature, national literature, and popular literature, as well as paradigmatic
figures like Hamlet, Don Quixote, and the figure of the dandy. According to several
contributors to the volume, *Weltliteratur* itself attests a "peculiar resonance of the
German concept *Welt* (world) and its not only geographical but also transcendental
importance . . . that is felt neither in the words *le monde* or *mondial*, or *universel*, or
even in *world* or global" (Lange 15).

In today's context the obviousness of that time appears strange when dealing
with closed systems of literature, while the "transcendental importance" will, at the
very least, cause surprise: it was an era of clear national and ideological boundaries

in which the paradoxes and uncertainties of postmodernity, the end of the "grand narratives," had not really penetrated to the surface. However, in 1954 Hans Mayer had already defined the distinction between "German literature and world literature" and he interpreted "national literature" as a political concept that initially served "a political thesis, which in fact suited the German democratic and national unity movement" (12). According to Mayer, against this "limited conception of the German nation and national literature" Goethe positioned the idea of *Weltliteratur* as "a mutual give and take" (16) and as "a diverse and pollinating exchange between the national literatures" (28). Mayer's use of the term is typical of the practice that prevails up to the present time of defining world literature in contrast with established categories such as national literature or popular literature, because apparently only in this way can the indispensable key differences be extracted. The result is either a qualitative cross-section of high-brow literature, the national literatures, and world literature as a subset of all literatures or a quantitatively defined expression in which national literatures form subsets of an all-embracing world literature. Both cannot satisfactorily accommodate in an epistemic way the present conditions with their multitude of hybrid forms.

In *Weltliteratur und Volksliteratur*, Horst Rüdiger posed a more future-oriented point as he explained world literature as a matter of comparative literature, and on the other hand—again, quoting Goethe—he claimed "to walk the path of synthesis, and . . . international cooperation," because only this direction promises success in view of the "technical and social upheavals which the standardised 'One World' has enforced" (44). In this requirement we read a sense of dissatisfaction with the self-sufficiency of individual literatures which were sorted according to standard languages and were no longer able to do justice to the diverse literary phenomena of the allegedly homogenized "one world." In 1995 Schmeling attempted a definition in the collected volume *Weltliteratur heute. Konzepte und Perspektiven*. Here, world literature is located beyond Eurocentric prospects around the entire world. Martin Brunkhorst notes in his contribution to the volume that in this type of canon formation "value conflicts inevitably arise and historical-geographical and sociocultural variables lead to permanent shifts" (33). With the example of Wole Soyinka's processing of ancient Greek tragedy materials, Brunkhorst demonstrates the problem that exists in a Eurocentric literary search for traces in non-European texts such as those in Soyinka's: "In the search for the continuing up-to-datedness of older examples of a world literature, the subject may not just be the passing on of European examples. . . . Integration processes, amalgamations, stratifications, bricolage, or overlay and displacement processes—or, put negatively: mongrelisation—lead to complex but often problematic situations in the canon of a possible world literature. But the recognition of these hybrid forms should also take place in the regional or national field" (33). Recognition as what? This question pops up almost automatically. As a subset of the national literatures? Or as regionally localized individual literatures? What is needed here is the problem of taxonomy, and that evades established monocultural and monolingual national philologies. To the same extent that Goethe's formulation expressed a political direction of impact, the term is equally not free from ideological complications even in the present: "a gray cloud concentrates at this point over world literature . . . In the current conflict between East and West, North and South, between postcolonial metropolises and neocolonial situations there is the danger that the idea of world literature could be drawn . . . to conflict" (Georgiev 78). Although Nikola Georgiev leaves his concerns without further precision, he hints at least at one problem, namely, that the impartiality of the Goethean era has been lost for us: where Goethe simply saw an intensified exchange between national literatures, today we connote the asymmetrical, hegemonic power relationship in favor of the West; and where Goethe celebrated economic and technical progress, we see global ecological failure. Goethe's "browsing about other nations" (Georgiev 78) seems degenerated to McDonaldization.

In this jungle of polyvalence, Wladimir Krysinski tries to save world literature by encircling it with the help of five actants: "the local, the national, the marginal, the institutional, and the universal. These are the actantial and semantic supports of a narrative of values which unfolds on a global scale and which guarantees for global literature its forms and contents" ("Récit" 151). According to Krysinski, a permanent area of tension is built between these actants, within which the preponderance may lie on each of the participating subfields. This descriptive attempt is problematic for two reasons, first, because it is neither specific nor placed on an empirical basis, and second, because it refers to Canadian facts which are not transferable to other hybrid literatures without modification. Krysinski is right in his claim that "Goethe's project should be reconsidered and put in perspective again" (151); however, he dismisses his readers by stating that world literature should be defined by "the heterogeneity of its works, the languages it speaks, and the passions that sustain it at the end of the century" (152), which just does not contribute to the operational efficiency of the concept. Walter Koschmal presents a different approach coming from Slavic studies. As the concept of world literature is virtually nonexistent in this discipline, Koschmal enters new territory and qualitatively describes "world literature—in the function of a canon—as a subset of the total of "national literatures" (102). Following Jan Mukařovský's *skopos* theory, Koschmal ascribes to the literary work three functions, a "national," an "international of the direct cultural context," and a "world literary" with each providing different cultural coverage. Thus he reaches a classification of epistemic competence according to which "comparative literature, but not the individual philologies, attain the world literature function of texts" (104). The *skopoi* can be differentiated from one another through their *signifiant/signifié* relation as the criterion of a common language—or, in the case of the Slavic languages, a family of languages—diminishes from the first, the national, to the third, the world literature *skopos*. Although the aesthetic-formal functions, that is the *signifiant*, form the primary object of analysis for Koschmal in the first two *skopoi*, this criterion takes a backseat on the world literature level in favor of the content, the *signifié*, because the expression plane of the sign is not translatable adequately or not translatable at all. Instead, as Koschmal argues, "the universal value appears to be dominant" (118). As with so many scholars before him, his survey also ends with aporia and we are, again, confronted with the unquestioned category of "national literature" as a starting point. And Koschmal's applied axiology is particularly dubious, because with the differentiation between aesthetic value on the expression plane and the universal value on the content plane, not only is the fundamental translatability of each text disputed, but also a canonization of monolingual texts is pursued that ignores the long tradition of literary multilingualism. Further, Koschmal does not do justice to the current language mixtures of different provenance. To look at world literature from a monolingual and monocultural aesthetic perspective of reception is one sided and, most of all, it produces no manageable tools for the description of literature under globalization. In addition, the reception aesthetics of world literature moves toward "normative values, canon-formation, or canon-rejection" and "universal validity" (Schmeling, "1st Weltliteratur" 159).

In 2006, Ida Klitgård and the other contributors to *Literary Translation: World Literature or "Worlding" Literature* investigated questions about the interrelatedness between concepts of world literature and translation, a research subject which is closely linked to Sarah Lawall's or Amily Apter's tenets for "reading the world." Lawall's and Apter's scholarship in comparative literature is concerned, in particular, with translation when students and readers in general do not have the command of languages other than English. In *Literary Translation* the concept of world literature is prominent and the internationalization of or in literature is thus a main feature. Indeed, internationalization is produced by the presence of more and more authors with a transnational background in the literary scene: "a literature emerges that is not bound to a place according to its origins, that roams among cultures and therefore is truly worldly" (Walstra 206). Whether this "literature on the move" (Ette) should necessarily be written in English, as the media and the publishing behemoths in London or New York often suggest, is a different question I discuss in chapter 2. What seemed to be the only conceivable consequence in 1995 has lost some of its vitality today, because to restrict world literature to works by V. S. Naipaul, Derek Walcott, Michael Ondaatje, and Salman Rushdie—as the most frequently cited names—seems shortsighted: I agree with Gert Mattenklott in his diagnosis that global migrations have caused the emergence of a world literature, yet it is surely more than a "symptom, if not a product of strife," which owes its "violent genesis . . . to war and exile" (612).

The concept of world literature has gained renewed interest in particular in the US starting in the mid-1980s and it remains prominent, even gaining since the mid-2000s (for a list of recent books on world literature, see Tötösy de Zepetnek, "Multilingual"; see also Tötösy de Zepetnek and Vasvári). One of the prominent scholars of world literature is David Damrosch, who defines the concept as follows: "world literature is not an infinite, ungraspable canon of works but rather a mode of circulation and of reading, a mode that is as applicable to individual works as to bodies of material, available for reading established classics and new discoveries alike" (*What Is* 5). In response to Damrosch's definition I refer to Stefan Blessin's critical attitude concerning the functionalization of Goethe's *Weltliteratur*: "there is no Goethe in a cross-cultural perspective, strictly speaking, because with his concepts of universality and productive adaptation he does not fall into this category—and what was envisaged in the term was also historically outside of his possibilities" (70). Thus—while in some instances the "new" notion of world literature as proposed by comparative literature scholars in the US may well be appropriate and useful—Goethe's notion ought to remain a matter of literary history.

In general, two major lines emerge: first, a general consensus that Goethe's concept requires new definitions in the age of increasing globalization and that his verification of most Western European literatures is anachronistic. Marián Gálik emphasizes the spatial and temporal dimension of all canons and other normative categories and makes us understand that world literature now refers to the entire globe. Hendrik Birus writes, "but what is world literature? The answer seems trivial: The literature of the whole world"—a laconic view but Birus gets to the point of the necessary expansion of Goethe's famous wording: "European, that is world literature" (1). Second, it seems that there is generally no longer any doubt about the fact that world literature should be an exclusive subject matter of comparative literature, not only because Goethe was the first "comparative literature scholar" recorded in the history of literature (see Hoesel-Uhlig 28) or because scholars such as Erich Auerbach and Leo Spitzer followed in his footsteps, but also because only a science that thinks beyond the national can live up to new standards in globalism. As Peter Goßens emphasizes in his study of the history of the concept in the nineteenth century, "world literature was and is a terminological fixed star, which has made it possible, while establishing its own position, to also blend alterity discourse structures and make them denotable" (10). Since new problems call for new methods, it is time to mark with the idea of a NWL both the connection to Goethe and at the same time the distance from him by bringing into view a changed cognitive grid of previously neglected research objects and linking them to one another in a manner different than usual (see, e.g., Amman, Mein, Parr; Gupta; Mitterer and Wintersteiner; Prendergast; Saussy). On the one hand, this accounts for the fact that world literature is a high educational ideal in the present just as it was in the nineteenth century, namely, transcending the narrow boundaries of national culture and the acquisition of knowledge in world literature. On the other hand, world literature has proven to be a more open and profitable discourse field for all processes in social, historical, or ideological thought (see Goßens 16–17)

Before verifying the performance of a modified concept of world literature at the transnational level in the field of hybrid literature, I present in the following an introduction to German-, English-, French-, Iberian Spanish-, and Portuguese-language discourses concerning "minority literatures." In addition, this schematic approach will once again make evident the artificiality or even the uselessness of classifications in national philologies.

Chapter Two

Hybrid Literary Texts and Philological Paradigms

In this chapter I present my thoughts about the relation of some philologies to their respective "small" literatures. Although the selection opted for almost automatically entails a charge of Eurocentrism, I consciously restrict myself to the fields where my command of languages allows me to have a substantiated opinion and this is why the Slavic languages, for example, are absent, although they belong to the traditional subjects of Western scholarship. The aim of these brief introductions to the intercultural literature of the German-speaking area, to English-speaking world fiction, to the fiction of the Francophony, Spain, Hispanic America, and Lusophony cannot be a detailed presentation of the respective research areas. They are meant only as a rough sketch of the developments in the last decades, when the originally monocultural- and monolingual-oriented philologies became confronted with an anarchic—from their perspective—literary production, the analysis of which renders their traditional tools largely useless. Particular attention is paid to the comparative fields of each respective philology, as the search for a reconfiguration of world literature is most pronounced in their ranks and scholars in comparative literature work as a rule today with the perspective of the Other. Therefore, it is not surprising that the first approaches toward the broadening of horizons beyond national philologies came from the discipline of comparative literature and that we are gradually on the way toward "comparative cultural studies."

When I decided to use the term "intercultural literature" I meant it as a tribute to the first comprehensive work in German scholarship—unmatched in its detail up to this day—*Interkulturelle Literatur in Deutschland. Ein Handbuch* edited in 2000 by Carmine Chiellino (see also "Interkulturalität," "Über"). Although we could surely discuss a few aspects of content, this book has actually become a handbook in the literal sense, a reference work for everyone who deals with hybrid forms of literature, at least in Germany. Chiellino's book constitutes a turning point, as he demonstrated for the first time the full range of this previously marginalized literature from the texts of the "guest workers" to those of Russian or Romanian Germans and exiles from Latin America, Africa, or Asia. And so the myth of the homogeneity of this "non-German" literature finally came to an end and its enormous diversity became visible. It was a long road to get to this standard.

The Adelbert von Chamisso Prize has been awarded in Germany since 1985 to authors of non-German origin who have opted for German as their literary language and have published in German. Well-known authors, such as Rafik Schami and Cyrus Atabay, rank among "Chamisso's grandchildren." After the initial euphoria over this award faded away, it is surprising from today's perspective that the primacy of the German language was declared as a principal point and the basic requirement for participation became the complete change of language to German. Harald Weinrich wrote somewhat patronizingly in 1992 that "when we meet the emigrants and migrants, we often forget that these migrants bring along not only their workforce but also their cultural memory and that they want to give to it an expression in the language of the host country, as was Adelbert von Chamisso's requirement" (10; on the issue of the use of the designation "migrant" instead of immigrant literature, see, e.g., Tötösy de Zepetnek, "Interculturalism"; in German-language scholarship the exclusionary concept "migration literature" instead of immigration literature is used throughout; for recent examples see Gramling, Kaes, Langenohl, Göktürk). Even if we ignore the fact that the author of these lines—Weinrich—obviously knew exactly what motives were responsible for the shift in perceptions, it is still amazing that he is also "informed" about what immigrants intend to express and in what language they want to do this. And it does not take a degree in sociology to identify in these statements a classic case of the "container paradigm." In other words, national affiliations are thought of as binary and consecutive. Mongrelization, contamination, language and cultural mixtures of all kinds—in short, hybridity—seemed to have no place in Germany in 1992. This is documented by the almost desperate search for a catchy name for this "other" literature in the form of such as "guest worker literature" (*Gastarbeiterliteratur*) (see Chiellino 389–91). Further, Weinrich reveals the hegemonic exercise of the German majority society's power over the Other by the praise of the "contributions of high literary rank . . . to which German literature owes some highly welcome enrichment" (10). Dieter Krusche functionalizes in a similar way the "literature from outside," as he calls it, when judging the works: "what they are able to add to our German literature will be seen all the more clearly the more one reads them" (13; note the "our"). It feels like we are reminded of Goethe's appeal to receive other literatures "from the outside" in order to escape the national literary ennui. German literature with a foreign cultural background is welcome, because this way there is something foreign in German culture that can inspire authors without the cost of translation: this is how we could interpret the message of such (no doubt well-intentioned) statements. In 1988, Horst Hamm claimed the authors among immigrants explicitly for the German market, because of the fact that "more and more authors [take possession of] the German language and so they document that they belong to the local culture. . . . The works by Saliha Scheinhardt interest only a German audience, the stories by Schami could hardly find a listener in the Arab world. The German literary market has taken possession of the genre" (164). Apart from the fact that such statements lack any empirical basis, Said would have had further evidence for Orientalist constructions in the West, because when we place a writer like Schami in a supposedly typical Oriental narrative tradition, the assumption that he would not be received in the Middle East just because of—or despite—his Oriental themes and forms is illogical, to put it simply. This is also obvious from the publisher's design of Schami's books, whose Oriental-themed designs would attract potential readers and have an impact on reception and readership. At any rate, it is impressive how Hamm concludes from the use of the German language—where it is being tacitly implied that it is the German "literary standard language," whatever this may be—the willingness of the authors for acculturation in Germany.

What is not being discussed are the texts themselves. The above-cited anthology, published by Irmgard Ackermann in 1992, is presented as a large number of literarily certified certificates, which will not leave the reader indifferent (Weinrich 11; see also Ackermann and Müller). This reflects the sociological exploitation of literary texts that was common as recently as the 1990s and according to which the texts could be read only regarding their authenticity and documentation, but whose aesthetic characteristics were ignored. This is the case first, because credit was not given to the authors for poeticity and literarity and second, because there were no standards available beyond the ones developed for a monolingual and monocultural literature. In addition, the preoccupation with marginalized literature offers the opportunity on the part of scholars to bring their own view into the spotlight through the solidarization and promotion of the "affected," as this view is morally "better" because it is not xenophobic. The emergence of the unfortunate categorization of a "literature of consternation" (*Betroffenheitsliteratur*) can be understood in the light of this (see Hamm 50).

The combination of the foreign cultural content plane with the plane of German-language expression helped researchers to reach some conclusions about the texts of the first generation of immigrants. However, with regard to the second generation it failed miserably, given the complexity and versatility of the many texts. In 1988 Hamm even dared to prophecize that there were "no new themes and impulses to be expected" by the second generation, because their writing, as that of the Germans, revolved only around "the search for identity," upon which "just the label 'guest worker literature' was imposed," and that "the melancholic nostalgia and tenacious sadness" in it were being published only "because one could do business with 'guest worker literature' at that time. With the label alone no literature will be produced in the long run, especially when German writers have described the same thing much better years ago" (165–66). Such sweeping statements are, of course, highly questionable and they rather indicate the view of the writer and the institutions that he represents than adequately analyze a research topic, howsoever defined. In addition, authors of the second generation such as Feridun Zaimoglu or José F. A. Oliver have objected to evaluations of this kind. Alev Tekinay argues that "at a time when German literature had come to a dead end and it had become a bit monotonous in terms of both narrative materials as well as language, the foreigners appeared as saviour angels" (28). Nevertheless, Hamm's book is interesting because it demonstrates the mechanisms of inclusion and exclusion in the literary world, where the literature of the Other has a right to exist only if it is able to generate interest by readers through "defictionalization" (Amodeo 41) and conveys the concerns of a group, be they homosexuals, women, or guest workers some of whom lived in Germany for two or more generations.

Thematic homogeneity is ascribed to the texts from the outset and so is the primacy of a moral and political claim over aesthetic criteria, which remain excluded because they are not located in the observer's point of view and therefore cannot be proven in the object of research. Immacolata Amodeo gives a good overview of published scholarship and deconstructs the "scientific" discourse of "guest worker literature" of the 1980s (12–74, 40–41), taking the reader into a horror of generalizations, trivia, and misinformation. The perception reduced to a binary perspective can record in the texts only the element of alterity, which in the absence of a criteria of evaluation is automatically assigned an inferior place in the canon of German-language literature, where the texts excel not by "linguistic mastery," but with the help of their "reduced vocabulary" by the "impressiveness" of the message (Ackermann 243). This certainly unintentional humor in Ackermann's statement is best matched with a reply by Yoko Tawada, who recaptures the nonliterary category of "loss of identity": "The buzz phrase 'loss of identity' has displaced the concept of transformation. Transformation, however, has been since antiquity—whether the Greek or the Chinese—one of the main motives of literature. Poetic transformations form a space between the yearning for a deadly transformation into a beast and the horror of the transformation into a man" (*Verwandlungen* 60).

Although my discussion above highlights the issue only briefly, it is nonetheless clear that the scholarly involvement with hybrid forms of literature in German-speaking countries had come to a dead end around 1990 when it was driven out by two relatively recent developments: first, around this time the first generation of scholars appeared on the academic market, who—as in the US and UK around the same time—because of their multilingualism and multicultural background could interfere in the discussion much more competently than the established, but less language experienced, generation of German philologists before them; and second, German studies in Anglophone countries gave important new impulses with reference to the debate on postcolonialism. These two parameters were complementary to each other and contributed in an intradisciplinary and interdisciplinary way to the improvement of the discourse, as they not only generated more awareness of their own literary action under the deconstruction of the claim for scientific objectivity and truth, but they also produced an opening to other philological fields including ethnology, anthropology, history, and sociology, not only in the German-speaking countries, but also beyond them, thus engaging foreign German studies even more in comparative literature and cultural studies than they had done through constant cultural contact.

As I mention above, Chiellino's *Interkulturelle Literatur in Deutschland* is a comprehensive survey of hybrid literatures that for the first time united bilingual scholars in a single volume and classified the phenomenon in a more expansive context. In this sense, Konrad Köstlin noted that "migration has lost its exceptionality in a globalized world" and that on the one hand it might mean a "new collective destiny," and on the other hand a "collective opportunity" for a "life in in-between worlds" (380–81). Chiellino and the contributors to his volume suggest that intercultural and hybrid literature—in German-language literature—ought to be considered as a point of departure for literary studies and stress that they should not be considered in the usual hierarchical manner that literary histories have constructed. Further, the contributors to the volume claim analyses of German-language intercultural and hybrid literature should include attention to aesthetics. The salient point is the beginning of an intercultural memory in Germany since 1964, which is embedded in each ethnic group of the cultures of the country and demonstrates the connectedness of German culture to Europe. However—with all due respect to Chiellino's and the contributors' work presented in the volume—I note that in these (and many other) points in his compendium the argumentation is precisely against that upon which his whole book turns. Thus, monocultural vision is predominant, where the starting point is formed by exactly definable, apparently homogeneous cultural and linguistic communities. To present scholarly argumentation about "imagined communities" is certainly not a promising method. Moreover, the frequently invoked factor of innovation in intercultural authenticity remains amorphous as a descriptive feature. In my opinion, the merit of Chiellino's manual does not lie in a consolidated theory, but in the presentation of unique and extensive material from primary and secondary literature. However, I would not agree with the Spanish philologist of German literature Ana Ruiz, who encourages the inclusion of the texts compiled in Chiellino in the canon of German literature, where she proceeds from a canon as a paradigmatic and normative institution "that provides moral standards and ideals of inspiration, transmits a certain heritage of thought, creates common frames of reference for a society and culture, allows the analysis of the relationships among the groups that propose it and those that are integrated for the first time in it, [and] offers the new vision of the society that proposes it" (46). The purpose of this integration should be "a step towards a self-understanding of Germany as the multicultural society that it is" (46), while in the opposite case—noninclusion—the texts would inevitably fall into oblivion, whereby Germany would maintain the fiction as a "unitary nation, identical to itself" (47). The problem of the two options available is, first, that they concede a positive effect to a national literary canon and second, that they attribute an integrating function to the canon, by which the "new rich" can also be admitted to the exclusive club of the old literary aristocracy and, finally, strengthen the apparently still doubted multicultural image of Germany, whereby the functionalization of minority literature through the mainstream society would take place afresh.

More representative of the younger generation of scholars more solidly grounded is, for example, Amodeo's study *Die Heimat heißt Babylon*. After a detailed and critical presentation of secondary literature, Amodeo discusses the difficult relation between the institutionalized national philologies and the "minor literatures" and notices that "because of their high deterritorialisation factor" they evade the mechanisms of evaluation that have been developed for national literatures and automatically sink into the "status of a 'lower' kind of literature" (93). By referring to Bakhtin's literary dialogics and Deleuze and Guattari's rhizome model she succeeds not only in demonstrating empirically the heterogeneity of this literature, but also in converting these properties as an aesthetic principle in a theory that brings the scientific discourse a decisive step forward (107). In addition, she reveals the principally "syncretic language profile" even in nonevident multilingual conditions in the texts (120) and notes the "transposedness" of this literature in relation to the respective national literatures (201) that requires "alternative description models" for the analysis of the "aesthetic process" applied in the texts (205; see also Blioumi on Greek German [im]migration literature). In this way Amodeo covers some part of the road along which I would like to walk further and in the course of which hybrid texts will be liberated from established national literary discourse.

Klaus R. Scherpe shows some understanding of the helplessness of German studies in dealing with foreign cultural productions, since they have "no culpable colonial history as does England or France, no multicultural involvement, which also questions the canon and the institutions of their own discipline, as in the US, no trend-setting migrant literature" (304). It seems only logical that innovations often come from scholars who are located closer to the corresponding discourses—from German studies abroad, especially in anglophone cultures. Thus, Petra Fachinger deals with the comparability of the German with US-American and English Canadian immigrant literature and comes to the conclusion that as German political reality is reflected frequently in German immigrant literature, in the same way much of the US-American and anglophone Canadian immigrant literature is characterized by the political and ideological reality of both countries and moves within the context of specific cultural expectations (53). Nevertheless, for Fachinger an "international aesthetics of migration writing" exists, and "similar texts strategies exist in the various national contexts" like the "re-writing or writing back to," that is, "the subversive rewriting of canonized texts, the estrangement of established genres, transtextuality, self-reflexivity, latent or evident bilingualism . . . moreover, female migrant literature seems to be characterized by a desire for cosmopolitanism, hybridity, and the denial to shelve the identity" in terms of Turkish German, Indoamerican, or Chicana literature (54–56). Her conclusion is that "literary studies have done so far too little work in the field of comparison of different migrant literatures" (56; in contrast to Fachinger, see, e.g., Cheesman; Pivato, Tötösy de Zepetnek, Dimić; Tötösy de Zepetnek, "Early German-Canadian," "Literary Theory"; Yildiz).

The proceedings of the 1995 international conference of German philology on (im)migration literature held in Vancouver were published in 1997 in two volumes (Fischer and McGowan; Howard) with the objective to reflect on "the general background . . . of the era of global mass migration" (Howard 9). Mary Howard, the editor of the volume, suggests that the study of Chicano/a literature or authors of Asian and Caribbean origin in the US or the UK is "in parallel relation[] to German-language (im)migration literature and its investigation appear[s] in a whole new light, on the one hand regarding their specific development, on the other hand in comparison to global developments" and she emphasizes the relevance of "food for thought from the social and cultural studies" (9). However, in none of the volumes is this ambitious claim realized, for despite the fact that many of its contributions go past the monocultural view and reflect at least bicultural conditions, we encounter only scattered references to standard authors of postcolonialism, such as Homi K. Bhabha, Frederic Jameson, Stuart Hall, and Edward Said, and comparative work on texts such as Chicano/a and Turkish German texts is absent (see, instead, e.g., Karakus; Yeşilada). In this respect, I can only say that the correct requirements arise precisely in the German studies of foreign countries, but that their redemption has not been decisively addressed. Consequently, some normalcy gradually ensues in the way that we deal with Other literatures on the basis of which in the *German Studies Yearbook* of 2003 (Lützeler and Schindler), for example, hybrid texts by Şenocak, Özdamar, Honigmann, and Tawada, progress beyond their special status as a subset of national literature and are treated together with monolingual German texts of contemporary literature, albeit in a separate section, "multiculturalism." It is important that the "cosmopolitan vision" (Beck) is noticeable in theory and methodology. For example, Şenocak's novels are no longer examined under German or Turkish ethnocentric points of view, but are read as alienated symbolic categories, as a "destabilization of real and imaginary boundaries," as a breakup of "binary oppositions," and as a trialog "through recourse to a third position, beyond binary polarities [where] new constellations are made possible in relation to different national and ethnic identities" (Dollinger 4, 19).

Similar conceptual new approaches can also be observed in comparative literature. Thus, Jürgen Wertheimer, editor of *Arcadia*, which since its first publication in 1966 has been committed to "Goethe's time and its world literature concept" (Rüdiger 36), heralds in 1996 the beginning of a new era, "now that the voice of the other is no longer a whisper, but a sensuous everyday experience, and so-called 'reality' floods us and thereby denies itself at the same time because *différ(a)nce* has become the aesthetic key term, and hybrid forms of existence and hybrid text forms are the rule. General and comparative literature studies should become what they are in substance: the most normal, the only appropriate methodological approach to dealing with literature and art as inherently international phenomena" (Editorial iii). Only a year earlier, an entire issue of the journal *Zeitschrift für Literaturwissenschaft und Linguistik* was dedicated to cultural conflicts in texts (see Schlieben-Lange). In Brigitte Schlieben-Lange's introduction to the special issue we detect a series of theoretical configurations including the break-off of national systems of regulation and their usurpation by the formerly subordinate level of nationalities or regions, as well as by the superordinate global level. She also points out the deficits in dealing with the "rapidly accelerating process of the emergence of new or new-old identities, hence, of course, of new conflicts along obsolete by now (ethnic, confessional) fault lines . . . there is little mention of the character and text-shaped aspects of these conflicts" and the "discursive constitution" of "emergent identities" gets little attention (1–2). Similar to Beck and Armin Nassehi, Schlieben-Lange highlights the relevance of the self-positioning of scholars as they produce "texts above texts" and who, as a result of this, "are constantly in danger of creating reality-constitutive texts, that is, of obliterating the difference between analytical texts and texts that must be analysed" and thus "of fixing reality" (2). In this context I include in the following chapter considerations on the "observer position." Another concern of Schlieben-Lange is the "provision of classifiers" in order to "by means of classification, make available the complexity of the world that is expressed through language" (3). The confrontation with radical new text forms is also the starting point for Thomas Wägenbaur's study on intercultural dynamics in Aysel Özakin's novel *Die blaue Maske*. For Wägenbaur there is an "ethnocentric exploitation of intercultural literature" in the actual task of literary studies in that the description and evaluation of the literariness of these texts can only be counterproductive as the issue is ultimately about "the specific literary implementation of a different culture and identity concept" (23) whose main characteristic is its hybridity.

The realization that the social sciences and the humanities have to be interdisciplinary and intercultural prompted Peter V. Zima to hold a conference in 1998 with the theme "Comparative Studies." In the edited volume of the conference papers Schmeling does not inquire after the real background or truthfulness of foreign cultural images, but after their position and function within a narrative system, because "otherness is no longer a definable, fixed quantity, just as there aren't, or shouldn't be, any distinguishable cultural entities" ("Literarischer" 195). Schmeling refers to Walcott and Soyinka as authors of "hybrid cultures . . . authors who essentially do not belong to a single culture, but embody the 'being on the road' between cultures. Their novels have neither territorial nor mental centralisation and thereby somehow illustrate Derrida's theory of the permanent suspension of meaning, of the floating being" ("Literarischer" 195). In view of such uncertain circumstances, Goethe's notion of *Weltliteratur* has to be revised "with the original, enlightened thought of the encounter between cultures and mutual fertilization" ("Literarischer" 194). Subsequently, Johann Strutz suggests a redefinition of the "object field" of comparative literature and its transformation into a "cultural studies metatheory" (202). By use of the example of the multilingual Alps-Adriatic region, Strutz demonstrates the necessity for the proper description of the "intercultural and interdiscoursive relationships of bicultural regions" that goes beyond individual philologies (202) and concludes that with the effective implementation of the theoretical configuration 'interculturality' versus 'reductionist concepts of unity' . . . the time of monolingual, national literary histories and individual literary teaching methodology should be over" (219). With a similarly cosmopolitan approach, Manfred Durzak, in his "Deutschsprachige interkulturelle Literatur—ein Phantom?" takes recourse to postcolonial theory (Said, Bhabha) and to authors like Rushdie in order to separate the texts of Schami or Özdamar from monolingual German literature, precisely because of their structural and thematic hybridity. From this position, the influence of German-speaking narrators—for example, in Sten Nadolny's *Selim oder die Gabe der Rede* or Uwe Timm's *Morenga*—can be seen, so that intercultural literature stimulates monolingual literature to obtain new forms (see also Durzak and Kuruyazıcı 33–36). And even Martin Walser's 2004 novel, *Der Augenblick der Liebe,* with its long, untranslated passages in English and numerous quotations in French, is a book that is hardly imaginable in its mixed lingualism without the familiarization with hybrid forms of literature.

In a 1993 article in the magazine *Der Spiegel* it is proclaimed that there is a new era of English-language literature: "The new star authors are Rushdie, Walcott, or Ondaatje; they come from all over the world—but not from England. With fresh foreign subjects, the heirs of the Empire help establish English, the world language, to a new world literature . . . the traditional idea of national literature had served its time. A global literature is taking its place, written and disseminated in English, the *lingua franca*" ("Die Schale" 232). For Goethe this would definitely be a surprising interpretation of his idea of *Weltliteratur* in that the Empire has been "writing back" already for a few decades and that it is hard to place English-language literature into national literature categories alone due to the numbers of its editions and their global dissemination. The worldwide success of novels such as *The English Patient* or *The Satanic Verses* and Nobel prizes in literature for authors like Gordimer, Morrison, Soyinka, Naipaul, Walcott, and Coetzee have allowed the classic model of the white, anglophone, British, or US-American, monocultural author to become obsolete. The *Spiegel* article also enumerates three generations of "ethno-authors" who range from Achebe and Naipaul to Erdrich and Walker and to younger ones like Kureishi and Phillips (233). The hallmark of this new literature, according to the *Spiegel* article, is the "defiance of space and time," "an inclination towards the non-rational," the conscious adoption of "traditions from their countries of origin," and a "Creolization" of the English language (233–34). Also in 1993 Wolf Lepenies reported on the foundation of the Académie Universelle des Cultures in Paris, whose main task was the abolition of the "Eurocentrism of cultural and intellectual life" in our age and "of enforced, desirable, and barely avoidable cultural contact" (132). This, according to Lepenies, manifests itself in literature, and specifically in the "world fiction" of the great metropolises of New York, London, or Toronto: "the international market opportunities for this literature of new, 'transcultural authors,' which in principle does not depend on translations, are high. Moreover, 'world fiction' has something of a utopia in itself: here the world's cultural periphery comes into its own and steals their hereditary meaning from the ancient centers of the intellectual world civilisation" (132; see also Kalogeras, Arapoglou, Manney).

Thus, "world fiction" serves a variety of interests: big publishing houses have a global market, anticolonialism-oriented readers have done something for their ideology with the purchase of a book written by a postcolonial writer, and bland "British contemporary writing" receives a "forceful push" through "uninhibited joy of fabulation" and "unusually sharp fare for the literary palate" ("Die Schale" 232). Here we are confronted again with the processing scheme for "intercultural" German literature and consequently hybrid forms of literature can be exploited for various purposes, with their own stereotypes of exoticism being projected on the new: Germans love the "Oriental narrative talent" (Şölçün 152) and the bored British apparently enjoy the spicy curry of the new food from India or Pakistan. As it is, the ideological shift from the "melting pot" to the "salad bowl" was consummated in the US and the actually existing multiculturalism was enacted in law (in Australia, Canada, and the United Kingdom, although not in the US). Showcase authors like Walker, Morrison, and Anzaldúa decorate the beautified self-portrait of the united and multifarious US. We grant to all these authors a "nonrationality" as a "tradition from the countries of origin" by means of which first, we devalorize the texts themselves through the absence of aesthetic evaluation; second, we deny all forms of the rational so highly rated in the West; third, we assign to them the position of the alterity and thereby we elevate the West and its cultural character to a universal measure; and fourth, we neglect the generation that has grown up in the country itself, because categories such as irrationality must necessarily come from the tradition of the countries of origin, where these too obviously have a single and well-defined container culture.

My above reading takes on the new tolerance of the wonderful "one world" makes one thing clear, namely, that they reproduce exactly the hegemonic discourses against which they supposedly write. Some analyze today's global domination of multinational corporations and organizations as a new form of colonialism (see, e.g., Miyoshi 1993), but in my opinion the triumphant enthronement of an English-language "world fiction" as NWL is, mainly, a matter of skilfull marketing and anything but a literary category or type of text. That scholars, for example in the US, are well aware of this is evident in the 1993 report by Kristin Ross in her capacity as "professor of world literature and cultural studies at the University of California, Santa Cruz" who launched with colleagues a course in "World Literature" with the objective "to study literature and cultural production in a global context" (667) and where the biggest problem is the bringing together of so-called "emergent cultures within the U.S. . . . with those non-Euro-American cultures, Islamic for example, that have traditionally existed within the university into a realm of specialized isolation" (667). Ross also writes that similar to courses with feminist approaches or gender studies, the word "world" should characterize primarily the interdisciplinary perspective as a "relational way of thinking about global literature and culture, such that students could not henceforth think about Europe or America in isolation from other global spaces" (670). At the same time, against the "postmodernist evacuation of the historical," great importance has been bestowed upon the historical factor, for example, in the comparison of the forms of slavery in ancient Greece and US-America. In this case, as Ross reports, the participating teachers noted after a while that they were always reproducing the binary postcolonial model of exploiters and exploited, even as they tried to escape it through the relationalization of alterity in research by exemplifying, for example, with the omission of Britain Asian modernism by reference to only three cities, Kolkata, Shanghai, and Tokyo (674). This conception is supported by the desire for a reorganization of research in dehierarchized and decentralized contexts; there are doubts, however, as to whether the method of

"Teaching What You Do not Know" (668) can truly lead to scientifically founded expertise. Ross cites the example of a colleague who refused the directorship of a seminar on South African literature on the grounds that he had not studied this field and argues that the typical advance in knowledge of university teaching staff cannot be considered as dogma when it comes to the creation of a principally unfinished research subject such as "world literature." To me, such an approach seems amateurish, for as we know, knowledge is observer dependent: all you see is what you know. In this sense, the euphoric attributing of any culture with the word "world" should certainly be viewed with caution, because the declaration of a global perspective, as with Ross, by no means generates automatically an adequate apparatus of empirical description or the analysis of specific texts on the basis of a solid theory.

By contrast, substantiated methodology and theory are found in broader studies, such as *Die Dynamik des Interkulturellen in den postkolonialen Literaturen englischer Sprache*, whose author, Bernd Schulte, situates his object of study at the outset directly in a context of research committed to a cosmopolitan outlook, since "the treated cultural-theoretical aspects . . . basically pertain to any literature that is afflicted by dynamic processes as a result of cultural overlappings or conflicts of occurred hybridisations. This is by no means limited to situations that are similar to the legacy of colonialism in the countries of former colonies: exiles, migrants, and highly mobile and less mobile societies can exhibit 'intercultural' characteristics and accept them in their respective stock of behavior opportunities (or refuse them)" (3). As in German-speaking countries, the problems begin with the designation of the new English-language literature, as Schulte demonstrates. A term overcome today, but most common in the 1960s and 1970s is "commonwealth literature" (Schulte 77), the propagation of which Rushdie is opposed to, because it is nothing but "an exclusive Ghetto . . . a chimera . . . an unreal, monstrous creature of the imagination . . . It is also uncertain whether citizens of Commonwealth countries writing in languages other than English—Hindi, for example—or who switch out of English, like Ngugi, are permitted into the club or asked to keep out" (63). Further, the newer term "emergent literatures" describes inadequately with a similar neocolonial point of view a group of texts whose "physical emergence" goes back to the 1950s (Schulte 80).

The data from Anglophone countries are indeed highly complex and I try to come to grips with them with diverse constructions on the part of literary studies: since the independence of former colonial territories, we have been classifying works usually according to the cultural affiliation of the authors, such as Anglo-Indian for texts of authors of British origin who thematize India or British life in India, or Indo-English for the literature written by Indians in English. Likewise, African English literature for the texts written in English by African authors, with the North African Arabic treated separately (Schulte 77). In the US, scholars get rid of this problem with "minority discourses" and speak of Hispanic American, African American, Italian American literature, and so on. These designations, however, are problematic: they imply bilateral, well-defined cultural conditions and thus lose their validity as deliberately introduced constructs in processes of acculturation no later than the second generation. They work with generalizations, which, in view of the highly complex lingual and social structures of India, Africa, and Central America can only be described as negligent. They defictionalize the texts by privileging the biography of the author and neglecting the hybrid or syncretic literariness of the texts, which is characterized by intercultural dynamics. They prolong colonial, asymmetrical, center-periphery power relations and therefore are usually unacceptable classification drawers of Western origin for the authors themselves: "For many writers and other intellectuals, the issue is about . . . the revaluation of the local today, which we wish to be a non-marginalised part of a diverse global culture(s) landscape. This means that what is sought is no less than the 'constant balancing act between regionalisation and globalisation' that individually corresponds to the cultural psychological and therefore identificatory ambivalence of the postcolonial writers" (Schulte 85, 147).

English-language authors move with their texts beyond all potential English-based canon configurations, which have ultimately been initiated in a high degree by Goethe's idea of *Weltliteratur*—a clear misinterpretation of Goethe's idea (Schulte 116) with the fatal result of entire cultural circles being excluded from the canon of world literature by criteria of normative qualities. At the same time, we attest maneuvers into paradoxes such as in the case of the US: the status of an independent literature was awarded to US-American literature at the middle of the twentieth century. The natural use of the attribute "American" for US-American is also striking, against which mostly Latin American intellectuals protest (see, e.g., McClennen). Another paradox is the fact that the English-language literatures of Canada, Australia, New Zealand, and that of the US, strictly speaking, should also belong to postcolonial literature, but are rarely referred to as such, as if it were only a question of the life length of a literature: since duration cannot constitute any literary category, hegemonic constellations prolong themselves in such designations or nondesignations. It is for this reason that Schulte requires—correctly, I believe—that "the acceptance of different literary forms of expression as equivalent versions of cultural behavior in the framework of alternative processes of human (cultural) existence" and notes a displacement of the "framework of reference for canon formation" (119), given the now obsolete national claim to exclusivity in the quality and quantity of world literature. As a consequence, Schulte reaches a different interpretation of the concept of postcolonial literature: "Subjects and texts of Western ("national") cultures blend with structures and contents of African, Indian, Australian, or Caribbean traditions into a complex world literature. However, now not as an integral component of previously held concepts of a canon of world literature as the Western scholars wanted to define it in an occasionally closer relation of the two terms canon and nationality. Instead, now understood concretely as a literature, which uses the cultural potential of the 'world' as it presents itself syncretically and as a result of culture clashes in order to create new texts (culturally-regionally differently contextualized) out of them. Thus, other forms of cultural or literary 'authenticity,' other concepts of reality are developed than those which have been processed in nationally and culturally defined literatures or held importance in terms of national literature" (Schulte 147).

Schulte outlines a conception of world literature which I consider a preamble to the one presented here, as it is still not made tangible with specific key differences, yet it is clearly distanced from the selective and normative idea of a sum of monoculturally defined high brow literatures and includes an other on equal footing in this category, which differs in its forms, but does not differ qualitatively. This new configuration of literary texts and systems of literature finds expression in the syncretic aesthetic of the texts solidified into an unmistakable style, an aesthetic that is not the expression of a synthesis, but is emerging from the harsh impact of the incompatible. Thus, Bhabha sees in world literature, in the style of Goethe, "an emergent, prefigurative category that is concerned with a form of cultural dissensus and alterity, where non-consensual terms of affiliation may be established on the grounds of historical trauma" (*Location* 12). Accordingly, Bhabha advocates "that transnational histories of migrants, the colonised, or political refugees—these border and frontier conditions—may be the terrains of world literature" (12) and thus presupposes the continuous presence of a certain potential for conflict in this literature of the displaced. Dirk Hohnsträter emphasizes Bhabha's merit in that Bhabha broke "the Manichean model of intercultural discourse" and has captured "the emergence of a new type of world literature" (63). Further, Bhabha's theoretical innovation is located in the "replacement of the dialectical logic of identity by the deconstructive or in the broadest sense post-structural logic of hybridity" (Wägenbaur, "Hybride" 27). The acceptance of hybridity as a theoretical configuration involves a determined rejection of holisms and "it questions the need for a nationalist option, as well as the inevitability of a 'clash of civilizations'" and suggests instead "an acting out in the framework of political, social, cultural, and economic interests" (Turk 12) at the center of which always stands the "translated" individual who, according to Rushdie, could possibly win something through the translation: "having been borne across the world, we are translated men. It is normally supposed that something always gets lost in translation; I cling, obstinately, to the notion that something can also be gained" (*Imaginary* 17). Thus, hybridity provides a theoretical construct that organizes entities in "tendential unlimited diversity" and offers a "realistic, ideologically sub-loaded program" (Turk 12; on hybridity, culture, and globalization, see Kraidy).

To embrace the logic of hybridity altogether and subsequently to accept it as a theoretical configuration is undoubtedly an achievement of postcolonialism, understood at first as a descriptive category, thus being close to Beck's vision of cosmopolitanism and also interpreted as a term that rereads colonization "as part of an essentially transnational and transcultural 'global process'—and it produces a decentred, diasporic or 'global' rewriting of earlier, nation-centered imperial grand narratives" (Hall 247). Postcolonialism does not simply represent a periodization in terms of a time after colonialism, but "it marks a critical interruption into that whole grand historiographical narrative which . . . gave this global dimension a subordinate presence in a story which could essentially be told from within the European parameters" (Hall 250). Thus, it is ultimately an epistemological paradigm shift and as such it is interesting also for countries with no colonial past similar to that of the British or the Spanish empires. Postcolonialism means the "reconfiguration of the entire field, in which the colonial discourse flows" and thus it should be used, for example, for German-speaking countries, because it examines sociologically, culturally, and theoretically the "real-historical phenomena of the postmodern world—mass migration, global circulation of goods, services, signs, and information" (Bronfen and Marius 8; for a similar and earlier take on this, see Tötösy de Zepetnek, "Post-Colonialities"). In his definition of the postcolonial, Paul Michael Lützeler works out the "description-term and the programme-term" as dominant aspects, which would only rarely be used in a differentiated way and included in an analytical and operational modus operandi: "the theory of the postcolonial is about the development of the intellectual tools so as to (descriptively) allow both the acquisition of former and new colonial dependencies, as well as the (programmatical) abolition of these same dependencies in a sense of a decolonization" ("Von der Postmoderne" 10). Whereas the concept of postmodernity has had the opportunity to develop since the 1960s into a general concept of periodization through continuous enrichment from various discourses, postcolonialism—despite its interdisciplinary nature—represents primarily a literary theoretical configuration whose intention is to read the literature of minorities and foreigners from postcolonial aspects (see Lützeler, "Von der Postmoderne" 11). Lützeler's prognosis—that the discourse of postmodernity along with multiculturalism and postcolonialism will gradually lead to a discourse of globalism—has come true in my opinion: he perceives Bhabha's rediscovery of Goethe's *Weltliteratur* explicitly as a conceptual point of connection of the strong economically and sociologically weighted discourse of globalism to cultural and literary studies (16). Steinmetz sees the relationship chronologically reversed as he perceives "the versatile complex of postcolonialism as the result of a globalization originally emanating from the West" (198). Since in both cases we deal with scientific constructs, it is basically pointless to strive for an absolute "truth": the fact of reciprocity is obvious. Fernando de Toro draws a difference between postcoloniality as a "cultural term" and postcolonialism as a "historical term inscribed in various temporalities and sites" (55); both terms need to be thought of as processual and unfinished.

Toro postulates that we are in a general "post"era and he believes that we entered a "post-theoretical condition" composed of four components: "(a) the dissolution of disciplinary boundaries, (b) the simultaneous elaboration of theory from conflicting epistemologies, (c) the theoretical productions from the margins, and (d) the search for a 'beyond,' a third theoretical space" (40). He calls for a radical change of thinking in scholarship, which should finally adapt to the changed relations under globalism: "today, the scleroticism of academic institutions amounts to a crisis that announces either its end or a new beginning: change or die" (41). Theorists such as Spivak, Butler, Cixous, Said, and Bhabha have triggered an opening of thought and contributed to the new space of "post theory" by having analyzed every research subject from different sides and from different perspectives, where the subject matter as well as they themselves constitute nomadic subjects with lost contour sharpness (Toro 42; see also Moore-Gilbert 34–151). Consequently, de

Toro—based on Bhabha's thought—rejects not only the formerly clear distinction between theory and practice, that is, between fiction and reality, and locates himself in a space "beyond"—a third, future oriented space of posttheoretical performance that includes both the here and the there (51). However, he also locates himself in a "strong antinationalist, essentialist position," as only this allows him to comprehend the literature of world regions with massive (im)migration such as Canada, which beyond the binarism of French and English has long since exhibited all forms of hybrid literature that escape binary types of classification such as Asian English. In this way, he writes, we can at last begin with a "global literature" (70). Toro suggests that representatives of such literatures are, among others, Ondaatje, Rushdie, and Fuentes, thus including texts outside of the Anglophone world. In this context, however, Natalie Melas questions the idea of nonspecific comparison in postcolonial contexts, arguing that after a long tradition of Eurocentric exclusiveness, the undifferentiated comparison of interchangeable objects contains the risk of fetishizing equivalence. For Melas, the process of comparing in a globalized age is characterized, on the one hand, by a particular form of incommensurality, which on the other hand does not present an obstacle to discourse or understanding. On the contrary, for a certain reading of the postcolonial condition, incommensurability is the necessary premise for a world in a network of relation.

Nomadic texts by nomadic authors question the authority of the canons of national literatures and this results almost automatically and with increasing intensity, as the residents of the third world gain in numbers as well as political and economic importance (for a bibliography of Hispanic scholarship in the US, see Gewecke). In view of this, it is no surprise that in the 1990s in US-American scholarship was characterized by a struggle for a "correct" literary theory and for a US-American national literary canon. In order to somehow manage the complexity that emerged in the course of revalued minority discourses, scholars in the wake of the conservatism of the Reagan era took recourse to normative world literature categorizations, such as the representativeness of the culture of origin, authenticity regarding the represented culture, or even the degree of mimesis of political relations as aesthetic criteria, as was the case in the Bernheimer Report of the American Comparative Literature Association in 1993 (see Bernheimer; see also Pozuelo Yvancos and Aradra Sánchez 28). It need not be emphasized that such categorizations seem like a last rearguard action of a long bygone era, but they are based on the container model of definable cultures and on a concept of mimesis that is already long overcome. Nevertheless, the canon debate is illuminating from today's perspective, because its intensity documents the sense of crisis in the face of numerous "new" literatures that cannot be grasped with traditional theories and methods (see, e.g., Guillory). That the ideal of a humanist-influenced, universalist world literature is complicated is evident in the efforts, for example, of Cordelia Candelaria to include Chicana poetry in a nonclarified high brow world literature accessible to all readers because of its themes like nature, death, or love (175). Rafael Pérez-Torres also moves in the same direction by according to Chicano/a literature an emphasis on difference, but then subdues himself to a criteria of evaluation of the majority culture: "this opening to difference, however, serves primarily to position Chicana literature in a universal relation to all world literature" (25). However, the Bernheimer Report has set in motion a fruitful discussion on the definition of the position of comparative literature in the US that is by no means completed and in its course we can observe at least an orientation back to literary texts as the exclusive object of examination, in contrast especially to cultural studies; and a new acceptance of theory seems to be established, because "simplifications . . . are the real danger of the discipline" (Virk 9). At the same time, we can observe at least the intention for an opening of canons of world literature and attempts to anchor them with solid foundations in university curricula in order to reach an "idealistic thrust of world literature . . . towards a more pragmatic and real-world turn, and the consequent process of reconceptualisation" (Gupta 141). In this sense, Pascale Casanova, in her *World Republic of Letters,* with an insistence on a system of national literatures of European provenance, reproduces precisely the reductionist and Eurocentrist perspective against which it actually takes up. An innovative contribution to the discussion has been made by David Damrosch (see ch. 1). Nevertheless, owing to the uncertainty of a "culture of origin" as a point of departure, the problem of classifying and placing cultural or linguistically hybrid texts remains unresolved. Damrosch faces this problem in his didactically oriented *How to Read World Literature*, where, among others, he deals with works of Walcott, Rushdie, and Murakami as examples of a "multinational narrative in a 'globalized' mode" (121), but he does not engage from an aesthetic aspect of national literature, hybrid literature, and world literature. Thus, Damrosch—similar to John Pizer, Sarah Lawall, or Michael Thomas Carroll—contributes to the US-American searching for a suitable concept of teaching world literature courses. More than on a determined canon of world literature, they focus generally on a metatheoretical approach, teaching the students "how world literature has been variously defined, and how they might seek to define it," thus enhancing "their ability to grasp the sameness/otherness, local/universal dialectic many of us clearly wish to inculcate in our world literature courses" (Pizer 22).

It is mainly scholars working in cultural studies who turn against the dominant internalization of the values of hegemonic canons with a broadly defined, nonnational concept of culture and conceive of culture "as the non-totalizeable amount of the ways of life and institutionalized practices and forms of representation in the multicultural society of the late-capitalist and postcolonial or neocolonial present. What especially needs to be kept in mind is the criticism of the hegemony of the Euro-American canon of 'high brow' literature, and the increased legitimization of minority discourses and self-articulation of non-Western cultures" (Goebel 533). Across the boundaries of nation-states, "contact zones" (Pratt) are identified as spaces in which different cultures overlap with each other or fight each other, but in any case they interact and produce innovative third spaces or liminal zones, as for example, the Caribbean, the urban agglomeration of Los Angeles, or the Río Grande between Mexico and the United States (see Lüsebrink 234; see also Anzaldúa; Herlinghaus and Riese; Riese). The approximation to the art forms of these globally scattered borderlands (Anzaldúa) is performed in cultural studies where "African American Studies," for example, offers a paradigmatic approach because it addresses a culture of hybridity that could be characteristic of the entire US. Nevertheless, Günter H. Lenz notes that "the inter-relations between African Americans and other minority cultures have to be given more attention" (101). And this is precisely the crux of the matter, for as fruitful as the many case studies of Chicano/a, African American, Chinese American, or Native American literature are for the respective minority discourses, they are not viewed in relation to one another, but are seen in relation to the traditional "white" national literature. Through this kind of contextualization, cultural translation takes place only under binary signs, and minority literature remains in the position of the Other. If we operate with the theoretical configuration of postcolonialism by employing chronological components (see Ashcroft, Griffiths, Tiffin 7), then the "utilization of postcolonial theories for the description of Chicana literature and culture appears virtually impossible" (Ikas 32). For this reason, an opening of postcolonialism toward an interdisciplinary theoretical framework or frameworks is needed, because "each colonial situation is unique, yet common to all are the conquest and domination of one people by another and a dominant, monologic discourse whose employment is linked to violence" (Arteaga 75). Only with an all-embracing cosmopolitan vision aiming for synopsis will minority discourses be brought out of their marginal position, something that can be achieved in cultural studies and comparative cultural studies and less so in literary studies. In the same line, Rey Chow poses fundamental questions about the acquisition of expertise in the humanities and argues for a shift from Eurocentrism to Pacific-focused studies: "How have we come to write in the manner we do in the Anglo-American world of humanistic studies today? How might this condition of writing be assessed against the larger forces of cross-cultural encouenters and entanglements—specifically, since the end of the Second World War? What might we learn by juxtaposing area studies, poststructuralism, and comparative literature—academic spheres which seem to lead separate existences but whose developments are closely tied to postwar North America, in particular the United States?" (1).

Franco Moretti also moves toward interdisciplinary, although from a different point of view. In dealing with the theoretical configuration "world literature" versus "close reading" he demands "distant reading," because "it allows you to focus on units that are much smaller or much larger than the text: devices, themes, tropes—or genres and systems. . . . Less is more. If we want to understand the system in its entirety, we must accept losing something. We always pay a price for theoretical knowledge: reality is infinitely rich; concepts are abstract, poor. But it's precisely this 'poverty' that makes it possible to handle them, and therefore to know" ("Conjectures" 57–58; see also *Graphs*). Thus, Moretti stands close to Beck's "cosmopolitan vision" and near to the systems approach (on which this study is based): only with complexity management can the supposed chaos be structured and turned into a manageable theory configuration. In the attempt to generate an operational and functional system for contemporary world literature, Moretti argues that "after all, literature around us is now unmistakably a planetary system" ("Conjectures" 54), and this raises the demand for new methods of analysis.

The conceptual approach, to not read any more but to read according to different categories, is certainly worth supporting, but the results to which Moretti comes are doubtful, because despite his impressive empirical basis of "four continents, two hundred years, over twenty independent critical studies" ("Conjectures" 60), it seems audacious to me to postulate with respect to non-Western literatures something as Moretti does by saying that "when a culture starts moving towards the modern novel, it is always a compromise between foreign form and local materials" ("Conjectures" 60). Hence the deconstruction of Moretti's approach by Efraín Kristal with examples from Latin American literatures. Kristal rightly rejects the generalization "Western form plus local content" and shows the influence of the "periphery" (see also Prendergast). Moretti presupposes as self-evident the one-sided and logocentric influence from the center to the periphery. However, his findings are based on philological studies. I submit that these theoretical configurations are not effective because of their binary view for the hybrid text forms of the inhabitants of the third space. In addition, a too coarse-meshed "distant reading" has its own perils, as is evident from Moretti's response to the attacks on his theory: the claim that literary innovations often start from the "semi-periphery," then receive some "improvements" in the "culture industry of London and Paris," and eventually begin from there a triumphant procession around the world, which can be demonstrated on the example of the picaresque novel ("More Conjectures" 78). This bears witness to a fundamental ignorance of the historical contexts of this genre in individual countries and shows how problematic is the situation of a scholar who relies exclusively on the expertise of others. Distancing, synthesizing reading, yes, but maybe better in the context of one's own knowledge and power of judgement.

The debate about Moretti's ideas on world literature makes clear that the Anglophone academic world is engaged in sounding the depths of turbulent waters. We can observe an extraordinary boom of English-language publications about "world literature" during the last decade—as I point out in chapter 1—and this scholarship is located in the spaces between globalization, postcolonialism, the study of ethnic minority literatures, feminist and gender studies, and so on. Surely one can perceive, for example, with Mary Gallagher a "perfect congruency of globalization and cultural studies" (7), but the question might be allowed whether the whole discussion, rather than leading to new knowledge, blurs or even conceals the boundaries of the subject in question? When Deborah Weagel writes that *Women and Contemporary World Literature* will "examine ways in which women in literature function within their particular culture and circumstances to confront the challenges they encounter. With a focus on power, fragmentation, and metaphor, it illustrates how some women in various countries throughout the world have exhibited resilience and power" (1), starting with Sor Juana Inés in seventeenth-century New Spain, which understanding of which world literature offers a theoretical or empirical framework for this kind of research? At least, in scholarship like Weagel's or Gallagher's, the pretension of an equivalence between English-language literature and world literature seems to be put to rest. In 2002 Jonathan Arac titles his article "Anglo-Globalism?" with a question mark and asserts that philology and comparative literature based on a national language do not answer the questions raised by the "globality of world literature and the diminishing place of the nation-state in our times" (45). Even the supposed global dominance of English, which we initially found reflected in the concept of world fiction in English, is not true in such absolute terms and certainly does not provide descriptive criteria (see, e.g., Orsini). Postcolonial theory formation has certainly the merit of having modified perspectives and prompted new questions, especially in relation to processes of globalization, yet lately, in the light of a theory discussion that has become a debate about the debate, a certain disillusionment regarding the efficiency and applicability of this same theory is detected (see, e.g., Goldberg and Quayson). According to Moore-Gilbert, the "downbeat tone of the debate over the current state of postcolonial studies [reflects] a more widespread atmosphere of disillusion in contemporary cultural criticism," which, after all this interdisciplinarity and opening, leads in some cases once again to a return to the "virtues" of a traditional literature historiography (186). Yet, at the end the balance is positive, because "postcolonial theory has helped to establish areas of inquiry, conceptual frameworks and tactical procedures which are now in fact variously extended, challenged, or modified by a new generation of critics" (187). However, the call for more intensive comparative work resounds here as well: "much more work could also be undertaken in terms of comparisons between the Anglophone and non-Anglophone worlds, and in work between vernacular and metropolitan languages" (187).

Tötösy de Zepetnek, with his framework of comparative cultural studies since the late 1980s, offers a suitable way out of this maelstrom of different approaches with their insufficiencies and that compete against one another. He endorses interdisciplinarity, which with the help of expertise from cultural studies, comparative literature, and contextual (empirical and systemic) approaches seeks to answer the question "what happens to products of culture and how?" The declared intention behind Tötösy de Zepetnek's ten-point program and its applications consists of, among others, the premise that the field is built on the theoretical and methodological postulate

> on evidence-based research and analysis. This principle is with reference to methodological requirements in the description of theoretical framework building and the selection of methodological approaches. From among the several evidence-based theoretical and methodological approaches available in the study of culture, literary and culture theory, cultural anthropology, sociology of culture and knowledge, etc., the systemic and empirical approach is perhaps the most advantageous and precise methodology for use in comparative cultural studies. This does not mean that comparative cultural studies and/or its methodology comprise a meta theory; rather, comparative cultural studies and its methodologies are implicitly and explicitly pluralistic . . . The focus on English as a means of communication and access to information should not be taken as Euro-American-centricity.

In the Western hemisphere and in Europe but also in many other cultural (hemi)spheres, English has become the *lingua franca* of communication, scholarship, technology, business, industry, etc. This new global situation prescribes and inscribes that English gain increasing importance in scholarship and pedagogy, including the study of literature. The composite and parallel method here is that because comparative cultural studies is not self-referential and exclusionary; rather, the parallel use of English is effectively converted into a tool for and of communication in the study, pedagogy, and scholarship of literature. Thus, in comparative cultural studies the use of English should not represent any form of colonialism—and if it does, one disregards it or fights it with English rather than by opposing English . . . And it should also be obvious that is the English-language speaker who is, in particular, in need of other languages. ("From Comparative" 260-61)

In my opinion, the main achievement of comparative cultural studies consists of the refusal of an a priori hierarchy in cultural or literary systems: "To 'compare' does not—and must not—imply a hierarchy: in the comparative mode of investigation and analysis a matter studied is not 'better' than another. This means . . . that it is method that is of crucial importance in comparative cultural studies in particular and, consequently, in the study of literature and culture as a whole" (Tötösy de Zepetnek, "From Comparative" 259). Suman Gupta underscores Tötösy de Zepetnek's interdisciplinary approach by referring to the relevance of market mechanisms. For Gupta, the "constant flux" of any kind of "boundaries" has resulted not only in a transformation of the academic and institutional dealings with literary texts and literary studies that takes place in a transnational space of world literature, but "ultimately the relationship between globalisation and literature is arguably most immediately to be discerned not in terms of what is available inside literature and within literary studies, but in terms of the manner in which globalised markets and industries act upon and from outside literature and literary studies" (170).

As an example of a transnational, interdisciplinary, and evidence-based scholarship I refer to Seyhan's comparative study (see also above) in her *Writing Outside the Nation* on Chicana and Turkish German literature: "narratives which originate at border crossings cannot be bound by national borders, languages, and literary and critical traditions" (4). Sayhan's target is to verify theoretical propositions such as Bhabha's third space and analyses texts by Castillo, Anzaldúa, Özdamar, and Özakin. In her analysis Sayhan focuses primarily on linguistic drafts of cultural memory, because, in her opinion, the zone of overlapping and blending—conceived by Bhabha as a third space—is constituted in the texts of said writers (15). A "comparative literature of comparative literature" ultimately arises out of this typological comparison, as I postulate above, one that would bring formally and contentwise hybrid texts in relation to each other instead of contextualizing them with monolingual and more or less monocultural texts: "the juxtaposed reading of Chicano/a and Turkish German forms of cultural expression and intervention allows for a differentiated understanding of the critical linkages between local and global cultures and linguistic transposition, bilingualism, and reimagined nationalisms. I believe that comparative readings of texts of different cultural traditions offer an enhanced appreciation of their respective positions by allowing them to be reflected through another. This process of reflection and counterreflection also accentuates differences in historical course, critical agendas, and modes of expression" (Seyhan 17–18).

In principle, Seyhan's work could justifiably have been presented in the section on German-language hybrid literature and this shows once more the contingency and artificiality of monolingually founded criteria and underlines the need to find a different solution for the classification of texts I discuss. Now that I move on to some observations on Francophone countries, I proceed again in consciousness of the shortcomings of this method, because precisely in this area, in the example of the Caribbean, it will be established again that a philological division according to individual languages cannot do justice to the object of research. A junction between Anglophony and Francophony already exists in the fact that the one term is just as suspicious as the other and that "Francophony" as an operative category that illuminates a particular literary discourse has equally clay feet as "Anglophony" or "German intercultural literature." Francophony has many facets: from a linguistic point of view, the term designates the totality of French speakers; in a geographical sense, it refers to the territories in which French is the first or second language, the common or administrative language; as a designation of a cultural entity it alludes to the affinity of speakers of French in relation to common values and ideals; and as an institution it covers a variety of international organizations and associations (see, e.g., Tétu). As in the previously described cases of transnational linguistic areas, the synoptic concept of Francophone literature also raises more questions than it answers and is at best an *étiquette commode*: "what is there actually in common between the situation of the writer from Québec, who is divided between contemporary French, the Québec vernacular, and English, which is very close to that of the African novelist who has to translate the emotions of his/her mother tongue in another language, which, however, is national, between the writer of Belgium whose French is the 'natural' language, and the Caribbean divided between *Créole* and French as *lingua franca*?" (Gauvin 6).

According to Lise Gauvin, the "linguistic over-conscience" is the element unifying French-language authors, that is, a special awareness in dealing with language in a linguistically complex environment, which, in turn, prompts numerous varieties of poetic strategies from absolute transgression all the way to total integration (8). The underlying reason for this is the absence of the use of a single written language, as is obvious for more or less monocultural and monolingual authors. The Francophone writer must win his or her language in struggle again and again, because he or she does not write French, but "in" French (Gauvin 8). This conquest of the language takes place in heterogeneous and complex contexts from where only an aesthetic of diversity can ultimately result as represented by the proximity to carnevalesque and baroque forms and with recourse to resources "of the hybrid, the in-between, the mixing" (Gauvin 13). The Francophone author becomes the Francograph *littérateur(e)* who mixes together his or her individual language in a language laboratory with infinite possibilities. Generally speaking, the issue of language in Francophone discourse holds a prominent position. Gauvin's metaphor of a "tamed Babylon" takes into account the plurilingualism existing in Francophone countries, but at the same time indicates the mastery of this potentially anarchic state (10).

Eduard Glissant sees in the awareness of the diversity and multiplicity of languages a characteristic of the present: "I think that in Europe in the seventeenth and nineteenth century, even when a French writer knew English or German, they would still not take it into account in their writing. The writings were monolingual. Today, even when a writer knows no other language, they take into account, whether aware of it or not, the existence of these languages around them in their writing process. We can no longer write a language in a monolingual way" (qtd. in Gauvin 11; on Glissant see also, e.g., Bermann). Glissant conceives with great precision the entourage of writing under globalization conditions, under which the knowledge of the simultaneity of an infinite number of events and the similarity of geographically separated phenomena can hardly be blanked out, even when an author deliberately has a "monogamous relationship" with only one language, as Durs Grünbein put it regarding his own relationship with the German language (46). In contrast to the monolingually writing author, the "polygamous" relationship of the postcolonial writer is almost always problematic, as every language and every dialect represents a complex sociocultural system. Patrick Chamoiseau describes this conflictual linguistic situation with the concept of "schizophony," because the author is always split between the "dominant language" and the "dominated language" (62; see also Albert on the relation of language identity and identity history with examples from many Francophone cultures).

Similarly to the English-speaking and German-speaking areas, different stages can be also identified for the Francophony. In the first phase of colonization, the French colonial power had an interest in the creation of an Indigenous (African or Caribbean) elite which owed its social advancement to the colonial regime, and from this elite emerged the first Francophone literature, logically more or less in conformity with the system. In the second generation as well, when a first attempt for the formulation of an African or other Otherness is articulated, this takes place within the French perspective: "The founders of *négritude* ideology—Léopold Sédar Senghor, Aimé Césaire, and Léon Damas—were educated in the French colonial system and were more familiar with the French language than with the *Créole* of Martinique or the Senegalese Wolof. The birthplace of black francophone literature is Paris" (C. Miller 242). These are writers who—far from being residents of the "third space"— were alienated both from their society of origin and the colonization society and therefore formed more deterrent examples for later generations (see Kom). Chamoiseau notes that "manifesting its love and hate within the chosen confinement of a dominant language, *négritude* proceeded likewise in its celebration as well. That language was becoming the vehicle of novelty, the main weapon of the liberating movement. But it amplified with a halo the dominance that it preserved intact" (60). According to Chamoiseau this struggle with regard to dominance ends in folklore and in self-decomposition (71). The way of appropriation passes through refusal, eventually ends in the exploitation of the French language along with a *regard neuf* (94), and results in dominating, multiple languages to the emergence of which all possible languages offered their contribution: "I circulate in the languages that are offered to me" (169). This new language is implemented through the acknowledgment of the *créolité* that Chamoiseau celebrates as the solution per se: "the Other changes me and I change it. My contact with it stimulates me and I stimulate it. . . . And this relationship with the Other opens up to me an infinite number of relationships with all the Others, a propagation which establishes unity and power for every individual: Creolization! Creoleness!" (202). In this way, Chamoiseau is also giving a definition of the *mestizaje*, whose characteristic is that the Other is merged into the Self without the Self being renounced, that is, always being at the same time someone else and oneself (see Ette 500).

The Caribbean space, with its accented *antillanité* (Fendler 5), is a kind of exemplary paradigm within the French-speaking world in *métissage* and is particularly interesting for my topic, because it can be inserted into the theoretical configuration of both Americas as a gigantic testing ground for culture and language contact. Ette ascribes to the Caribbean all qualities of a nonhierarchical third space, in the sense of Bhabha, that presents itself as a new hope beyond the bipolarity of Africa with its anticolonial discourse and Europe with its colonial discourse (463, 513). There is absolutely no synthesis to be understood under this; on the contrary, the texts of the Caribbeans speak of the many conflicts along the fault lines of cultures and languages always running elsewhere, and *métissage* or *mestizaje* is mostly a concentration of differences always in struggle for a sensitive balance. Antonio Benítez-Rojo describes the Caribbean islands as a perpetuated chaos, a "black hole of social violence," as alterity par excellence: "The literature of the Caribbean can be read as a *mestizo* text, but also as a stream of texts in flight, in intense differentiation among themselves and within whose complex coexistence there are vague regularities, usually paradoxical. The Caribbean poem and novel are not only projects for ironizing a set of values taken as universal; they are, also, projects, that communicate their own turbulence, their own clash, and their own void, the swirling black hole of social violence produced by the *encomienda* and the plantation, that is, their otherness, their peripheral asymmetry with regard to the West" (Benítez-Rojo 27).

The French-speaking world with its chaos-related literary diversity is a challenge for the study of literature, yet the main task has always been to bring order into the apparent anarchy of texts by arranging them into manageable systems of genres and subgenres (Mura-Brunel 125). Nevertheless, there have always been works which escaped any classification or at least have made this more difficult. A case in point is Aline Mura-Brunel's work—about *oeuvres migrantes*, as she designates them, some of which she locates from the seventeenth century to today. However, she confines herself to monolingual texts as she focuses on themes and literary topoi. Still, she notes the need for a "coherent typology which provides the new text with a past, a destiny, therefore a sense" (133). In addition, she argues that "it is necessary to accept the birth of new genres and new modes of enunciation" (134), whereby she approaches the theory of the existence of an unprecedented kind of literary production, one that calls for a reorganization of fictional spaces and locations at a global level. According to Jean Bessière, this task can be performed only by comparative literature, because literature theory is always a work on a literatury text and simultaneously on its methods of analysis: "in literary studies passing from a national context to an international context, from a monolingual context to a plurilingual one, from one history of literature to multiple histories of literature, from a formalism which adheres to the dominant works of a given place at a given time, of a given literary school, and the like, to a formalism which adheres to many eras, many countries, many schools, does not eventually seek to suggest a certain essence of literature, certain definitional paradigms but to conceive the methods and the discourse which would be able to perceive the literary object within various realisations and situations of the literary object" ("Des Equivoques" 293).

According to Jean-Marc Moura, this challenge of the globalized present can be dealt with by "cultural studies, postcolonial criticism, mythology, reception studies, and research on the notion of literary space" ("L'Imagologie" 188; of note is that in French scholarship, in general, cultural studies is being discovered only in the last few years [see López-Varela Azcárate and Tötösy de Zepetnek]). According to Moura, cultural studies impart an operational basis that goes beyond the exploration of a national image and the awareness of cultural contexts which are not necessarily identical with the national. Moura's second point is most relevant for my project, namely, postcolonialism studies, that in his opinion pertain to a literature that should be classified by specific qualities of theme and form, whereby Moura stands at a short distance from the here-proposed major differences. As representatives of postcolonial literature he names those of the commonwealth, Lusophone, Francophone, and Hispanophone literatures and at the same time notes that so far little research work has been done on the postcolonialism grid regarding the Lusophone and Hispanophone literatures (189; on Lusophone literatures see Vieira, including a sizable bibliography). Much of the "cosmopolitan vision" is felt in this approach and he takes into account that a theory and methodology of literature that is still rooted in the nineteenth century is no longer able to do justice under conditions of globalization, for a literature typologically comparable in global standards needs to be confronted with globally operating examination methods, too.

Such transnational philological configurations are attested to more decisively in Bessière's work than in Moura's. First, Bessière refers to the foundations of Anglophone postcolonial studies in Francophone theorists from Fanon to Foucault, but he turns sharply against the option of comprehending Francophone literatures of whatever origin under a label such as world literature, because he sees in such a view a reduction of transnationally conceived works on the expression plane in the French language and as an inadequate, simplistic categorization of literature ("Littératures" 7–8). Moreover, the asymmetry in the center-periphery relationship as the only conceivable theory is questioned. Thus, Bernard Mouralis demonstrates by the example of African literatures in French that from the moment in which the French colonizers created a school system, the colonized were able to set against the colonial discourse their own discourse and to generate an Indigenous literature, in which both their own (oral, regional) traditions as well as innovative forms of European literature at the beginning of the twentieth century were processed. Through this interaction arose the *négritude* of the 1930s, for example, or the journal *Présence Africaine*, published in 1948, that together with a variety of African literary works exercised a strong influence on contemporary French intellectuals (Mouralis 17–21). The transition of the former colonies to, more or less, independent, demographically heterogeneous nation-states provokes—in the face of repressive regimes and economic misery—not only an enthusiastic support in the form of a strictly anticolonialist, anti-French, and pro-nation-state literature; on the contrary, the authors keep a critical distance and are unfortunately often themselves victims of the dictators (Mouralis 21–22). As for the 1980s and 1990s, Mouralis detects in many writers of African descent a new thematization of the colonial era, but not from the perspective of resistance; instead, he sees a historiographical balance within which French colonization represents only one major piece of the jigsaw on the total area of collective memory. The past is recontextualized and at the same time relativized: "Thus, the history of African literature may appear like a succession of questions concerning the type of domination which Africa was subjected to and the way Africans feel they are its inhabitants. In this succession, independence is an extension but also a rupture, since the territory that becomes independent is henceforth a national space whose dimension is considerably inferior, in most cases, to that of the huge political constructions put forward by the colonists" (Mouralis 25). In the light of this, Mouralis observes not only a reserved attitude of African writers toward national or pan-African appropriation, but also a general African and non-African internationalization of the works, which is thematically expressed in permeable boundaries and multiple centers (25).

Charles Bonn demonstrates similar trends in the literature of the Maghreb, which since the 1980 has given up its focus on resistance and anticolonialism in favor of steering toward other matters which are by no means apolitical, but bring along a widening of perspective. At the same time, the number of writers has multiplied and many new publishing houses have marketed and distributed the works of Maghreb writers in the French-speaking world. In particular, the "great ones"—for example, Assia Djebar, Mohammed Dib, Rachid Mimouni, and Tahar Ben Jelloun— are no longer seen as a group within minority literature, but their texts are of equal value next to the ones by important contemporary authors in France (Bonn 32–34). Nevertheless, this normality also involves a danger, namely, that of the philologization of the study of literature through categorization based on the linguistic expression plane. Glissant rejects this as an appropriation and a cancellation of the special element and sets a higher price on his identity as an inhabitant of the Caribbean, his *antillanité* that connects him to the Créolophones, Anglophones, or Hispanophones (see Gyssels 240). Therefore, Kathleen Gyssels proposes a shift of focus from the various linguistic realizations to the homogeneity of the texts from the Caribbean, the *créolité* which manifests itself as a common cultural heritage. In a further step, a Caribbean canon—qualitatively defined according to Chamoiseau—could be formed, which would enrich the world literature with aesthetically innovative works (Gyssels 250). That the Caribbean, in spite of all its heterogeneity, is seen as a single cultural space is evident from the literally exploding—since the 1990s—study of the Antillean Island world across the disciplines (Gyssels 252–54).

The fact that the transfer of analytical methods from postcolonial studies can be profitable in the case of some French-language literatures is now generally accepted. For example, Moura brings in the case of French-speaking Canada, Creolophone areas (the Antilles, Haiti, Guyana, Mauritius, Reunion, and the Seychelles), the regions of Africa with French as a lingua franca (French sub-Saharan Africa, Madagascar, the Maghreb, Lebanon), as well as territories of the former Indochina and the Middle East with French linguistic remnants (Moura, "Sur quelques" 165). The study of these literatures require close cooperation with scholars of postcolonialism in order to put their methods and results to use for the French-speaking world. For the rest, the differences between the Commonwealth and Francophony are bigger than their similarities, as in the Commonwealth—in contrast to the Francophony—the will for financial cooperation pushes the cultural aspect aside (see Tétu 235–47): "this way, there could be a hybridization of Francophone and Anglophone Studies before approaching the larger fields . . . especially of Lusophony and Hispanophony" (Moura, "Sur quelques" 165). According to Moura, such an interdisciplinary approach would have the decisive advantage of being more fair to these new literatures (166). Rushdie points to the same direction when he opposes the category of Commonwealth literature, which, in his opinion, denotes a narrowing and depreciation of "English literature" and "is a topographical, nationalistic, possibly even racially segregationist" concept (63). Albeit a certain delay in postcolonial, gender, or cultural studies in French-language scholarship, these fields are now being paid attention to in general and in comparative literature in particular (see Tomiche). Interdisciplinarity in the study of hybrid literatures is relevant because the realization that transnational literatures cannot be approached with methods of traditional philology has become obvious.

The Iberian colonial empire of the sixteenth century evolved over time in different directions: after the Latin American wars of independence of the nineteenth century, the Spanish empire was virtually at the brink of destruction with the loss of Cuba, its last colony, in 1898, but Portugal was involved in bloody battles in Angola and Mozambique until the Carnation Revolution of 1974. In 2000 Portugal returned Macao to China and was involved in the conflicts over East Timor up to recently. In this respect, the colonial history of Spain temporally lies, in contrast to Portugal, relatively far back, so that in the case of Spanish America we can no longer speak of a postcolonial relationship with the "mother country," just as in the case of the United States and the United Kingdom. Portugal, however, comparably to France, carries up to the present the burden of accounting for colonialism. However, the

larger Iberian area not only holds a special position in relation to the previously discussed cases in terms of colonial past, it also exhibits—unlike the German-speaking
regions, France, Great Britain, and Portugal—a long-standing tradition in dealing
with cultures of alterity, religions, and languages. As is well known, Jewish, Arabic
Islamic and Christian forms of culture were present in Spain in changing asymmetric
relations from 711 (e.g., the arrival of the first Berber military forces from Morocco)
to the expulsion of the last *moriscos* in the seventeenth century. The process of elimi-
nation of the medieval coexistence of three cultures that resulted in a unified Spain,
especially in the eighteenth and nineteenth centuries, was gradually dragged to the
surface only in the second half of the twentieth century by authors exiled under the
Franco regime, such as Américo Castro or Juan Goytisolo.

This denial of perception is all too evident in the light of the third feature of
Spain: while France and Great Britain were almost homogeneous in comparison to
Spain at the moment of their appearance as colonial powers, centrally administrated
states with a clear nation-centered cultural program, Spain always had to fight with
the opposition of the so-called "historic nations" of Catalonia, the Basque Country,
and Galicia. In the post-Franco Constitution of 1978 the official status of the Catalan, Galician, and Basque languages was established next to the Castilian or Spanish,
and not a few also wanted to see the Andalusian dialect and the Asturian as separate
languages enshrined in the Constitution. In any case, the democratic, federal Spain
has, since 1978, offered an interesting test case in the practice of accommodating
behavior, namely, "the acceptance of linguistic diversity and the recognition of otherness as one of the characteristics of modern-day Spain" (Hooft Comajuncosas 42).
We should, of course, add that this acceptance of the plurilingual reality by no means
implies an actual equality of the four languages at all levels, as the other three official
languages, despite government support policy, have not grown economically in the
Spanish cultural market and, especially, the book market that operates globally in all
Spanish-speaking countries, but also in the US or Canada, with a public that reaches
millions (see García Canclini). Thus, the result of an investigation on the situation of
peripheral systems of culture in Spain is hardly surprising: Catalan, with its ten million speakers and a literary tradition that goes back to the early middle ages, can hold
its ground at best next to the Castilian, and it also is the language with the most translations into Castilian, but there is no translation activity of the minority languages
among one another and this demonstrates the fixation on the majority language with
the more lucrative market (Hooft Comajuncosas 70).

Linguistic relations within Spain, in comparison to countries such as Germany and France, are complex from institutional, social, cultural and historical perspectives: a high percentage of the population is bilingual or plurilingual. However,
González-Millán rightly cautions against examining literature as a form of cultural
practice only as a "slavish manifestation of social reality" and instead he calls for an
interdiscursive approach that focuses on "its active [i.e., the literature's] participation to the organisation of social relations," and therefore examines "literary production as a means of articulation, representation, and appropriation of social relations

together with other institutional agents and the corresponding discursive formulas"
(16). The importance of the interaction of literary discourse with other discourses is
evident, for example, in the function of the Catalan inferences in the Castilian Car-
valho series detective novel by Manuel Vázquez Montalbán: the Catalan insertions
in his earlier works such as *Los Mares del Sur* (1979) most notably indicate social
differences between the wealthy Catalan bourgeoisie and the marginalized Andalusian immigrants, so this polarization resolves itself with an increasing "normaliza-
tion" of Catalan as the first language and is replaced by an ironic narrative attitude
to both groups of speakers since no subversive (anti-Franco or anti-hegemonic) or
social indicator function is any longer assigned to the use of Catalan in the 1990s
(see Sturm-Trigonakis, "Großstädtische" on the language as an identity marker; on
the urban novel of Barcelona in Castilian and Catalan, see Sturm-Trigonakis, *Barcelona*). Catalan as a literary minority language has lost its former role as a counter-
discourse through the consolidation of its institutional and sociocultural status. In
the case of the Galician dialect as well, González-Millán comes to the conclusion
that the use of Galician alone in contemporary literature guarantees "neither the reli-
ability of the representation of the Galician reality nor its efficiency as an act of appropriation" (22). Instead, since the 1980s there is a "multiplication of the new forms
of representation" and "the relative diversification of the appropriation modi of Galician literary discourse" that is "an important indicator for the examination of the
hypothetical entry into a new phase of its institutionalization" (González-Millán 24;
on matters Galician see also Vilariño Picos and Abuín González). The widespread
criticism of a literature that previously preferred typical Galician rural settings and
now produces bestsellers with forms of the crime novel or of women's literature
demonstrates that the transition from the declared "resistance literature" of minority
subalterns to the commercialized and mass-produced book is not readily acceptable.
Given the general democratization in the sense of a "diversification of the producer
and the recipient community," and the increasing commercialization and technologi-
zation, González-Millán calls for a "radically new literary discursive logic," which
will take into account the interaction of these parameters (37).

This discourse change could, with the help of the postcolonial perspective
gain in depth and this is also the reason for the above undertaken analysis of intra-
Spanish relations. On the one hand, a radical settlement with the Iberian colonial and
neocolonial tradition has taken place in the Castilian language since the 1960s in
the work of Goytisolo by a favoring the displaced Jewish Islamic heritage, a settlement that can be analyzed with the methods of Anglo-American postcolonialism
(see Armbruster 227). On the other hand, "a repression of collective identity designs
in favour of the textual registration of an individual alterity awareness" can be established in the literary production of Galician, Catalan, and Basque contemporary
authors (Gómez-Montero, "Ambivalenzen" 334). This registration is also the characteristic feature of the hybrid forms of literature discussed here. The subaltern writing against a hegemonic power, such as Castile, or a colonial "mother country" like
Britain has been replaced by a self-evident coexistence of nonhierarchized "nodes of

ences. In accordance with globalism theorists like Giddens and Beck, García Canclini detects a significant transition from postmodernity to globalization in the 1990s, which on the one hand has created global goods markets, money, communication, and (im)migration, has made national borders insignificant in many areas, and in addition to the traditional mixed zones of commerce and politics has advanced the hybridization of the cultural sector. On the other hand, it has provoked new lines of division, inequality, and an accentuation of local particularities. A world in which local traditions—from the Bavarian sausage to the Argentine tango—can ubiquitously be registered in global relations, can be dealt with only with new questions, as the old dichotomies of global complexity—between McDonaldization and retreat to Macondo—are no longer appropriate. How, for example, can we still think in national concepts, when a fifth of Mexicans and a quarter of Cubans live in the US, Los Angeles is the third largest Mexican city, and Buenos Aires the third largest Bolivian city? At the same time, such figures expose the stereotype of the "nomadic planet," because the approximately 130 to 150 million people who migrate each year to other countries are only 2.3% of the world's population (see García Canclini). In view of these relations, complexity management begins—as Reinhold Görling claims—with the fact that there is a "clear [difference] between a real diversity of cultural forms and the processes of producing cultural difference" (Görling 162). It is not just that the nations are "imagined communities" (Anderson), globalization also runs the risk of becoming again Lyotard's long unmasked "grand narrative" as an "imagined globalization," as García Canclini calls it.

As far as the Portuguese case is concerned, I begin from different premises than Spain. First, the Arabic presence in Portuguese territory was less intense than in Spain, as already at the end of the twelfth century the *Reconquista*—the reconquest of the land by the Christians—had been completed and so a relatively peaceful coexistence of the Jewish, the Muslim, and the Christian populations followed. Around the middle of the thirteenth century the region was "turned into a homogeneous, national Portuguese entity" (de Oliveira Marques 108; see also Zimmermann), that is, to the formation of a sense of a national common identity. With the Spanish domination of Portugal between 1580 and 1640 this awareness of the Portuguese nature was reinforced in order to distinguish it from the larger and ever-threatening neighbor Spain. In the fifteenth century the Portuguese began their maritime expeditions that bestowed on small Portugal a vast colonial empire. Thus the course of Portugal's colonial history differs in a remarkable way from the history of Great Britain or France, a difference whose negative consequences are reflected until the present day in literary production. I emphasize the important global role of the Portuguese language, which occupies the sixth or seventh place on the list of most spoken languages (Kuder 37). Portuguese is the official language not only in Portugal and Brazil, but also in Angola, Mozambique, Cape Verde, the islands of São Tomé e Príncipe, and the small state of Guinea-Bissau, and it is also used in Asia in Macau, Goa, and East Timor: "it is remarkable that such a small nation . . . was able to transfer their language to about 200 million people" (Kuder 34). Since 1996, following a Brazilian initiative, these countries have been united in the *Comunidade dos Países de Língua Portuguesa* which in practice pertains less to the cooperation at a linguistic-cultural level than it does to economic and political issues, particularly of the African member countries (see Baum; Kuder). The term *lusofonia* is relatively recent: it appears for the first time in the 1960s in a Portuguese dictionary and reflects, just like the terms Francophony and Hispanophony, the idea of a culture and community of values based on the common language (see Baum 99).

Unlike France or Britain, in the nineteenth century Portugal was not in a position to "build a social and economic structure in its African overseas territories which would have made them competitive in comparison with other European powers" (Graf 67). Apart from Lisbon's lack of political interest in efficient administration, this was in large part owing to the fact that immigrants from Portugal in the nineteenth century usually came from the uneducated and poor population strata or were prisoners and exiles, while the industrialized countries England, France, and Germany sent "intellectual and technical management staff" for the systematic exploration and exploitation of the colonies in the African overseas territories (Graf 70). In the 1930s the ideology of *lusotropicalism* appeared, propagated by the Brazilian sociologist and anthropologist Gilberto Freyre, as a "Portuguese separate path" of the peaceful coexistence of different ethnic groups and cultures, over the course of which the superior Portuguese civilization should be brought to the African territories "over the 'biological process of assimilation' and the 'sociological process of cultural symbiosis'" in order to produce there similar successful "lusotropical" societies such as in Brazil (Graf 68). This myth of the happy coexistence of the African (and American) people with the tolerant Portuguese served as a justification of the colonial regime under the Salazar dictatorship up to the 1960s (Graf 68). A significantly negative factor for the development of a literary tradition was the generally low level of education in the African colonies of Mozambique, Angola, Guinea-Bissau, Cape Verde, and São Tomé e Príncipe. Since 1953 the African territories had been organized in a two-class society, headed by the *assimilados* with Portuguese citizenship. The *assimilados* used the Portuguese language orally and in writing, accepting Portuguese culture and thus leaving the traditional tribal association. This restrictive policy resulted in the 1960s in an illiteracy rate of 97 percent in Angola, 98 percent in Mozambique and nearly 100 percent in Guinea-Bissau (see Kuder). The situation was slightly better on the Cape Verde islands, with a rate of 78.5 percent (see Laranjeira). Regarding the reading habits of the colonial society, Pires Laranjeira draws a depressing conclusion:

> The black population of the Portuguese colonies almost didn't read newspapers—not to mention literature. The literary texts actually read were only those that the "assimilated" had access to in school, without any continuity in literary reading that could mean a reading public of European texts. Much less could one consider, within this context of such cultural paucity and clear European preponderance, the existence of a hypothetical public formed in an African taste, that would have effectively had access to Afri-

can texts (and of all aesthetics, languages, and peoples) . . . For the colonists (or better yet: for their children, who could, in fact, continue their studies) or the civil servants and transient workers, African or black literature could not be of interest because it presented itself as a body foreign to their sensibility and comprehension. (26-27)

The low level of education meant that in the linguistically heterogeneous colonial territories of Africa the Portuguese language could not play to the same extent the identity-establishing role of a lingua franca as English or French did in Nigeria, Kenya, and Senegal. São Tomé e Príncipe and Cape Verde were the only colonies where a Portuguese-based Créole, used by everyone, was produced in the nineteenth century and has now become the national language (see Chabal 6). In addition, the much-cited influence of the metropolis on the few educated people naturally turned out to be more restricted in the case of Lisbon than in world cities like Paris or London, especially because the repressive Salazar regime with its strict censorship of the press managed to survive as far as the Carnation Revolution in 1974 and thus all intellectual opening was successfully obstructed.

According to Patrick Chabal, the historical context of Portuguese colonialization is characterized by five differentiating factors: "1) The distinctiveness of the Creole island cultures of Cape Verde and of São Tomé e Príncipe; 2) the poor colonial integration, uneven economic development and the complex racial and social mix of Angola and Mozambique; 3) the social and cultural impact of the regime of the Portuguese dictator Salazar (the *Estado Novo*, or New State) on the African colonies; 4) the dynamics of nationalism, the effect of the war of liberation and, for Angola and Mozambique, of the 'civil' wars which followed; and 5) the impact of outside cultural, intellectual and literary influences on the development of the literatures of Lusophone Africa" (12–13). Brazil, on the other hand, since its independence from Portugal in 1822, has walked a steady path to becoming a successful nation-state, and with its modernist and regional neorealistic literature has exerted a great influence since the beginning of the twentieth century on emerging African literatures, where Brasilianisms encouraged African authors to let local structures and words flow into their Portuguese: "many writers from Portuguese-speaking Africa explicitly acknowledged their debt to Brazilian literature and stressed how relevant that model had been for their own literary quest" (Chabal 27). Although such schemes are necessarily simplistic, Chabal's chronology on the various stages of Lusophone African literature gives a good overview: "assimilation, resistance, assertion, and consolidation" (10) characterize in his opinion the main phases of development whereby this scheme is also applicable to Francophone or Anglophone literatures or generally true about writing under colonial and postcolonial conditions. In a similar way, Gerhard Schönberger draws a difference for Mozambican literature between a first, European-influenced phase (1925 to 1945–47) and that of the "literary return (1945-47 to 1964)," which is replaced by the "anticolonial and nationalist-revolutionary literature (1964-1975)," and finally leads to the ongoing "phase of the national literature since independence (from

1975)" (293). For it is logical that the educational system imposed by foreign rulers leads initially to an adjustment to discursive configurations in literature. *Négritude* is a classic example of this type of assimilation. It is just as inevitable that resistance will follow "hand in hand with nationalism and the struggle for independence" and in Lusophone Africa this led to a conscious rejection "of metropolitan values and a deliberate attempt to redeem African culture" (Chabal 11). The third phase begins with independence and can either bring along the autonomous self-assertion of the artist as a creative individual or a search for the repositioning in the postcolonial context, the latter often going hand in hand with a critical examination of the new rulers. In the fourth phase "there comes a period when writers feel secure, even if not safe, in their position as writers and become concerned above all about the consolidation and future development of literature in their country. That is not to say that writers are self-consciously working to affect the evolution of the 'national' literature—although some are—but rather that what matters to them is their place in that literature in the world. In other words, their concerns are the concerns of writers the world over" (Chabal 11).

Given the colonial history of Lusophone Africa, it is not surprizing that the literatures of these young nation-states are concerned especially with the processing of the past and an intensive search for an own literary discourse that reconciles the present with the African oral tradition. Therefore I think it is not appropriate to compare the successful Mozambican writer Mia Couto to Rushdie, as Chabal undertakes: he sees in both of them "a writer of modern literature who is steeped in a non-Western culture" (85). This statement is certainly true as a lowest common denominator—and it would be for almost every postcolonial writer—but it does not capture the reality of the individual texts. For where Rushdie, for example in *The Satanic Verses* or *East, West,* creates linguistically hybrid forms and thematically and structurally transforms both transnationalism and local solidarities and traditions, Couto positions at the heart of his work the collective search for identity of the Mozambican society that is traumatized by foreign dominion, bloody wars, and repression in the name of communism (see Chabal 81; Laranjeira 312; Schönberger 189). Couto's concern is not the stretching of a third space in which hybridity can develop playfully, parodistically, and yet autonomously. Rather, he is defiant, and it is exactly for this reason that his syncretic reconfiguring of different literary discourses seems to overcome the confines of national literature. This seemingly inevitable scrolling through various stages of development is present in David Brookshaw's representation of the Cape Verdean literature that looks back to a tradition and remains up to the nineteenth century: "that rootedness in an area has given way to a desire for rootlessness" (204). Following this view, Klaus-Dieter Ertler in his study on the "differentiation of peripheral regions" of the Romanic "-phonies" (297) presents as an example of Lusophone texts of the author Sergio Kokis, an expatriate from Brazil to Québec, who processes his Brasilianity especially in his first two novels, written in French, *Le Pavillon des mirroirs* (1994) and *Negão et Doralice* (1995). Kokis works not only thematically, but he also assimilates "inter-textual or

trans-textual borrowings from the Brazilian and Latin American literature classification" and so arrives at a "fictionalization of Lusophony in a foreign form" (Ertler
409), a strategy of cultural hybridization practiced, for example, by Özdamar in the
German-speaking space with great success.

Chapter Three

New World Literature and a Systemic Organization of Hybrid Fiction

In humanities scholarship there has been much discussion with regard to reality and its images; while the former has by no means been objectifiably revealed, the latter are thought of only as a staging of cultural practices at a given time. Nevertheless, the relationship between the two components is not dichotomous per se; rather, it can be described with the words of Günter Abel as "revolving door-like," where "any individuated and specific reality is always constituted in signs and conditioned by interpretation; any substantial and non-accidental experience is always an experience of reality" (13). Abel believes that "our signs, our spirit, and our experience deal directly with reality and relate directly to it" and thus the talk of a basically deficient relation between sign and reality, or of a "gap" between the two that has to be overcome is absurd (13). On this premise, he notes that in the current era of the globalization process we "are confronted with new problems and urgent challenges, for which we have as yet developed no mechanism of appropriate and orientating reacting and acting" (59). When faced with a radically different social and cultural situation compared to the 1960s and 1970s, the question of the nature of literary production and its study arises afresh, because scholarship is no longer interested in the supposedly objective approach to the object of study. Literary studies have lost their innocence, their boundaries have become blurred, the objects of their observation present themselves in previously unprecedented diversity and escape the established methods of analysis. Given this diagnosis, it is time to modify the therapies, and this can only happen if we apply interdisciplinarity to sharpen the eye for comparable phenomena in other fields. I confront the weariness with theory by undertaking on the following pages an excursion into systems theory in order to provide a basis for the drawing up of the category NWL.

Elisabeth Beck-Gernsheim's description of the situation is applicable to literary studies: next to the more or less monocultural and mononational mainstream society, we now live in "increasingly and rapidly growing groups whose basic experiences are structured differently, meaning that they are stretched between many different countries, cultures and centres"; consequently, they move in a "transnational system of coordinates," one that cannot be processed with a monocultural and mononational perspective (17). Now, this negative assessment is certainly too bold and not entirely accurate, as the systemic frameworks of Niklas Luhmann (sociology), Siegried J. Schmidt (literary and media studies), and Itamar Even-Zohar (literature and translation) have long bid goodbye to the national homogeneous "container paradigm of literature" (Drechsel, Schmidt, Gölz 6; among the several US-American books about world literature and systems, see the recent books of *On Literary Worlds* [Hayot] and *Against World Literature* [Apter]). The fact that the mononational outlook offers no adequate reference system for many literary texts I have demonstrated in the preceding chapter. In my opinion it is worth applying sociology and systems theory—not in order to functionalize the literary texts, but for a recovery of hybrid literature.

The applicability of systems theory for literary studies is based on the fact that it contains a social component that has been lost following the deconstructive approach. And compared to the "monolithic postulate of a cultural poetics," it offers the advantage of conceiving subsystems of society with functional differentiation, such as those of literature and art (De Berg 137). The transfer of Luhmann's, Schmidt's, or Even-Zohar's operative methodologies is of less relevance compared to the thought configurations of their followers, because the propagation of system theoretical knowledge sharpens the search for the similarity of problems in crisis-ridden literary studies (see, e.g., Van Peer, Hakemulder, Zyngier). We cannot deny that—as the construction of supposedly self-contained nation-states has become obsolete—internally homogeneous "power containers," national-philological literature studies, or a combination of them, as comparative studies, can also no longer adequately analyze former national-literary defined spaces. Therefore, Beck's "cosmopolitan outlook" as a cognitive schema is useful, as it allows the perception of spaces of action and strategies which the national vision does not allow. According to Beck, the national and the cosmopolitan outlook should not be regarded as mutually exclusive either/or perspectives, but as both/and configurations, as he claims for the policy of second modernity. Beck's theory allows the perception of the problem field as such, but in a further step the problem posed must be descriptively addressed before we can attempt to find solutions. In the present case, the "cosmopolitan outlook" has directed attention to the existence of transnational or hybrid forms of literature and the issue now is to build a theoretical framework that will allow us to identify the specific nature of these texts and configure a category for them. To this end I draw on Nassehi's theory of closedness versus openness with which he tries to overcome the conventional "ontological knowledge paradigm . . . of the observer-independent existence of a being" and thus paradoxically opens "thinking spaces" which "point to closedness" (*Geschlossenheit* 32). Nassehi understands his concept as a test of the "system theoretical design at a case of application . . . a kind of field test" that demonstrates "that the theoretical form of systems theory can gain all forms of openness, from connectivity, construction of forms, world perspectives, and the like only from the special perspectives of concrete operational closedness" (*Geschlossenheit* 14). This theoretical configuration is the justification for the drawing up of NWL, which at a first glance may be obsolete in the face of already existing ones, such as postcolonialism, national literature, or intercultural German studies, but on closer inspection is revealed in the facts that, first, it closes a gap in the established theory structure and second, that thanks to its operative closedness it remains open for the other configurations and offers log-in spots. The concept of system is initially based only on the interrelation of the separate elements among themselves (Nassehi, *Geschlossenheit* 65), where system building "always [takes place] from below," and must "derive upgraded category-performances from the accumulation of real-time events, which means that it must derive them empirically and not simply presuppose them" (*Geschlossenheit* 163). Starting from this idea I draw up the NWL as a category on the basis of empirical, differentiating theoretically obtained data.

The category of NWL I attempt to establish is not to be thought of as a homogeneous and stable system, just as the term "society" in Nassehi is nothing more than "the initially disorderly, chaotic, anything but 'conscious,' unplanned and in real-time operating entirety of all possible social actions, communications, processes" (*Geschlossenheit* 162). According to Luhmann and Schmidt, society is based on communication and as such it should be thought of as a globalized form of the social (see also Willke, *Atopia*). This does not mean homogenization, but the "radicalism of social and cultural inequalities and the explicit non-uniformity of living conditions as a contingent social phenomenon . . . on the floor of a worldwide process of differentiation" (Nassehi, *Geschlossenheit* 163, 214). Globalization plays here more the role of a "cognitive schemata" than concrete reality (*Geschlossenheit* 197) and it refers to the "process of intensification and dynamization of the social processes in the global social context, which eliminated neither spatial nor social boundaries, but rather provoked them" (*Geschlossenheit* 196). These considerations perhaps have given rise to more *aporiae* on the inevitability of this theory design than eliminated the doubts. A fundamental feature of the systems approach is its high awareness of its inherent contingency, "that the classification of a system could turn out this way or the other" (Willke, *Systemtheorie* 3: 256). In principal, systems are created if two conditions are met: "When, on the one hand, through the creation of borders opposite the chance of contingent events in the world, islands of reduced arbitrariness or partial order are created, and on the other hand, when the relations between the circumscribed parts cannot be fully realized for reasons of time and therefore, according to a particular search pattern, only certain selective relations are preferred between the parts" (Willke, *Systemtheorie* 3: 256).

Helmut Willke designs a third option—*heterotopia*—as an expression of the "crisis of classification of modern societies" and thus complements his description of atopic society with its crisis in global knowledge as *dystopia* with its transnational "lateral world systems" (*Atopia* 136). These he defines as "functional systems of the traditional nation-state limited society" that "grow into global relevance" by transnational interdependence. He names as examples "organised crime, . . . transnational institutions and organisations in fields such as commerce . . . sports . . . globally outreaching university systems . . . media companies, operators of satellite networks, global information agencies such as Reuters" (*Atopia* 136–37). It is characteristic of these systems that they have arisen in recent years with a tremendous dynamic and that they escape any nation-state control. In *dystopia* Willke diagnoses dynamic chaos as a normal state of the globalized world and proposes solutions for managing highly complex systems in the form of a "post-trivial, federal class," an "elaborate ramble walk on the seam line between the dynamic imbalance and chaos" (*Heterotopia* 36). His theoretical configurations are directly transferable to the problem posed here: if we place hybrid forms of texts as a dystopia of an already atopic society, we can configure them again as a category using the heterotopic construction of system. A presupposition for this is the acceptance of disorder, which has already been for Theodor W. Adorno a *conditio sine qua non* of artistic forms of representation: "The task of art today is to bring chaos into order" (qtd. in Willke, *Atopia* 71). In line with this, I claim that the task of immigration, migrant, and similar "minority" literatures is to bring chaos into the neat categories of national canons and national literatures and further into established national philologies. Willke's theory is to generate "chaos in the sense of an orderly resolution of order and thus in terms of a transition to a new order, the special feature of which should be to be competent in dealing with heterotopia. The chaos itself is already there. It is waiting to be furnished with a structure and linked to a new form of order" (*Heterotopia* 255). But the question is not to generate order as a "light" version and to subject the highly complex system of hybrid literatures to trivialization. The case is, rather, that "only dramatically improved theories, models, and tools of dealing with irreducible heterogeneity and uncertainty help against the hyper-complexity of systems" (*Heterotopia* 255).

It may be a truism that any form of scientific knowledge production is involved in a social and historical process and is therefore characterized by contingency: "science now appears like the other aspects of social life also as a cultural artefact, the *a priori* privileging and context-independent validity of scientific knowledge is contested," as Eberhard Berg and Martin Fuchs stress in the introduction to their book on the "crisis of ethnographic representation" (16). In this sense, it is the meta-scientific intention of this book to make a few brief reflections on the relation between the position of the observer and the object of research, so that "the object of observation does not just come up for discussion, but actually comes to speak itself" (Willke, *Atopia* 212). For literary and media studies, "objects, themes, [and] environments" exist only for the observer, who constitutes them by means of "differential management as meaningful entities"; moreover, these objects do not exist simply in the ontological sense, but form phenomena, "that is, observer functions and time-bound results of empirically conditioned, sensorimotor, cognitive, and communicative processes" (Schmidt 35). Hence the consequence that literary scholars do not speak about texts, but about "socio-culturally conditioned observer problems when experiencing literary phenomena in literary defined social situations" (Schmidt 35). In other words, when we bring this down to the common denominator, "it is not the text that means, has effect, says, etc., but we ascribe texts (out of good sociocultural reasons and by no means arbitrarily) to interpretations . . . The texts are not sorted into canons; instead the observers rank the texts in alternating hierarchy positions" (Schmidt 42).

Nassehi suggests that the "self-referentiality of the inquiring gaze" even with supposedly objective research results based on empirical observation (numerical data, polling, etc.) exists as a modeling of reality and not a "reflection of a factual reality" (*Geschlossenheit* 31). Thus, knowledge does not stem from objectifiable facts, but always has its origin in "interpreted observations" which "are based on the processing of differences" and are an "internal operation of the observing system," where selection and perception of the differences are again observer dependent (Willke, *Systemtheorie* 3: 253). Ever since Luhmann, "observation and self-reference" have been the two pillars of systems theory thinking (Willke, *Atopia* 116) and the awareness of this constellation is useful also for my presentation of the problem. In order to avoid phenomena of triviality during research, "the one who sees only the objects does not observe wrong, but sees only the trees and not the forest" (Willke, *Atopia* 115). My goal is to describe the functioning of the forest, at least by approximation, and this must be specified through the position of the observer and the knowledge standpoints neighboring it as an observation in the second degree or an observation of the observation with simultaneous and equal observation of the object of study, in this case the hybrid texts, where the observation in the first degree depends directly on the capabilities of the observer.

Knowledge is created when "observers in a communicatively constituted and communicatively mediated social practice meaningfully bring data and information into a meaningful context," which consists in the "confirmation or revision of an existing practice or in the creation of a new practice," where "practice" is an "ensemble of social practices," "that serve the accomplishment of a concrete task" (Willke, *Dystopia* 22). In compliance with its embedding in concrete sociocultural contexts the resulting knowledge is time bound: "knowledge is knowledge only for a particular time" (Willke, *Heterotopia* 324). This reduction of knowledge to a temporal dimension makes up a good part of its inevitable contingency and leads to ever changing and fruitful readings (i.e., new interpreted observations) of the same (old) texts in literary studies. On the other hand, it illustrates the futility of literary study. Maybe this is positive, but in the incompleteness and absence of "absolute truths" there is also an opportunity for improving and revealing so far unimagined perspectives. One of the connection points between systems theory and literary studies is that scientific practice has nothing to do with problem solution and identities, but with the constituting of phenomena and problems by observation, that is, with differences, as any constitution of objects ensues "by means of distinctions and definitions" (Schmidt 34). The temporal sequence is of crucial importance, because "we cannot make an indication without drawing a distinction" (Wägenbaur, *Hybride* 35). Luhmann and Schmidt defined this idea when they characterized every system as a form that necessarily excludes a certain type of environment and where operations join operations and in this way define which operations are still connectable, so that we can perceive differentiation as a "system formation in systems" (Luhmann 19). Therefore, any combination of subsystems would be a form of differentiation and this is all that matters in our context. Because, logically, an inclusion can only exist if exclusion is also in play and the task is now to consider these two components not as mutually exclusive but complementary, in other words, "to relate the difference between inclusion and exclusion to the needs of the construction of a system" (Luhmann 20). For the polycontextual world, this and/both principle is of enormous relevance and the issue of multiple identities or multiple affiliations is by now the standard social science practice, unless we insist on the rigid mononational outlook as a relic from earlier times. This is why Beck emphasizes the complementary nature of concepts such as nationality, transnationality, and localism and in place of "exclusive differentiation" he calls for the "mode of inclusive differentiation" as a main objective of second modernity (Beck, *The Cosmopolitan* 4–5).

When this is transferred to my current task, the establishment of NWL as a theoretical literary category, it means that multiple affiliations of texts with various homologous categories are perfectly permissible and even desirable. Thus, for example, texts by Oliver can at the same time fall into the category of German national literature, Alemannic dialect poetry, and, as hybrid texts, into NWL—depending on which bundle of features prevails in relevance. Other texts—certainly the smallest group—may belong exclusively to a single subsystem. What is of interest are the points of intersection, the connection points between individual subsystems: in order to find these points, the differences must be identified, because without operative closedness there exists no openness of a system. We must note that "a process of exclusion underlies all system processes" through which "first, order [emerges], unambiguities and meanings . . . and such stabilities are generated, and their paradoxes are removed by the fact that they suspend the view on their operative genesis" (Nassehi *Geschlossenheit* 64). Order is nothing but the "limitation of contingency . . . a shortage of reference possibilities, the randomness of which would render the structure formation impossible" (57). On the other hand, it is necessary, as in a recursive loop, "to generate orders in order to get to differences" (56). In order to resolve this operative paradox, I establish a "theoretical model" with the help of which the "relevant properties of an object, process, or system will be worked out in a set of assumptions and equations" in order to serve "the preparation, the classification, and evaluation of data" (Abel 373–74). The model rests on the three characteristics of multilingualism, phenomena of globalization, and regionalism or localism as the main specifics of the texts. Further, the existence of these features of course presents a primary positioning gained through empirical observation, which as I have explained is indispensable.

Beck's cosmopolitan vision or Willke's "lateral world systems" are system theoretical configurations, which, when transferred to the study of literature, can shed light on the relationship between the national, the global, and the local or regional by demonstrating the coexistence of these components under dehierarchized conditions: the revaluation of the global and the local on the one hand, and the loss of importance of the national on the other, have led to the breaking of exclusive regulation at the national level: which national corpus of laws would prevent a transnational giant like IBM, for example, from making independent decisions of global proportions? Which authority could prosecute criminal activities on the world wide web and possibly even take action against them? It is obvious that traditional national regulation systems fail in view of the flows and actions of transnational human, commercial, financial, and information actants, at least in the West. Aihwa Ong, in *Flexible Citizenship,* shows that this diagnosis is true only for the West: developments and practices in Asia demonstrate that transnationalism, flexibility, and difference represent consequences of globalization, but they are by no means accompanied by more democracy or civil rights. On the contrary, economic globalization has led to almost early capitalist labor relations and a strong polarization between the rich and poor (and this is at times exploited by multinational corporations of the West) (see Sturm-Trigonakis, "Pikareskes"). Importantly, national philologies are no longer able to work with their traditional instruments. If we take as a basis the "revolving door" metaphor I refer to above to deal with realities and their images, this is only a logical consequence of the globalization age, and it would be a paradox if the study of literature did not respond to the new challenges. Therefore, monolingual—or rather monocultural—texts coexist today with those characterized by plurilingualism and inter- and multiculturalism, the fictionalities of which outline transnational dimensions. National philology and even bilateral or trilateral comparative literature, however, miss the point in toiling with such border-crossing texts if they do not adapt and adopt to the new configurations of literature and literary production altogether.

Systems theory deals with classifications as theoretical configurations, which it develops by means of theoretical models based on difference management. The object of this venture is to manage the contingency and complexity of the world, but without resorting to simplification and trivialization. Therefore, the exact amount of order is constructed that is necessary for the perception of distinctive features, so that eventually we come to open systems with an operative closedness. The trick of this is the exploration of connections with adjacent systems under symmetrical conditions. Thereby, systems theory allows for a different theoretical design for literary studies than national philology. At the moment when hybrid forms of literature are coordinated as a connectable, independent artistic system to an equally connectable, independent system of national literature we avoid the current unsatisfactory classification of hybrid literatures under designations such as "minority" literature or (im)migrant literature as a subset of a national literature. By configuring a separate category for hybrid literatures, the latter are liberated of their asymmetric hegemonic relationship with national literature and can be analyzed impartially and in compliance with the structural and aesthetic characteristics relevant for this category.

I utilize another assumption from systems theory, namely, that systems in principle have self-referential and autopoietic properties, from which results a sensitization in dealing with difference: first, the handling of bundles of features gained by empirical observation is a condition for the configuration of a new category, but in the following it is exactly the cause of an increased awareness toward another difference (see, e.g., Schmidt; Schroer). Systems theory is but one (scientific) discourse among others and it follows that systems theory can occupy no objective observer status outside the system; thus, each observation implies at the same moment an observation of a second degree. This way, every blind belief in theory is put to rest and the inevitable result for research is a critical distance from ontological theoretical concepts. If we continue to accept the construction of a second modernity (Beck) as a cognitive scheme for the description of globalism-buffeted post-postmodernity, then the time for the comparative cultural study of culture and literature is now. Formerly popular discourses such as intercultural literary studies, postcolonialism, and deconstructivism should be subjected to a test and synthesized at a global level. It is clear that this is a field test, a scientific construct that bears its contingency within itself, and its raison d' être is located in the fact that it is global, transnational, and applicable. It is for these reasons that I propose to "reanimate" the idea of world literature Goethe failed to complete and that somehow got lost in the discipline of comparative literature owing to its adherence to the national and the Eurocentric (see, e.g., Tötösy de Zepetnek, *Comparative*, "The New"). Thus, the three principal pillars on which the structure of NWL can be established are as follows. First, periodically, NWL begins at the time of Goethe (i.e., in the West); second, its trail is sketched out in current aporiae and developments, especially in comparative literature, but also in various philological approaches; and third, it can be derived from efforts to arrange new categories following the impact of globalization in the context of systems theory.

Following my discussion in the previous chapter, I argue that scholars of comparative literature—especially in the US—produced much scholarship regarding the questions of the canon and canons of literature. Contributors to the Bernheimer Report, for example, take the view that through the contextualization of literary texts in discourses of gender, ethnicity, culture, and ideology the research object can no longer be restricted on literature (see Bernheimer). While this development is ongoing in the discipline, I do not to align myself with comparative literature (i.e., the US-American type), because "even if a literary text is read with cultural and scientific interest, it requires the tools of literary scholarship in order to be unlocked" (Nicklas 42). Eva Kushner thinks in the same direction when she concedes that the impact of cultural studies is welcome in order to restructure the landscape of humanities disciplines where the study of literature is a focus, but warns of the associated risks of the identity loss of the discipline and demands the preservation of the priority of the study of literature per se. As I argue above, it is precisely the analysis of literariness that has fallen behind in previous readings of hybrid texts, because through the strongly culturally oriented interpretation the formal and aesthetic features of such texts have been neglected in favor of a privileging of cultural conditions. And I repeat that in the case of German-language scholarship, the literary production by non-Germans has been read up to the present day particularly as a "document" of social realities, something that Chiellino and his colleagues opposed repeatedly, but with little result.

The dealing with various versions of cultural studies is illuminating, especially as the presentation of the problems turns out to be suited for parallelization. If a recognized cultural studies scholar such as Doris Bachmann-Medick also begins the search for a new understanding of world literature and underlines that "European criteria are not sufficient for dealing with non-European literatures" and that "European literary theory is a very local, but not a universal phenomenon" (Bachmann-Medick, "Einleitung" 55; see also Bachmann-Medick, *Cultural Turns*), then—with the call for an ethnologization of literary study—she places herself in the company of literary scholars who are discontented with the current ways of the study of hybrid texts. Bachmann-Medick aims at an "expansion of the literary canon into non-Western literatures" as a "main objective of postcolonial approaches" (55). However, if we conceive the canon as a qualitatively defined exclusive club of the world's best high-brow literatures, it is likely that today there is probably no doubt about the fact that authors such as Naipaul or Walcott are admitted into the canon. It also seems to me that the discussion about world literature is no longer pointed to a "third world literature debate" with the danger of this discourse being in turn administered only by Western scholars with high salaries (Bachmann-Medick, "Multikultur" 267). On the contrary, the discourse about world literary discourse is, in my opinion, both globalized and distributed to several locations outside Western centers. In this respect, I agree with Bachmann-Medick when she writes that "typical examples of world literature . . . would be (literary) texts which are localized in world relations and in which cultural position determinations are reflected and developed (such as in Rushdie, Naipaul, Achebe, and others). The foundation of such texts is more than ever the processing of truly experienced otherness and self-experienced cultural conflicts that goes far beyond a mere literary imagination of foreign worlds, far even beyond an imaginary, museum world 'archive' of literatures" ("Multikultur" 273).

A key concept is hybridity, as it marks the sphere "in which we subject ourselves to the culturally other within the web of cultures, which means that the tough traditions, to which the own self-understanding is in each case attached, can be quasi liquified" ("Multikultur" 279). The result, according to Bachmann-Medick, is that world literature "is developed, closely following the 'homeless' in-between-existence of the postcolonial subjects," where "the recognition of cultural differences [not cultural dichotomies!] is negotiable as well as practically differentiable" ("Multikultur" 279). As an example of this concept of world literature she takes Rushdie's *The Satanic Verses*, because the novel "is on the one hand engaged in a self-reflexive, critical involvement with controversial global issues" and on the other hand, the Qur'an is decanonized and relativized "by reference to the world system of other secular texts" ("Multikultur" 284). In this way we abandon the paradigm of "culture as text" with the potential translatability of cultures into another, but we put in its place "culture as translation" as a new paradigm "that emphasises the negotiating character in the constitution and assertion of cultures, the 'trading' [in Goethe's sense] in the problematic search for cultural commensurability and at the same time local-historical association" ("Multikultur" 287). Further, the term "culture" in the current globalization debate has experienced a "gradual shift from essentialism to hybridity" (Rosendahl Thomsen 64), and this shift finds its literary equivalent in minority literature discourses. Here—despite my misgivings about comparative literature—the discipline can called into play, because only this can work out the differences in literary texts which antagonize tendencies of homogenization as perceived and denounced by cultural studies: "we will, then, be prepared to measure the dialectics of difference in a world increasingly 'globalized.' This has always been the aim of the discipline of comparative literature and it continues to be so" (Parkinson Zamora 7).

In addition, striking similarities with the social sciences concerning the form and extent of the processes of globalization can be revealed, especially if we set hybrid literature as a separate functional system with specific characteristics. These characteristics are, on the one hand, the result of observations on the text corpus and, on the other hand, based on deficiencies in philological study, which is unable to do justice to new paradigms in methodology and theory formation. The awareness of these shortcomings now leads to an attempt to constitute hybrid literature as a separate system, as I postulate above. This type of difference management is based mostly on definitions made by Schmidt in his framework *Empirische Literaturwissenschaft,* namely, "theoreticity, empiricity, and applicability" (see, e.g., "From Hermeneutics" 4). It is a micro-system and, according to Schmidt, we can position as its superordinate macro-system a "literary system . . . embedded in the media system of a society" ("From Hermeneutics" 6), if this does not reduce it to the national or the European. A macro-systemic "world-system that is a capitalist world-economy," according to Immanuel Wallerstein, is "a historical system, that is, it has rules that govern its operations (which makes it a system) and it is constantly evolving (which makes it historical)" (1). Interestingly, while the macro-system approach has been taken up by a number of US-American proponents of world literature (e.g., Damrosch), the concept and its applicability are criticized now (see, e.g., Conrad, Eckert, Freitag). Opposite to such system constructions I give preference to "literatures of the world" (i.e., plural) a superordinate system as the sum of all currently circulating literary texts and literary production in which NWL is located as a subsystem with the following criteria:

> 1) The first criterion is bilingualism and/or multilingualism, for, despite all appreciation of the literature written in African, Indian, and other non-European languages, we discern a tendency to language mixtures in the widest sense. Multilingual texts, literary code switching, and related phenomena have always existed, so I am primarily concerned with the explanation of the differences from earlier texts with more than one linguistic register and with the understanding of plurilingual writing as a specific text strategy. Thus, focus is shifted from the hitherto overstressed, in my opinion, question of the linguistic competence of the author to the performance of language(s) in the actual text.

2) The second criterion is content and thematic nature, which refer to the phenomena of transnationalism typical of globalization: they range from border-crossing and transgression of all types over multiple identities including such as exile, (im)migration, and spatial movements, etc., and give rise to the fictional exploration of the third space. Movement is also understood here as temporal, because clashes of different eras can often be found next to spatial constellations. Generally, the subject is difference and incompatibility out of which, under certain circumstances, something new arises, which, however, may exist also as various forms and ways of dissent.

3) The third criterion includes poles provoked by globality and transnationality and including the regional and local, with which we leave the level above the national and find ourselves at the level below the national. Topics such as clothing, food, or religion are processed here as an expression of local cultural practices. The same goes for concrete places or cities and real and mythical past layers which, in turn, have certain relations to the global.

The decisive factor in my construction of NWL as a separate subsystem of the literary system is the interaction of the above three differentiating parameters, because the distinctive moment that makes this literature unique and contrasts it to all other systems and subsystems of literature (such as national literature or feminist literature) appears only in the form of this interaction. What I emphasize is that NWL is a subsystem of literary production as based on the writing of such texts, because the name-dropping of authors—common particularly in discussions on postcolonial literature—cannot be a substitute for clear criteria of differentiation. An author like Rushdie can definitely be classified as a postcolonial author, but in my opinion this represents a restrictive perspective that does not do justice to the diversity of his work: while the short stories *East, West* and the novel *The Satanic Verses* are perhaps well described with the label "postcolonial," this is surely not the case for his novel *Grimus*. By contrast, the first two works are representative NWL, because they comply with a broad definition of multilingualism and present both local affiliations and global phenomena. However, I would not classify *La Nuit sacrée* by Tahar Ben Jelloun as NWL because—despite the presence of the Arabic use of metaphors in this French-language text—in the text itself the oscillation between the transnational and the local has not been registered for all the metamorphoses and the border-crossings of the protagonist. A system can be successful, that is, closed and at the same time open, only if its defining criteria are fairly strictly met; this by no means excludes multiple affiliations. Similar to Rushdie's short stories in *East, West*, Assia Djebar's novel *Nuits de Strasbourg* also allows a postcolonial reading, because the text works on the results of the French colonization of North Africa and particularly Algeria. At the same time it can be read under the aspect of gender or as a feminist novel. It is also a book about European collective memory, in which the European enmities and reconciliations are processed since the formation of national consciousness in the nineteenth century. However, as the text meets the three criteria required by NWL, it is placed here in this discoursive context.

My theoretical design of NWL can form an operative base for the intention of descriptively and analytically coming to grips, against all simplifications, with the complex hybrid forms of literature of the last twenty-five years. It is narrow enough so that it can be applied only to certain texts and broad enough to be transferable to other texts.

Chapter Four

Forms/Types of Poetic Multilingualism and Interferences, Metamultilingualism, and Transtextuality

A Brief Survey of Poetic Multilingualism

"'In dulci jubilo.' Nun singet und seid froh! / Unseres Herzens Wonne / Leit in prae-sepio / Und leuchtet vor der Sonne / Matris in gremio. / Alpha es et O!" (qtd. in Forster 10). When this Christmas carol was written in the fifteenth century, the poet was hardly concerned whether anyone would feel confused or discriminated against because of the mixture of languages: Latin as the language of church and scholars was used as a matter of course alongside the vernaculars, depending on the situation. The same bilingual naturalness has only recently been achieved again through songs by—mostly English—popular artists: centuries lie in between where literary bilingualism or multilingualism in the Western cultural environment was subject to changeable fates.

Uriel Weinreich conceives bilingualism and multilingualism as the ability of an individual to use two or more languages depending on the context, that is, to code-switch between different language systems, usually national languages (15). We will see to what extent this approach can be modified for NWL. In the history of multilingual texts two important facts are apparent: first, that the phenomenon of multilingualism in written form can be traced back to a long past and second, that the evaluation of multilingual texts from an aesthetic aspect has always been depen-dent on the respective social and political contexts in a given culture. In this respect, the present study is integrated with a long line of potential approaches to such lin-guistically hybrid texts and at the same time demonstrates once more contingency in dealing with multilingualism in literature: "since Antiquity, dialects or foreign languages appear in literary works," underlines Paul Goetsch, who lists the marking of the difference between the written and the oral text, the different social prestige of the languages, the recipient target-group, as well as the expansion of the means of expression, among others, as the causes which can motivate an author to use more than one language in a literary text (7). This enumeration has not lost its validity and applies to current conditions, even if further factors come into play. Antiquity called mainly for linguistic *puritas* in its writings on rhetoric and allowed the insertion of foreign language items in Greek texts only from Greek dialects and in Latin texts only from ancient Greek, and this only frugally (see Knauth, "Multilinguale" 269). Knauth suggests that "the codification of mixtilingualism as a stylistic barbarism had endured approximately two millennia and thus considerably contributed to the marginal status of multilingual literature" ("Multilinguale" 269; on multilingualism see also Cruz; Grutman; Knauth, "Translation," "Weltliteratur"; on US-American English and foreign languages, see, e.g., Miller, Joshua; Sollors).

Brian Lennon's 2010 book, *In Babel's Shadow: Multilingual Literatures, Monolingual States,* is an interesting case where the concept of world literature and translation is explored. Lennon writes that "world literature is less a system, suggesting a set of relationships exposed to research, than it is a scene—a focus of new or renewed attention by writers, critics, scholars, and other professional read-ers—that generates such relationships as much as (or more than) it discovers them" (xvii) and in this he follows Damrosch's definition (*What Is* 5). Further, Lennon suggests that the "cultural 'scene' . . . is to impute a certain level of organization, of pattern . . . and to mark the start of its incorporation into official culture" (171). Len-non's designation that world literature is a "scene" which then is institutionalized followed by its location in "official culture" is curious, because especially in the US there is no "official" culture and in Europe this is also a question despite the fact that in some countries like France or Spain there are "official" directives by ministries of culture or education. Lennon also writes that world literature is "kitsch" because of its "mixed quality and the contradiction it embodies" and because of "the partial opacity or illegibility of the kitsch object" (xvii). I understand in this proposition that Lennon argues for the hierarchization of literature, something I object to. What is true in Lennon's argumentation is that ideological factors play an important role in literature altogether, and in NWL in particular, because linguistic purity has al-ways been an expression of an imperial claim to power from the *Imperium Roma-num* to the European nation-states and their colonies. Add to this "linguistic and political principle of unity" a mythical yearning for the primordial human unified language, which was lost due to the Babylonian confusion of languages described in the Bible, so that multilingualism is tarnished from the start with a kind of divine curse (Knauth, "Multilinguale" 270). Writers in antiquity concerned themselves with "mixtilingualism" (i.e., intratextual multilingualism), that is, foreign language insertions within a closed text. In contrast, the term multilingualism or synonymous terms such as polyglossia, plurilingualism, interlingualism, or colingualism could mean both the intertextual switch between different languages in different texts by the same author and mixtilingualism within single texts, whereby interlingualism often also undergoes a specialization of meaning in the direction of mixtilingualism (see Knauth, "Multilinguale" 266).

Pursuant to the rejection of mixtilingualism in "high" literature by ancient tradition, a mixture of languages was mostly accompanied by a burlesque intention—prime examples can be found in macaronic poetry since about 1500, where scholarly Latin is spoofed with a Latinized Italian (see, e.g., Forster 14). In this way, a typical situation of the diglossia of a prestigious Latin and a less esteemed Italian with vernacular variations is converted into poetic strategy, which had to have been so successful in its time that it found imitators again and again: Rabelais's *Gargantua et Pantagruel* can be called macaronic-like in the broadest sense and even in Molière's *Le Malade imaginaire* the medical profession is ridiculed with a pseudo-Latin-French doctorate award ceremony. In the twentieth century, Dada and concrete poetry are by all means to be regarded as late successors of the macaronic. Despite the partially disrespectful handling of Latin, its usage—the lingua franca of Europe in the Middle Ages—played a hardly underestimated role as a written language. The fame of Erasmus of Rotterdam, for example, was based mainly on the fact that his writings were penned in Latin and accessible to every scholar from Scandinavia to Sicily. Even Martin Luther, who was known as a great advocate of the German vernacular, in his after-dinner speeches switched from German into Latin when discussing theological questions (see Forster 10). As a rule, the choice of language was genre and addressee specific, so that Latin and the European vernaculars—which in the course of the fifteenth and sixteenth century developed into more or less standardized literary languages—led a peaceful coexistence.

Since the Middle Ages, the Iberian Peninsula had been one of the regions of Europe where numerous languages were present in everyday life: alongside classic Arabic of the Qur'an, Arabic dialects were used, Hebrew as the language of the Sephards, Latin as in the rest of Europe as the language of the church and scholars, and to these were added the Castilian, Catalan, Galician, and Portuguese, as well as the Basque vernaculars. Still in the *Libro de Buen Amor* by Juan Ruiz, Arcipreste de Hita (Archpriest of Hita), published in 1433, numerous Arabic insertions—as well as of other Iberian languages—are to be found within the Castilian text, which indicate that the public of the time could understand at least some terms in the Arabic colloquial (see, e.g., Haywood and Vasvári). Arabic-Hebrew-Romanic poetic forms, such as *jarchas* (*harǧa*) and *moaxaja* (*muwaššaha*) preceded this, as well as a specialization in specific language forms depending on the genre. Medieval Castilian epics were written in Castilian, as, for example, *El Cid*, while Alfons X "the Wise," King of Castile in the thirteenth century, modeled his songs dedicated to the Virgin Mary after the example of Arabic love songs, but wrote them in Galician Portuguese, the language of lyric poetry at the time (see Knauth, "Multilingualisme" 270). The *Minnedichter* Henric van Veldeke created a lyrical style similarly genre specific, the relevance of which existed in Low German as a medium of expression and was imitated in the entire German-speaking area: "the idea that certain languages were proper for specific purposes lasted into the sixteenth century when Charles V, King of Spain, Emperor of Germany, and Duke of Burgundy, maintained, so it is said, that French was the language to speak with one's ambassadors, Italian with one's women,

German with one's stable boys (according to another version, with one's horses) and Spanish with God" (Forster 17).

Language loyalty in Europe was not a subject of debate until far into the eighteenth century; it represented the medium through which a poet wrote texts for a specific occasion, and those who could do so in more than one working languages were not few (see Forster 35–38). This is the context within which *Pentecostal polyglossia* is also to be regarded: on the basis of the biblical Pentecostal wonder, through which the twelve Apostles were made competent in all languages in order to proselytize in all parts of the world, the Catholic Church launched the propagation of its doctrine on a global scale, whereby Latin was upheld as the language of theology and the rites, but homilies and the catechesis were articulated in the respective vernaculars. Mixtilingual texts of all kinds came thus into being, from songs in Latin and a European vernacular, such as the poem "In dulci jubilo" I refer to at the beginning of this chapter to educational dramas, songs, or Bible translations in the Latin American territories to be proselytized, whose authors did not use only Latin, Spanish, or Portuguese, but also Indigenous languages such as Náhuatl, Tupi-Guaraní, or Quechua (see Knauth, "Multilinguale" 271).

In the course of the seventeenth century a process of ousting started, during which Latin was not entirely given up as the language register of science but was increasingly displaced by French as the language of the most powerful and splendid European power of that time, France. It was mostly upstarts, such as Prussia and Czarist Russia—both little respected with regard to culture—which adopted French as the epitome of the modern and of worldliness. Both Frederick the Great and the Russian nobility expressed themselves mainly in French, and nineteenth-century Russian literature bears traces—sometimes in the form of entire passages—that the Russian elite up to 1917 communicated in French even among themselves. Leibniz gradually replaced the Latin of his philosophical writings with French and wrote little in German (Forster 52) and still around 1800, August Wilhelm Schlegel wrote the most part of his critical work in French and was clearly not worried about his readership (Forster 54).

The Romantics of the nineteenth century raised the status of the national and discovered "that languages had souls," that each language, each dialect is unmistakable and unique; "the energies of writers were devoted to the production of 'national literature'" (Forster 55). Even Goethe's idea of *Weltliteratur* was by no means conceived as mixtilingual but within the framework of increased translation among national languages through which "in Goethe's opinion a foreign language coloring of the literary national language could take place" (Knauth, "Multilinguale" 272). In no case was the aesthetic ideal of a "primary native language identity of high literature" given up (273), which, in comparison to previous centuries, equals a paradigm shift in the area of poetic language:

> After the pre-romantic raising of the status of the mother-tongue to the 'mother of language' (Jean Paul), multilingualism is, however, connoted completely differently: it appears to point either to an "infidelity" toward

the own linguistic "homeland" or to "homelessness." Since, by means of
the "transcendental-hermeneutic" turn in the history of reflection on language, we were made aware of the meaning of linguistically constituted
and conveyed world "pictures" and world "views" and the dependence of
the reality experienced by a community of speakers of the words that make
it accessible and the grammar, both the shift from one language to the other,
as well as the combination of components of different languages present
themselves as something fundamentally distinct than a mere play with external forms. (Schmitz-Emans, *Die Sprache* 57)

If we examine this turn to a single and uniform national language during the
nineteenth century within the entire structure of literary text production, it turns out
that the existence of a national literature in a single national standard language is a
fairly short episode in the long history of literature, since monolingual and monocultural texts, as we have seen, were certainly not the norm before the nineteenth
century and were again subject to fierce attacks since the turn into the twentieth
century. The intensive debate about national languages in the course of Romanticism created not only outward boundary mechanisms toward other nation-states, but
also had as a consequence the discovery of multilingualism in individual countries.
This was the case, for example, in the young Latin American states which had just
recently become independent, where the Brazilian José de Alencar already in 1865
claimed a mixtilingual national Brazilian literature with Portuguese and the Tupi
language in the opening of his novella *Iracema,* and thus wrote the first manifesto
of a national Indigenous multiculturalism (see Knauth, "Multilinguale" 273). This
trend also met with approval in Europe in the 1920s and 1930s and exactly because
of its archaic-anarchic features it met there with surrealism and Dadaism, two movements which also experimented with mixtilingualism and multilingualism as an expression of a deeply felt linguistic scepticism. Alfons K. Knauth summarizes this
avant-garde direction under the superordinate concept of "simultaneistic polyglossia" ("Multilinguale" 273) and emphasizes its cosmopolitanism and consciousness
of global ubiquity and omnipresence: "the contours of a new world literature thus
became apparent, which are not characterized anymore—as in Goethe's time—by
a translated multilingualism but, rather, by a non-translatable mixtilingualism or a
mixtilingualism to be universally understood" ("Multilinguale" 274).

In Europe multilingual authors such as Stefan George or Rainer Maria Rilke
experimented with French and other languages. Rilke stands out in that he published
such an extensive opus in French that he also made a name for himself as a French
poet (see Forster 69–71). Samuel Beckett leaves behind an extensive oeuvre in English and French, and Joseph Conrad and Vladimir Nabokov consciously decided in
favor of English as their literary language, both representing a much-cited example
of a complete language shift. However, these examples also illustrate the difficulties linked to a language change. Conrad's decision to use English as his literary
language had always been for him the second best choice, since he had a better
command of French, and without the help of his co-author Ford Madox Ford he was

not capable of literary production (see Szegedy-Maszák 97). Nabokov passed down to us his complaints about English as his literary medium: "the absence of a natural vocabulary. . . . Of the two instruments in my possession, one—my native tongue—I can no longer use, and this is not only because I lack a Russian audience, but also because the excitement of verbal adventure in the Russian medium has faded away gradually after I turned to English in 1940. My English, this second instrument I have always had, is however a stiffish, artificial thing, which may be alright for describing a sunset or an insect, but which cannot conceal the poverty of domestic diction when I need the shortest road between warehouse and shop. An old Rolls Royce is not always preferable to a plain jeep" (qtd. in Szegedy-Maszák 98). Beckett was often attacked because of his "bad" French and also made his first French attempts with the help of various co-authors; his self-translated versions deviate thus dramatically from their respective original so that we should consider them new creations (Szegedy-Maszák 101–03). Beckett's endeavor to eliminate language culminated in the silent movie with the title *Film* and thus a circle was closed: "Bilingualism may lead to silence. That is one of the possible conclusions one may draw from the career of Samuel Beckett" (Szegedy-Maszák 104).

T. S. Eliot, Ezra Pound, and James Joyce are classic examples among modern writers who do not use their multilingual abilities in their texts consecutively, but utilize them simultaneously to produce mixtilingual literature. It is no coincidence that the turn to literary multilingualism starts exactly when European imperialism is at the highest point of its aggression and in this phenomenon a form of "resistance to the pressures of militant nationalism and militant monolingualism as apparent for example in the theory if not the practice of an arch-modernist like Marinetti . . . Significantly, with the waning of empire and extreme nationalism after the Second World War, literary modernism too wanes" (Firchow, "Literary" 61; see also Forster 74). This would, incidentally, also be a plausible explanation for the poetic boom in Alsace-Lorraine shortly before World War I: Yvan Goll, René Schickele, Hans Arp, and Ernst Stadler countered both French and German nationalism with a deeply European, nationally and internationally multilingual work, that, with its explicit crossborder properties of setting within fixed sovereign territories, removed itself from language and the nation state.

A multilingual work such as *Finnegan's Wake* not only speaks a deeply rooted linguistic scepticism that arises from the knowledge of the arbitrariness between the *signifiant* and the *signifié*, but also broaches the issue of the meaning potential of the unintelligible—as in Pound's *Cantos*—and underlines its extensiveness, so that the materiality of language receives a new dimension of meaning. In the German-speaking areas, this line is continued after World War II in concrete poetry and the novel. Thus, Ernst Jandl, on the basis of foreign language, fantasy language, dialectical and onomatopoeic set pieces, writes poetic texts whose surface structure, as well as the "arrangement [of words] and the principle behind them" produce a "Babylonian disaster" (Schmitz-Emans, *Die Sprache* 72, 83). However, where "the 'Babylonian Theme' asserts itself in literature, a reflection is articulated, at least indirectly, on the deficiency of language in its unfoundedness and disparity, on its inability to mediate between people and things, or even between people among themselves without losses, concessions, and damages. Modern literature is in many ways affected by 'Babel'" (Schmitz-Emans, *Die Sprache* 81). On the other hand, exactly therein lies the opportunity, because through the staging of the unintelligible, borders are opened and potentials made accessible which monolingual texts can barely even fathom. Or, as in France in the 1950s, *spatialisme* arises, at the same time as in Brazil and Japan, as part of concrete poetry in which languages and various artistic media are mixed and this softens previously accepted boundaries between idioms and media (see Knauth, "Multilinguale" 279). In a comparable manner, Guillermo Cabrera Infante, for example, with his novel *Tres tristes tigres,* set in Havana, continues the tradition of novels such as *Don Quijote, Gargantua et Pantagruel, Finnegan's Wake*, or the complete artwork of stories by Jorge Luis Borges, and "in the consciousness of a world-literary and world-speaking simultaneity" stages a literary Babel of the most various linguistic registers (Knauth, "Multilinguale" 283; see also Steiner 195).

What had been only a tributary of literature until around the second half of the twentieth century has become, in the course of the last three decades, a wide stream: while colingualism at a regional level—as for example in the Alsace or Switzerland—has a rather peaceful character and mixtilingual texts do not necessarily take sides in favor of or against one side or the other, in other parts of the world in the course of migration, decolonization, and changing political conditions a potential for language conflict develops and this leaves its mark directly on mixtilingual and multilingual texts. Thus, in the postcolonial context almost every word in Wolof, Berberic, or Urdu can be read as a political statement against the respective former colonial power France or Great Britain. It is along these lines that Glissant develops his theory on the Creolization of languages and cultures on a global scale (see Bermann; Knauth, "Multilinguale" 279). US-American Chicano/a authors search in Spanish-Náhuatl-English mixtilingual texts their imaginary and real past before and after the arrival of Columbus and place themselves linguistically in the conflict-laden borderlands between Mexico and the United States. Seyhan differentiates, with regard to border-cultural literatures, between three stages that partially overlap or simultaneously exist next to one another: in the first stage of a diaspora situation, a thematical tendency toward the representation of the individual fate or the collective (im)migration history can be observed, and this is expressed by means of the authors' first language. In the second stage, a language shift into the idiom of the "host country" takes place, where the texts focus on "an aesthetically inscribed field of social observations, critique, and innovations and use of the target language" (Seyhan 107). And in the last phase the phenomena of hybridization and Creolization can be found: the texts produce a "borderland of different languages, rites of passage, and negotiations of myth and reality, memory and presence, madness and reason, and factual account and revolutionary experimentations in language and style" (Seyhan 107).

For NWL, the latter phase is relevant because in the majority of cases the three key situations—multilingualism, transnationalism, and regionalism—manifest themselves exactly at this liminal area between national literatures. This, of course, does not rule out the use of multilingualism in other stages as a poetic strategy. In general, however, such multilingual border territories with their "'luxuriant' and 'nomadic' participation in multiple cultures" call the understanding of literature into question: Strutz rightly derives from his analysis of the pluricultural Alpine-Adriatic area the demand to give up the "reductionist concepts of uniformity" in favor of a "principle of multiplicity close to reality" because in the direct present "the age of the monolingual, national literature histories and the single literature didactics should be over" (219). Demographic statistics by themselves already point to the same direction, as the already existing plurilingual conditions in broad parts of Africa and Asia start to also gradually spread in Europe so that multilingualism develops, here as it already is elsewhere, from being a special case to being normal (Bickes and Bickes 98). A number should help illustrate: in 2001, 21% of children in Germany, a country normally categorized as monolingual, had at least one foreign parent (Extra and Verhoeven, "Immigrant" 6). By now, around 30% of the population in Western Europe has (im)migration backgrounds (see Extra and Verhoeven, "Immigrant" 6; for further information on the European situation see Currle; Sassen).

From one-word interference to metamultilingualism and transtextuality

In the light of these rapid changes of demographic conditions, conventional definitions of bilingualism and multilingualism lose their meaning, because they are based on "two separate and isolated language competences" (Rickheit 327). This configuration is not only as far from reality as the container paradigm I discuss above, but also proves to be impracticable regarding hybrid texts, which rarely use two languages equally. Newer classifications are more differentiated, "but certainly do not make easier a concrete allocation of a specific bilingual speaker to a specific category of bilingualism" (Rickheit 327). Gert Rickheit discerns (without priority) between "linguistic competence, cognitive organization, age at the beginning of language acquisition, presence of a second language community in the environs, the relative status of the two languages, as well as group membership and cultural identity" (326). How and where these criteria influence text production remains unclear. A transfer to written texts is even less possible, because—while linguistics explore multilingualism mostly in the person of a speaker or in concrete utterances—more complex circumstances exceeding this become relevant for written text analysis (see Bhatia and Ritchie). The presentation of single philologies with their minority discourses has revealed that these are up to now overtaxed regarding the analysis of these complex text forms. In that respect foundations are to be laid and Schmitz-Emans's and her contributors' distinctions—between nations, states, regions, cultures and multilingual texts including pictoral, verbal, and nonverbal—in *Literatur und Vielsprachigkeit* is suitable for this as an operational basis. Conrad and Nabokov are examples for language shift, while numerous authors of the text corpus examined here illustrate second-language use.

Thus it can be established that the only decisive criterion for NWL should be multilingualism inside the text, that is, varieties within a specific language. The result is a "fundamental multilingualism" in the sense of Amodeo, a "syncretistic language profile" where multilingualism can appear in the text in concrete forms of "multiple discernable languages," but also in latent forms (120). Amodeo ascribes to such texts a "fundamentally inherent dialogicity" which already manifests itself, for example, in the "foreign name of the author," but can be detected more explicitly in interferences at lexical, grammatical, syntactical, or metaphorical levels (120). However, such a text ranges strictly at the performance level. According to Ray Jackendoff, human language can be examined at a competence and a performance level, whereby competence denotes "the functional characterization of the 'data structures' stored and assembled in the f-mind in the course of language use" and performance means "the use of these data structures in the course of language perception and production" (34). By choosing here the performance level as the subject of examination I attempt to avoid the confusion of different observer perspectives—where statements of the authors themselves regarding their texts also belong—and to achieve a degree of objectivity in analytical statements about the texts as much possible. In connection to Spivak's critique on "the Native informant," Venkat B. Mani describes in view of Özdamar's texts the mechanism of fetishism of the author as creator of social documents: "In their well-intentioned endeavor to recognize these immigrant narratives as contributions to the diversified social text of the West, cultural critics began to consider works by minority authors as sources of objective truth about minority communities. While attempting to understand the struggles of collectivities through these largely autobiographical individual narratives, scholars tend to turn these authors into the undisputed representatives of their communities—indeed, into native informants who provided the coveted authentic voice for the trials and the tribulations of ethnic minorities" (32; on Özdemar see also Milz; Rankin).

Nor can we be concerned with working with the self-limitations on the artistic configuration of a *langue*. Rather, in the context of hybrid literature, instead of reducing the complexity—as would have been done at the level of *langue*—it has to be allowed at the level of *parole* and made manageable by classification. It is exactly the emphasis on the contingency between *langue* and *parole* that characterizes "dynamic, self-descriptive, complex, and environmentally differentiated communication systems" (Giesecke 13). In connection to this, the question arises as to "which phenomena are to be sensibly designated as 'language'; not vice-versa: there is no path from the unusual model of 'langue' leading to communication and comprehensive communication systems" (Giesecke 13). The model of the nation-state was constituted with *langue* as a foundation of its identification structure, but with the prerequisite that hybrid literatures represent a counter-discourse to the established national ones, neglecting *parole* as an expression of border-crossing, the transnational, and anarchy would be absurd.

Next, I attempt by means of concrete examples from the text corpus first to capture descriptively the rhizomatic meshwork of interferences between matrix language (ML) and embedded language (EL) in their diverse manifestations. These two concepts provide a useful model for the description of code-switching whereby the idea is that "basic words and constituents from one language (the embedded language, EL) are inserted in a matrix provided by another language (ML). This has proved to be an adequate point of departure for the description of many bilingual text corpora" (Boumans 281). As a second step I examine the mechanisms of interference and analyze them with regard to their functions and recipient orientation. Interferences are regarded classically, following Weinreich, as "instances of deviation from the norms of either language," whereby this definition of course raises the problem as to what extent we can assume a norm in the context of poetic language. Still, I am keeping this term for purely practical reasons, as well as code-switching as the alternating use of two or more languages within an utterance, although code is in fact the equivalent to *langue* (Martinet 33). Despite these shortcomings I keep these terms, because they are fixed components of linguistic terminology and because code-switching is paradoxically as a rule defined and examined at the level of spoken language and is—to some extent—transferable to written texts: "code-switching is the alternate use of two (or more) languages by the same speaker within the same conversation" and differentiate further between intersentential (at sentence boundaries), intra-sentential (within a sentence), and extra-sentential (with isolated elements, exclamations, etc.) code-switching (Extra and Verhoeven, *Bilingualism* 42; see also Callahan). Drawing on the research of Ernst Rudin on the English-language Chicano/a novel, these linguistic differentiations are expanded for text analysis, so that a descriptive schema with the following parameters is generated: 1) one-word interferences, subdivided according to different contexts; 2) multiple-word interferences up to the sentence level; 3) multiple-sentence interferences up to entire passages; 4) grammatical interferences, forming of analogies, and neologisms in the ML with EL background; 5) metamultilingualism, as speaking about different languages; and 6) transtextuality.

The above description includes at least a large part of the phenomena observable in the text corpus, so that the manner of embedding EL interferences into the ML can be outlined in the next steps in order to arrive at their poetic function in the overall text structure. In order for this first descriptive part not to get out of hand, I am limiting myself to a few examples from the corpus where the existence of similar paradigms from other works is implied. The variety of form of literary multilingualism in hybrid literatures takes center stage here, whereby it cannot be emphasized enough that it is simply a temporary schema of description with the goal of creating an inventory resulting from the observations in the text corpus. Further text examples from other cultures require an expansion and modification of the principal differences in order to include their linguistic specifics. The texts used here are written exclusively in inflectional languages as MLs, to which mostly either other inflectional (e.g., Spanish) or agglutinative (e.g., Turkish) language types are added, while other groups, such as tonal languages (e.g., Sino-Tibetan), are not included at all.

According to Rudin's research on Chicano/a literature, the most frequent interferences are "single word entries," which in turn are 95% nouns (110). This finding correlates with the observation already mentioned by Weinreich that vocabulary is much easier borrowed than the phonetic or the grammatical and this holds true especially for isolated words, which represent culture-specific things or relationships (79). From the texts examined here, one-word interferences can be detected as follows.

Types of interferences

One of the most frequent occasions a foreign word is used is in discussions about food. For example, in *The House on Mango Street* by Sandra Cisneros, the names of the young protagonist's friends are given both in their English and Spanish version, where in a nonsense nursery rhyme in the English text "cold *frijoles* / Mimi, Michael, Moe. . . / Your mama's *frijoles* / Your ugly mama's toes" (37–38), a typical Mexican dish—beans—appears, seemingly completely unmotivated. In Jhumpa Lahiri's collection of short stories, *Interpreter of Maladies*, the dinner scene of a newly married couple is outlined: "Shukumar put the rice on the table and the lentils from the night before into the microwave oven, punching the numbers of the timer. 'You made *rogan josh*,' Shoba observed, looking through the glass lid at the bright paprika stew" (10). The student Maya in *The Middleman* by Bharati Mukherjee is invited to the home of her Bengali professor and is served "mutton croquettes, fish chops, onion pakoras, ghugni with puris, samosas, chutneys" (103). In the trilingual poetry volume *Duende* by Oliver, the Alemannic carnival-*Striebele* are given both in the standard German and the Spanish version (8), while the Spanish sardines *boquerones* are not translated into either Alemannic or German (26).

In Monica Alis's novel, *Brick Lane*, young Bengali Nazneen is married off to London and there painstakingly learns to stand on her own feet: her clothing items are almost always given in Bengali: "Nazneen felt the letter inside her choli" (183) or her husband Chanu is sprawled on the sofa "in lungi and vest" (184). Trini, the heroine of the novel of the same title by Estela Portillo Trambley, is usually wearing a *hilpa* and wakes up every morning in her hammock; her *petate* and these designations are kept throughout the text. *Trini* is generally a linguistic rhizomatic meshwork of ML, which is in part foreignized through grammatical interferences from the Spanish or through pidginization and from Spanish vocabulary in almost every sentence or—to a lesser extent—from the Mexican Indian language Tarahumara, such as the designation *raramuri* for a holy man, *tehueque* for guard or escort (65), or *ahau* for a village elder or leader (19, 71). Even geographical proper names, such as "El Cerro Minaco" or "Peña azul" (66) are always given in the original in this novel. In Djebar's *Fantasia: An Algerian Cavalcade* we read about the *sarual* Berber girls wear or the ankle chain *khakhal*. Anil, the protagonist in Ondaatje's *Anil's Ghost* lets us know right at the beginning that English is her main language and that, after fifteen years in the West, she speaks and writes only little of the Sinhala of her native

Sri Lanka. Nevertheless, a series of Sinhala words, such as "diya reddha cloth" (90) or "some brinjals, this is my pride" (95) are woven into the text. On the whole, this area proves to be resistant to language change. Clothing and food are acquired cultural practices which can easily be transferred to other cultural contexts in situations of (im)migration and function as brought-along identity markers for the homeland, just as geographical designations do.

In *Trini* there are numerous examples of interpersonal relations little susceptible to language change, so that there are many Spanish interferences in ML. For example, *mamá* and *papá* or *tía Pancha* as the closest familial designations are kept as such in the entire novel and the same holds true for terms of endearment such as *pollito* (17), *chinita* (27, 31) or the neutral *chavala* (46). Even negative emotions or curses fall under this rubric, whether it be *puta* (180) or "that *borracho*" (40). In *The Middleman and Other Stories*, too, in the circle of Indian Americans the curse is cited in Hindi: "Something about eunuchs not knowing their place. 'Don't ever go up there again, *hijra*-boy'" (Mukherjee 144). In Naipaul's *A House for Mr Biswas*, the address form *mai* for the mother and head of the Tulsi clan is maintained in the entire book.

Another kind of relationship is built between the lyrical "I" in Oliver's poetry volume *Vater unser in Lima* and his Peruvian partners—who address him in the entire book with the pejorative term *gringo* or *gringuito* (14, 16, 30, 40)—and this is narrated with regard to the loathed US-Americans or rich Germans as cultural alterities of Western imperialism. An absent "you" is also addressed in the poems by Ilma Rakusa in *Love after Love*, where affectionate forms of address alternate with insults, mostly in lengthy form: "Du Charmeur, du Blender, du / Kräfteverschwender, du Seelenfresser. Oppressor. / All these lovely words: I'm lucky to have you. / Remember, I care. / I caress you. / Das Karo ist leer./ Keiner. . . . Verzieh dich! / Leave me, lover. Belagerung beendet" (12–13). In another instance there is, "Wie zählt man den Sand? / you're kidding yourself, idiot / wahr ist: Kinder des Winds / du ein warrior und ich / eine Närrin der Sehnsucht" (20). Yanick Lahens's *Dans la maison du père* tells of Alice Bienaimé's youth between French school, Catholicism, and Haitian Vodou. The housekeeper "Man Bo" and her stories belong to her child world, as well as the old beggar "Man Lolo" (31); the resolute Man Bo gives her orders mostly in the Haitian *Créole* such as "*Chita la* and stop moving" ("*Chita la* et ne bouge plus" 34). As a rule, they are affective laden terms of the immediate environs of the fictional characters or a basic vocabulary of elementary social ties which resist place and language change and are therefore presented in the literary texts in EL, particularly when it concerns the fiction of a first language of the characters.

Another area that shows numerous interferences includes all kinds of higher powers, which are often linked to a mythical past or one presented as real. Thus, Vodou vocabulary plays an important part in *Dans la maison du père* and is always given in *Créole*, a typical case of interference stemming from the need to name new things, phenomena, and facts which the matrix language does not provide lexical categories for, as for example the *Créole mitan*, the axis of the world: "Prior to this image there is no beginning. The image is central. It is the axis of my life" (14, 97). In a description of a Vodou mass, not only designations of the persons acting are given in *Créole*, such as *hougenikon* or *hounsis* (97, 98), but also chants sung during the ceremony are quoted where the expressions stand out visually by being italicized. In Naipaul's *A House for Mr Biswas*, too, the evil Hindu powers remain an interference: "'You will be hearing from my solicitor,' Mr Biswas said. 'And those two *rakshas* you have with you. They too'" (350).

Anzaldúa's *Borderlands/La Frontera* treats the revival of the world of Aztec gods as a mythical past of the Chicanos/as and as a consequence the text is interwoven with Aztec gods, such as Coatlicue as the fusion of birth and death (42): "*Tlazolteotl, diosa de la cara negra*" (74), or the "*Virgen de Coatlalopeuh*" (75), and more. One of the poems at the end of the volume, titled "Canción de la diosa de la noche," is about the search for the goddess: "I seek *la diosa* / darkly awesome. / In love with my own kind. . . . The moon eclipses the sun. / *La diosa* lifts us. / We don the feathered mantle / and charge our fate" (198–99). The world of Aztec gods also plays an important role in the novel *Trini* by means of the identification of the main character with the goddess Tonantzín: "Tonantzín was smiling at her! . . . The drums were in Trini's blood now, finding tributaries carrying light into oceans, worlds whispering, seed waiting. Tonantzín spoke and she listened" (74, 149, 225). To the Native American universe of animated magical nature also belongs *El Enano*, the "dwarf," who regularly appears out of nothing and supports Trini (13, 191, 228). Further, Tía Pancha's numerous prayers are always given in Spanish, as, for example, "Tía Pancha's gentle voice leading the children in Ave María. 'Ave María, ruega por nosotros'" (58). Such passages exceed one-word interference as a rule and the one foreign word serves as a point of entry to the religious sphere that is then outlined in detail in the ML, as also happens in Ali's *Brick Lane*: "Chanu had brought her tasbee. She held the beads and passed them. Subhanallah, she said under her breath. Subhanallah, subhanallah. When she passed the thirty-third, her fingers loitered on the dividing bead. She breathed deeply and ploughed on. Allhamdu lillah. Thanks be to God" (130).

In the examples above, it has already been shown that code-switching often enough exceeds the length of one word or that a combination of both is present. Particularly in extremely multilingual texts which transfer quantitatively linguistic material from the EL into the ML, longer intrasentential and intersentential expressions are found, as is typical in Feridun Zaimoglu's *Abschaum. Die Geschichte des Ertan Ongun,* where the first-person narrator uses the *Kanaksprak* "invented" by Zaimoglu as a positive reevaluation of the deficient immigrant: "Ethem's a drug addict gipsy from Turkey, Türk çingenesi, Kasımpaşa, belalı, and Fatih from Konya's my friend. . . . By the way, he's in the slammer now, he shot two guys. So, Ethem yells: Ulan parayı vermezseniz sikerim sizi, fuck you, if you don't gimme the money" (98). Arnulf Depperman's study on the language of youth is informative here:

> A large part of the linguistic development of the young people in the ghet-
> tos takes place outside the paths of educational institutions. This includes

the self-determined, undirected acquisition of Turkish by children who are not of Turkish origin. Linguists Inci Dirim and Peter Auer discovered that in multi-ethnicity Hamburg districts, German, Croatian, Bosnian, Tunisian, and other youngsters learned Turkish through leisure interactions with other children and young persons. Their competence ranged from a few morsels up to almost accent-free command of the Turkish language with a significant repertoire for expression. Turkish is used here by young persons of varied origins matter-of-factly alongside German and German-Turkish language mixtures in peer group communication. (75)

Every story in Zaimoglu's novel is written in the above explicated style where the German slang-imitating oral discourse is interwoven with Turkish expressions which are mostly left untranslated, although their meaning can sometimes be gleaned from the context. Anzaldúa's *Borderlands/La Frontera* reveals already in its title a multilingual work: it is a hybrid text in every sense that disregards genre boundaries as it also neglects thematic and linguistic unity. In particular, parts of poetry are written for the most part in Spanish while the documentary-like ones are written in the English ML, where italicized Spanish or Náhuatl words lend the text two-dimensionality: "at the beginning of the sixteenth century, the Spaniards and Hernán Cortés invaded Mexico. . . . By 1650, only one-and-a-half-million pure blooded Indians remained. The *mestizos* who were generally equipped to survive small pox, measles, and typhus (Old World diseases to which the natives had no immunity), founded a new hybrid race and inherited Central and South America. *En 1521 nació una nueva raza, el mestizo, el mexicano* (people of mixed Indian and Spanish blood), a race that had never existed before" (5). A special type of multiple-word interferences are proverbs, which play a preeminent role in Özdamar's texts. A rendering into German usually follows the original without any loss of their didactic aspect. One of the many examples can be found in Özdamar's collection of short stories, *Mutterzunge*, where where she narrates the search of the protagonist living in Germany for the Turkish language of her mother and the Arabic of her grandfather.

In Oliver's poetry we encounter further exampes of multiliguality and imagery: "Despierto. / De madrugada despierto. / Despierto los anhelos. / Es la noche que llega. / Su mano de fuego. / Llega a tocar las puertas de mis casas. / La despierto. / Mano que busca el olor del olvido. / Olvido transparente. / Velos fugitivos. / Las aguas. / Su memoria. / Oh, pardon . . . / Ich vergaß, / dass ich in Deutschland bin. / Ich wache auf" (*Gastling* 10). Here, the lyrical "I" wakes from the smell of the houses of Turkish residents set on fire in autumn 1992 and lets his thoughts wander to other conflagrations, such as those of the Spanish Inquisition. The "I" moves associatively from one smell of fire to the other, declares his nonbelonging to these countries pervaded by fire to neither Spain nor Germany and tries to make for itself a neutral place, a peaceable in-between. As the arson attacks in Solingen evoke others in Spain, so the one language elicits the other quasi automatically. However, this is not in parallel to the emotions described but is diagonal to the text meaning and thus destroys deceptive uniformity: code-switching enhances the atmosphere of anarchy and chaos spread through the text and functions therefore as a multiplier of the text message in this poem.

Peter Turrini, in his play *Ich liebe dieses Land*, brings several languages to the stage via Beni, the asylum-seeking Nigerian, and Janina, the Polish cleaning lady: German is the language of the civil servants holding him in custody pending deportation and of the police physician, as well as of the young journalist. Janina, who works there as a cleaning lady, speaks in part German with the typical interferences of a person whose first language is Polish, mixed with Polish one-word and multiple-word interferences, in part Polish. Beni, the Nigerian, first attempts a sentence in his West African language (19) and then shifts into English in order to tell his story of persecution and torture in detail (46). In German he has command of only one sentence: "Ich liebe dieses Land" ("I love this country") that he repeats over and over to make the German civil servants be friendlier toward him (as he was told to do) and this is, of course, in stark contrast to his treatment and impending deportation so that the sentence turns from increasingly ironical to cynical in the course of the play.

In principle, insertions of texts of substantial length are rare in hybrid texts since they make reading by a nonmultilingual public difficult. In Turrini's play, translations are added for the longer passages in a foreign language. However, they have little use in this form unless they are performed as part of the play's production. But they achieve their purpose, that is, to localize every speaker linguistically and culturally and to mark the levels of communication and noncommunication where it is shown that the two characters, Beni and Janina, who do not share any linguistic intersection with each other, come closer.

In Martin Walser's *Der Augenblick der Liebe*, the numerous English passages remain untranslated, and code-switching often enough seems to take place without motivation: "Had this sentence had consequences in Europe from 1750 to 1900, Freud, whom she, proselytised by Madelon Pierpoint, called the great Vienna-Victorian novelist, would have, for ever relaxed, been able to lie himself down onto his couch in the Berggasse. *When she left Dr. Douglas's office last time, she felt like a jerk. She had rambled, talked in circles. It becomes apparent that their relationship caters exclusively to her need for confidence, reassurance, emotional stability . . .* When she then had, with tipsy courage, pushed a letter in the letterbox, pushed so, as if this push had to transport the letter over the ocean, the letter started to shout" (71; emphasis added to indicate the English-language passages in the German-language text). If any compliance to rules for the language shifts can be detected at all in this text, where French and Latin also occur, then it is that the scenes which take place or have taken place in the US in English are those which mostly provoke code-switching. This technique not only interrupts text coherence in an abrupt manner, but also should—owing to the number and extent of the English EL parts—make the reception by a German monolingual reader impossible.

While multilingualism in Turrini's play reproduces oral language and in Walser's text indicates a change of situation or perspective, in Anzaldúa's *Borderlands/La Frontera* the Spanish-language parts are often poetic texts which raise thematically the flow of prose to a higher poetic level and encapsulate in a concentrated and synoptic fashion what was said earlier. This technique is a reminder of classical Arabic literature: In Ibn Hazm's *El collar de la paloma,* for example, prose in colloquial language of the Al-Andalus of the time alternates with poems in classical Arabic, which condense the antecedent narration. However, in Chicano/a literature—in contrast to the situation in Germany and Austria—we can assume a considerable Spanish-English bilingual readership, which makes the threshold of inhibition toward the use of extensive EL portions clearly lower than, for example, in a German text with Turkish insertions or a French text with insertions from West African languages. The insertion of longer, untranslated passages in EL bears the risk, from a readership-reception view, of making the text hermetic.

I now present some thoughts on transfer phenomena not considered in the above mentioned schemata of lexical interferences. Under grammatical interference, Weinreich integrated the adoption of morphemes or grammatical relations the "change in function of 'indigenous' morpheme or category," the "abandonment of obligatory categories" (pidginisation), and the "integration of loanwords" (Weinreich 64), phenomena, that is, which are all more or less provable in the texts of the corpus. An example for the violation of grammatical norms is, for instance, the incorrect English used in the letters of Nazneen's sister, Hasina in *Brick Lane.* It is a kind of Pidgin that makes due without temporal and personal markers and that uses the English continuous form and the like incorrectly, and generally presents itself as an oral style with many instances of incorrect syntax. In Hanif Kureishi's *The Buddha of Suburbia*, the demand that the protagonist Karim speak English with a Bengali accent, in order to lend his role as Mowgli from Rudyard Kipling's *The Jungle Book* more authenticity, throws Karim into depression, because for him and his Bengali father it is exactly accent-free English that represents the expression of their British identity. The novel's first sentence outlines the social self-contextualization of the hero: "My name is Karim Amir, and I am an Englishman born and bred, almost" (3).

A whole series of rule violations pervade the volume of poetry by the Chicano Juan Felipe Herrera, *Border-crosser with a Lamborghini Dream.* For instance, the English "I" is spelled in lower case on principle, there are numerous incorrect endings or phonetic spellings, and the Spanish words do not carry the obligatory accents, as in the poem "punk half panther":

> Lissen
> to the whistle of night bats —
> oye como va,
> in the engines, in the Chevys
> & armed Impalas, the Toyota gangsta'
> Monsters, surf of new world colony definitions
> & quasars & culture prostars going blam
> Over the Mpire, the once-Mpire, carcass
> Neural desires for the nothing. i amble

Outside the Goddess mountain. Cut across
The San Joaquin Valley, Santiago de Cuba,
Thailand & Yevtusenko's stations. (2-3)

In the rendition of Turkish proverbs in Özdamar's *Mutterzunge*, some words
are translated into a kind of immigrant worker German, where the conditional con-
junction and the corresponding obligatory inversion of the verb in German in subordinate clauses are neglected. In Turrini's play *Ich liebe dieses Land,* the cleaning
lady Janina speaks German with an East Prussian tinge that is occasionally interspersed with Polish words or expressions. Whereas this variety is thus widespread
through the refugees who migrated to Germany at the end of World War II, the native
German-language reader almost automatically imagines the characteristic pronunciation when reading. A considerable number of similarly typical "errors" are to be
found in *Trini*, where a cry such as "That Tonio!" (25) is formed in analogy to the
Spanish "ese Tonio," although it is inconsistent with the English standard. Oliver,
in contrast, uses morpheme transfer to form words such as "renovember" from the
Spanish iterative prefix *re-* and the German name for the month November (67). In
other examples he modifies word gender and thus, in the volume *Heimatt* in 1989,
he comes up with a "Mondin" (the word *Mond*—moon—in German is masculine,
here with the ending of feminine gender) in analogy to the Spanish *la luna* (69)
and in *Duende* with a "Meerin" (*Meer* [sea] in German is neutral, here with a the
ending of feminine gender) in analogy to the Spanish metaphorical "la mar" (42).
These two terms, along with numerous "pure" German neologisms, are components
of the poetic idiolect of this poet from southwest Germany. The foreignizing effect
is not brought about only with the change of grammatical gender, but because of the
image itself, since a Germanic masculine moon is turned into a Romance-language
feminine one. A similar reaction between foreignization and humor is provoked by
the rendition of proverbs, as in Kureishi's novel, when Haroon, the father of Karim
the protagonist, in the face of the chaos caused by renovations in the house, flings a
curse at his family: "May you have the builders," which is countered by his bother-
in-law with a "Haroon, I'm kissing the joy as it flies" (112). This scene is comic owing to the reference to two completely different discourse contexts: Haroon uses in
his curse an image that does not exist in English and at the same time does not make
any logical sense (after all, the workers are already there), while his brother-in-law
thinks he is making him happy by referring to one of the lessons of Haroon's medita-
tion evenings, which is equally inappropriate in this case.

These few examples should be sufficient for the documentation of grammatical interference in diverse forms. Undoubtedly, along with lexical interference, it
is the most widespread method for the production of hybrid text patterns and the
joining of different worlds in a text. Gürsel Aytaç, in her examination of language
in Özdamar's novels, reaches the conclusion that Özdamar "writes against the usual
rules of translation by not thinking like a German but like a Turk. . . . What this author is doing, according to the German Philology taught in school . . . is incorrect;

artistically, however, she has created something magnificent because she overcomes the rules of translation and writing in the foreign language and writes German with a Turkish language feeling" (176). Even if we cannot always presume to have authors with a clearly definable "language of origin" in the texts examined here, we can at least presume bilingual or multilingual circumstances which find their way into the texts as a poetic strategy through violations of rules, neologisms, metaphor transfers, and other methods. Further, grammatical and lexical interferences—along with the phonetic, which are here only marginally relevant, as in Turrini—are best analyzed as phenomena of the *parole* of bilingual or multilingual individuals in countless linguistics studies (see, e.g., Auer; Milroy and Muysken; Myers-Scotton). However, they are not sufficient as key differences for the examination of literature, because they do not cover the poetic strategies inscribed in the texts. Therefore, I am addressing two more criteria beyond the morphological level, which I consider indispensable for the description of literary multilingualism: metamultilingualism and transtextuality.

Metamultilingualism and transtextuality

Metamultilingualism denotes speaking about languages in the broadest sense, because—in view of the selection options authors have at their disposal—it has to be considered as part of the intention for polyglossia when the reader is being informed in which language a specific scene happens. This information is an important component of the creation of a fictional world and takes place at a more abstract level than does the production of an outlined foreign world, mimetically created through a foreign word, an interference. In this respect we have reached the point where the linguistic definition of multilingualism is not sufficient anymore and literary multilingualism is to be understood by means of additional categories of description.

The most common ways to bring into play different types of discourse are *inquit* formulas. In Naipaul's *A House for Mr Biswas*, for example, the reader is almost always informed which character in the novel speaks in which language at any time: Mrs Tulsi speaking to a customer uses "English in a slow, precise way which surprised Mr Biswas and filled him with apprehension"; her daughter, Shama, on the other hand, Mrs Tulsi reprimands sharply in Hindi for her impolite behavior toward that same customer: "Mrs Tulsi spoke some abuse to Shama in Hindi, the obscenity of which startled Mr Biswas" (76–77). In principle, the shift into English always takes place when it comes to a confrontation, for example, when Mr Biswas thinks to have finally escaped his wife's family and tries to be alone with her in a rundown shop named "The Chase," or when she expresses the wish for her brother-in-law, Hari, to bless the shop—which would mean more expenses—Mr Biswas reacts with an outburst of rage: "He was taken completely by surprise, and lost his temper. 'What the hell you think I look like!' he asked in English. 'The Maharaja of Barrackpore?'" (133). When it comes to legal matters, Moti, Mr Biswas's interlocutor, shifts into English in matters of fact, although the people involved usually speak Hindi, "using English, the language of the law" (158). While Hindi represents the language of intimacy, family, and the sense of well-being, English represents the official and marks in the entire novel the distance between Shama and Mr Biswas, as in the scene where Mr Biswas, after a long separation from his wife, meets his fourth child, for whom his wife's family had already chosen a name: "'Her name is Kamla,' Shama said in Hindi, her eyes still on the baby. 'Nice name,' he said in English. 'Who give it?'" (299). With this English answer Mr Biswas expresses displeasure and grief that he had been excluded from the birth and the name-giving. The reference at every instance to the language used also informs us about the relationship of the people involved and is therefore part of the text's discourse strategy.

Another language constellation marks social differences in Shyam Selvadurai's *Cinnamon Gardens*. Instructions to servants are given in Tamil in Colombo or in Hindi in Bombay, while the members of the colonial upper class speak English among one another. The partially incorrect English with typical pronunciation errors of the Sinhalese Mr Jayaweera corresponds to his poor suit and dubious descent. Balendran's wife Sonia, who is the daughter of an Englishwoman and grew up in England, is, because of her inadequate language skills, attributed a certain positive special position as progressive and socially active on the one hand, but on the other hand, she remains an outsider. A situation of diglossia is devised, where all languages are socially subordinate to the correct English of the Ceylonese upper class. At the same time and at a further level of meaning, criticism is leveled on this acculturated group that sacrifices its own language in order to plunder the country alongside British colonial rule. Cases like this serve for the determination of location of the inner-textual world, that is, the narrator functionalizes the linguistic relationships for the clarification of the relation between the persons acting in the text. At the moment, however, when at a metalinguistic level speaking about languages becomes itself the topic, the world outside the text comes into play, since the author is incorporating at this location a metanarrative and self-reflexive component in the text that exceeds the narrative strategy, whereby both can occur at the same time (on this, see Braunmüller 18). This means that the text not only informs us about who is making use of which language at which point, but it also raises considerations on the meaning of individual languages for each person. Exemplary in this respect are the novels by Djebar, where language issues are tirelessly debated and different viewpoints are adopted.

In *Fantasia: An Algerian Cavalcade*, Djebar tells the story of Algeria's conquest by the French at the beginning of the nineteenth century contrapuntally with the autobiography of the first-person narrator, who is trying to find herself within a multicultural environment under French colonial rule. This happens for the most part through contentions with a complex mesh of Algerian, which is made up of Berber as a medium of oral tradition, Arabic as the language of religion, and school French as the language of the oppressors, as well as the language of a freedom unusual for an Islamic region. And add to these the Turkish of Algiers's former Ottoman rulers. The protagonist has a close relationship to the first three languages, which transport access to different worlds explained in detail in the text. Thus, she comes to know French as the language of love through a friend's older sister in the home of the French gendarme of the village, where the mocking manner of the French girl toward her absent fiancé deeply impresses her: "'Darling Pilou'; words followed by bursts of sarcastic laughter; what can I say of the damage done to me in the course of time by this expression? . . . An innocuous scene from my childhood: but later, when I reach the time for romance, I can find no words, I cannot express my emotions. Despite the turmoil of my adolescent dreams, this 'darling Pilou' left me with one deep-rooted complex: the French language could offer me all its inexhaustible treasures, but not a single one of its terms of endearment would be destined for my use" (27). Consequently, it is later impossible for her to lend an ear to a man who tries to woo her in French, because the French love words "formed a mask which the interlocutor had willy-nilly to adopt in the opening moves of the game" (*Fantasia* 128). When she reverts to her mother tongue after that, it is a gesture of being open to every possibility, otherwise she prefers the distance-creating French. On behalf of so many others on whom the French school system of the colonies left its mark, the heroine of the text summarizes the schizophrenia of her presence:

> I write and speak French outside: the words I use convey no flesh-and-blood reality. I learn the names of birds I've never seen, trees I shall take ten years or more to identify, lists of flowers and plants that I shall never smell until I travel north of the Mediterranean. In this respect, all vocabulary expresses what is missing in my life, exoticism without mystery, causing a kind of visual humiliation that it is not seemly to admit to . . . Settings and episodes in children's books are nothing but theoretical concepts; in the French family the mother comes to fetch her daughter or son from school; in the French street, the parents walk quite naturally side by side . . . So, the world of the school is expunged from the daily life of my native city, as it is from the life of my family . . . I do not realize, no-one around me realizes, that, in the conflict between these two worlds, lies an incipient vertigo. (*Fantasia* 185)

The relationship to the French language that began in this manner remains difficult, because it never stops being "the enemy's language," a language that was "formerly used to entomb my people," which the autobiographer exposes herself to as "a fire which may consume me" (*Fantasia* 215), because it is the only tool at her disposal.

Colonial circumstances also shape the relation of the lyrical "I" to the English language in Walcott's cycle of poetry *Midsummer*, where the passing of a year between the homeland in the Caribbean, the US, and the UK is described: the changing topographies evoke the languages belonging to them. The "I" in these poems poses similar questions about the placing of the self in the thicket of languages as Djebar's Algerian protagonist:

> I heard them marching the leaf-wet roads of my head,
> the sucked vowels of a syntax trampled to mud,
> a division of dictions, one troop barfooted,

the other in redcoats bright as their sovereign's blood;
their feet scuffled like rain, the bare soles with the shod.
One fought for a queen, the other was chained in her service,
but both, in bitterness, travelled the same road.
Our occupation and the Army of Occupation
Are born enemies, but what mortar can size
The broken stones of the barracks of Brimstone Hill
To the gaping brick of Belfast? Have we changed sides
To the mustached sergeants and the horsy gentry
Because we serve English, like a two-headed sentry
Guarding its borders? No language is neutral. (*Midsummer* 128)

The problem of the potential shift of allegiance by deciding in favor of the language of the colonizers is examined again and all languages are denied innocence, because they always transport power relationships. In another poem in this volume, Walcott sketches the heavenly landscape of the Caribbean, which is "named" after and also destroyed by the conquistadores' chain mail and arrows, so that the desperate question is raised from the point of view of the conquered: "Was evil brought to this place with language?" (56).

The situation of the expatriate can also give occasion for metamultilingual text passages, such as in *Bait* where the Serbian author David Albahari discusses autobiographically the loss of his home country, Yugoslavia, and his arduous acclimatization attempts in Canada, while he traces the last fifty years of Balkan history through tracking his mother's life. The first phase of exile is shaped by feelings of absolute loss and helplessness regarding the unknown environment, which are translated into language categories: "I'm . . . infinitely far from everything that once made me what I am, or what I could have been, or what I was. And that chaos of grammatical tenses confirms to what extent I find myself outside life, in which only the present tense exists and there is no grammar" (76). Just as Anzaldúa places a powerful "I am my language" (59) in space, so the protagonist in *Bait* is afraid that losing his native tongue will also result with his existence coming to an end: "In two years a language can be forgotten; in sixteen it can vanish from the face of earth, and when it vanishes, we, too, are no longer" (9). This panic about losing his mother tongue makes him eavesdrop on his fellow countrymen, to crowd them in the street, running the risk of making a fool of himself or being taken for a thief, only to be "enveloped in the softness of their Bosnian pronunciation, the drawl of Vojvodina or any of the mimical forms of my language" (76). Only through a slow process does he accept the other identity, which takes gradually hold of him by means of the English language of his exile (40), because "thanks to someone else's language, I was finally beginning to feel like someone else" (106).

Yoko Tawada's volume of short stories, *Überseezungen*, gives us the topic of the book already in the title, which depending on the accentuation can be read as "translations" or "overseas tongues" or even "sole fish." The linguistic point of departure for the protagonist is her statement that she speaks "only Japanese, my mother's language, I have never changed mothers" (48). On this is based a variety-rich, 150-page long contemplation on dealing with languages other than Japanese, from computer difficulties when transcribing Japanese ideograms, to Latin characters (16, 33, 49), to the adoption of Japanese proverbs or metaphors in German, which leads to comical expressions, such as "being unfavourably in love" (46) or having a "mute car" (a defective one) (69). The learning of yet another language, Afrikaans, throws the protagonist back again into a child state, when the incorrect use of the new language is followed by a prompt punishment: "The tongue that failed was cut off. But no worries, all pupils had multiple tongues behind their lips" (89). Despite the admonitions of the teacher, correct sentences will not come together: "maybe it was because we were somewhere else and from there transferred the sentences interlinearly, we translated from the language we had never spoken to a language that didn't exist" (90). Only after laborious classes does the protagonist suddenly feel a "new tongue" in her mouth: "it was cold and tiny" (90). The new language arrives, still restricted and unfamiliar. Tawada's reasoning on the foreignness of the German (and the other) languages moves the German in the position of alterity and opens for the native German-language readers unusual dimensions of their language, because it is viewed with different eyes; their supposed own language becomes thus foreign and unfamiliar (*unheimlich*), and the shift of position forces the German recipients into the situation of a foreigner.

On the whole it can be observed that most hybrid texts deal with the issue of language at a metalevel. The language—or rather, languages—are the decisive medium on which identities, places, times, emotions, and relationships are inscribed. Language is at the same time the archive of the past and the staging of the present. Since here we are dealing with forms of a multiple world generation, fed by multiple cultural sources, it would really be surprizing if the languages participating every time were not to flow into the texts. And as it clearly follows from the passages on interferences, different idioms are present concretely as bodies of sound and meaning, but the self-reflexive characters in hybrid literature also extend themselves to the metalingual dimension, so that speaking about languages often enough almost takes up more space than the very performance of these languages. In some authors this metalingual debate occurs throughout the entire work and examples include Özdamar, Tawada, or Djebar, who make their protagonists reason about language. Every language also always transports further texts; therefore, in the following passage, transtextuality will take center stage, which also represents literary multilingualism at a metafictional level to a measure equal to metamultilingualism.

Gérard Genette uses the term "transtextuality" in order to speak about relationships between texts in general, whereby it includes intertextuality, paratextuality, metatextuality, architextuality, and hypertextuality (2–5; on the history of intertextuality, see Juvan). Within our context we are first concerned with intertextuality, which represents the least abstract, lower level in Genette's five-type system and which he takes to mean "the actual presence of one text within another" (2): "In its most explicit and literal form, it is the traditional practice of *quoting* (with quotation marks, with or without specific references). In another, less explicit and less literal guise, it is the practice of plagiarism . . . which is an undeclared but still literal borrowing. Again, in still less explicit and less literal guise, it is the practice of allusion: that is, an enunciation whose full meaning presupposes the perception of a relationship between it and another text, to which it necessarily refers by some inflections that would otherwise remain unintelligible" (2). That which in Genette's explanations appears under the rubric of allusion should in the present case also expand to the mention of the authors' names, since they often enough represent a language or a country as well as their texts, so that in this case we could speak of an allusion in the second degree.

An example would be the numerous mentions of Federico García Lorca in the work of Oliver: starting with "homage to Federico García Lorca" in his second book *Heimatt und andere fossile Träume* (1989) (47)—where for the first time García Lorca's famous first line, "Verde que te quiero verde" ("Green, how I want you green"), from the poem "Romance sonámbulo" in *Poema del cante jondo* is quoted as the only Spanish interference next to the title in German—the name of the Andalucian poet appears in almost every volume following, up to *nachtrandspuren* (2002), although his poems are never used concretely as quotations. Instead, the figure of García Lorca functions by synecdoche for places, eras, ideologies, or poetic discourses: with his violent assassination by the Spanish falange in 1936, he symbolizes every kind of fascistic reign of terror (*fernlautmetz* 45–7) and offers explanatory models for the xenophobic violence in the fall of 1992. In addition, the name García Lorca places the poet in a multilingual, transnational poetic universe, to which Octavio Paz, Pablo Neruda, Rafael Alberti, or Luis Sepúlveda also belong and which also expands to include Friedericke Mayröcker, Reiner Kunze, Paul Celan, or Nelly Sachs. Thus Oliver's texts correspond intertextually with the experimental lyrical poetry of the twentieth century that is shaped by an antifascist commitment and takes a political position against totalitarianism of any persuasion. The mere name—García Lorca or Reiner Kunze—calls up an overall context with the potential meaning that belongs to it and thus the reader also thinks about the individual texts of the poets mentioned despite their absence.

Özdamar's title *Seltsame Sterne starren zur Erde* suggests an intertextual reference to a poem by Else Lasker-Schüler. Texts of the Jewish German poet permeate the entire book of Özdamar as a leitmotif and include also excerpts from works by Bertolt Brecht and Constantine Cavafy, quotes from a book by André Müller about the director Benno Besson, and a song from a CD with pieces by Kurt Weill. All quotes are identified as such and are listed in detail at the end of the book, so that the meaning potential of the insertions is fully developed on the reception side and is capable of referring to the intellectual environs of the Turkish first-person narrator. Next to these explicit quotes there are also countless allusions to theater plays or films of the 1970s, titles from newspapers, or even weather reports, all of which are combined as a kind of collage that lend the text historical authenticity and outline the measure of foreignness. In *Trini*, however, one of the major characters, Tonio, is singing a love song that cannot be identified further while performing some house-work. "En tus ojos tiembla mi destino. Y mi suerte en labios tan divinos. . .' His voice was clear and strong" (26). This song interrupts the text coherence twofold: first be-cause it is marked as a quote with quotation marks and second through the Spanish. This song is characteristic of the happy-go-lucky Tonio, who will later become Tri-ni's husband, whom she will never be able to rely on in precarious situations, because he will have turned to other women or gambling or has simply disappeared. In this respect, Tonio is from the start portrayed by what he says as an unreliable character.

In Walcott's *Tiepolo's Hound*, a kind of poetic biography of the impressionist painter Camille Pissarro, more intermedial indications of European painters appear rather than intertextual relations, due to the nature of the subject. Nevertheless, even in this poem, they serve the poetic strategy of constantly contrasting the two lan-guages English and French, the Old and the New World, as well as the blaze of color of Provence with the silver-gray of Paris. It says in one instance: "Our landscapes emerging in French though we speak / English as we work. My pen replaced a brush" (19) and then goes on to evoke Stendhal's *Le Rouge et le noir*, which resurrects the French countryside even in the English translation: "Even in translation a crisp-ness in the Stendhal / shone from the barrack's gamboge arches, a prose / bracing in its width; so every village cathedral, / with its rusted zinc roofs through clumps of almonds, rose / in inheritance from Stendhal or Cézanne's L'Estaque / the im-pasto indigo bay, the ochre walls of Provence" (19). Paris, on the other hand, evokes "Baudelaire's *fourmillante cité*, a bursting anthill / of crowds and carriages, quick strokes made them move, / in time with bell and whip, stanza and canticle" (42).

Another type of transtextuality in Genette's theory is the architextual relation, which means "a relationship that is completely silent, articulated at most only by a paratextual mentions . . . but which remains in any case of a purely taxonomic nature" (4). As a rule it manifests itself in an awareness of belonging to a genre; this in turn "is known to guide and determine to a considerable degree the readers' expectations, and thus their reception of the work" (5). In this case we are dealing less with genre-belonging *in stricto sensu* but with the manner of narrating: in Jusuf Naoum's *Kaffeehausgeschichten des Abu al Abed* as well as in Schami's novel *Die Sehnsucht der Schwalbe,* the texts serve Orientalist expectations by incorporating a basic plot in the style of the tales of a thousand and one nights, which now and again gives the opportunity to interrupt the narration and to return to the basic plot and comment on the narration at a second level. Both books are written in German by immigrants from the Lebanon (Naoum) and Syria (Schami); nevertheless, their narrative strategy refers to the Arabic cultural environment. However, they do not simply assume those patterns; rather, they stand in an ironic distance to them and present themselves at times as a playful pastiche and at other times as a satirical caricature in both directions: when Schami narrates events from an illegal milieu set in Frankfurt like a robber story from the desert, it not only satirizes the Arabic narrative pattern, but also the clichés in the minds of the native German-language readership, who expect exactly such a pattern from an author with the exotic name of "Rafik Schami." The publishers' marketing takes it a step further by happily providing books by Schami, Naoum, and Özdamar with jackets in the style of naïve paintings with Oriental motifs.

Rushdie's short story "Yorick" from the volume *East, West* can be defined as hypertextual according to Genette, that is, a hypertext "derived from another pre-existent text" that was produced through the "transformation" of a hypotext, in that it does not necessarily have to refer to this hypotext explicitly (Genette 5). At least two hypotexts can be detected in "Yorick," namely, Shakespeare's *Hamlet*, where the court jester is named Yorick, and Laurence Sterne's *The Life and Opinions of Tristram Shandy*, where Yorick is the name of the priest. The text unfolds veritable fireworks of transformations, in part by narrating Hamlet's story in the garrulous style of *Tristram Shandy*, in part by presenting it as a drama in dialogue form, rewriting the tragedy into a comedy. At the end, the author breaks the contract of fiction with the reader, since he exposes everything as a lie: "Yorick's child survives, and leaves the scene of his family's tragedy; wanders the world, sowing his seed in far-off lands, from west to east and back again; and multicoloured generations follow, ending (I'll now reveal) in this present, humble AUTHOR; whose ancestry may be proved by this, which he holds in common with the whole sorry line of the family, that his chief weakness is for the telling of a particular species of Tale, which learned men have termed *chanticleric*, and also *taurean*" (94–95). In *The Satanic Verses* Rushdie reaches even further and sets his novel in a hypertextual relationship to the Bible, as well as to the Qur'an, where he satirizes Mohammed's life story (and that of other religious characters). Another clear hypertext is Etel Adnan's *In the Heart of the Heart of Another Country*, whose title and structure are directly taken from William H. Gass's volume of short stories, *In the Heart of the Heart of the Country*, as the author explains in the epilogue, only that the stories take place in other settings.

On the whole, most of the texts examined here show one type or other of transtextuality or a mixture of them, so that we can place them next to text types "of maximal intensity" such as the parody, or single texts such as *The Waste Land*: "In those texts, given texts or discourse types are not simply used, but they are being referred to 1), the intertextual references are intended and marked and of a great communicative relevance 2), a self-reflexive awareness of intertextuality is articulated in more or less explicit metacommunication 3), the quotes and allusions form structural patterns 4), individual texts or specific structures of text groups are cited emphatically and concisely 5), and all this serves the application of textual difference and dialogical relativisation of words, texts, and their underlying systems of norms 6)" (Broich and Pfister 30). This qualitative bundle of criteria is complemented by the quantitative factor and here I risk the claim that hybrid texts are eventually more open to widely scattered transtextuality, simply owing to the fact that their authors can draw from a bilingual or multilingual reservoir. For the time being it should suffice that the texts examined here present a broad spectrum of transtextual phenomena which are often marked by code-switching and therefore predominantly belong to the marked or explicit type of transtextuality. According to Jörg Helbig's definition, an "intertextual insertion"—transtextual according to Genette's terminology—is always marked when it is "brought into the perception focus of the recipient through emphatic use" appearing in the form of a "linguistic and/or graphic interference" or "clearly revealed as an intertextual reference . . . through the linguistic conveyance of information" (93–94). In the texts of the corpus—as in all other texts—nonmarked insertions can of course also appear, which would logically have to be written in the ML in order to meet the criterion of implicitness.

In sum, the existence of transtextuality should be established as a manifestation of multilingualism that either manifests itself concretely as an EL quote or as an allusion to texts, genres, styles, or authors and should in its capacity as a differentiated part of the text always be categorized as marked.

Chapter Five

Multilingualism as Poetic Strategy

In this chapter I discuss how literary multilingualism in hybrid texts is performed in the above presented types of multilingual texts and how such texts ought to be analyzed with regard to their aesthetic and reception characteristics. My point of departure here includes linguistic perspectives as well, according to which language contact is realized through code-switching as a rule and whose functions can be defined as follows: "a referential function: lack of knowledge of one language or lack of facility in that language on a certain subject; a directive function: exclusion or inclusion of one or more interlocutors; an expressive function: emphasis on a mixed ethnocultural identity; a metaphorical function: highlighting the information conveyed; a metalinguistic function: commenting directly or indirectly on the languages involved; and a poetic function referring to the literary register of a text. These functions play different and partially overlapping roles in various contexts" (Extra and Verhoeven 43).

The above functions are partially transferrable to literary texts, although only when applied to text unity instead of the code-switching of a single speaker, and on no account are these functions to help interpret intentions of the writer. Thus the "referential function" of the above model should not be interpreted as a statement about the writer—because we cannot judge his or her language competence—but as a text strategy, such as in a scene of the Chicano novel *Trini*, where Trini's father, José Mario, names the price for the flowers he wants to sell in Spanish, because—as follows from the text—he has no command of numbers in English (243). Thus, code-switching turns the recipients' attention to the character's poor English skills and indirectly to the small chances of integration for the older generation of immigrants, which, of course, has nothing to do with the writer's language competence. Another function is aiming at readership or reception, since multilingual texts live off exactly this tension between inclusion and exclusion, whereby both the production aesthetic and the reception aesthetic functions are touched upon.

Earlier, I described metalinguistic functions under the term metamultilingualism, and here it seems to me that the linguistic point of view is not transferrable to texts. Even if it is actually the case in daily bilingual speech—when discussing certain subjects in connection with a specific L2 language or discussing the L2 itself—bilinguals "switch" from L1 to L2 (i.e., language 1; language 2), this phenomenon as such could not be proven in the texts; rather, "speaking about the other L2 language" serves its visualization since the text, for whatever reasons, is not written in this L2 but in a L1. The last of the above mentioned functions, the poetic one, is far too general for application to literary structures and could at the most be applied to transtextual phenomena. But those are not always, as was shown, linked to code-switching, but often convey the L2 text in a translation, as a paraphrase or in a summary. Thus, my conclusion is that the above linguistic model is capable of offering bases for the examination of functions of polyglossia in hybrid texts, but that such a model is too simplifying and is not capable of managing satisfactorily the complexity of hybrid texts. Unlike code-switching in bilingual speech—which is often ungoverned and subconscious—code-switching in hybrid literatures always has to be interpreted as a component of a poetic strategy since just as with genre, style, plot, or setting, a selection is made from infinite possibilities. Consequently, the search for the reasons for each decision is interesting, because only thus can text strategy and the "model reader" inscribed in the text be detected (see Eco, *Im Wald* 27). And so we arrive at the second parameter without which, while irrelevant for linguistics, no text realiszation can take place: the reader, whose role is ambivalent, especially in multilingual texts. In this sense Gary D. Keller notes, in his study on literary strategies of bilingual Chicano/a authors,"that code-switching in literature need not, and usually does not, reflect code-switching in society" (263), so that we should differentiate between sociolinguistically analyzable, mimetically motivated code-switching and literary code-switching (269). Because language switching within a text represents such a radical "foregrounding" that it focuses attention on the language itself, "each and every code-switching must have a definite (be it explicit or implied, thematic or stylistic, etc.) aesthetic function in order to justify itself" (283). Therefore, Keller rejects placing different kinds of texts, such as drama, poetry, or novels, next to one another as subjects of examination, because code-switching is context dependent to a high degree (302). Although I would join this claim in principle, the corpus examined here includes different text genres, because the fact of using multiple languages in a text as a general characteristic for NWL matters to me more than the functional details within a specific text or genre. For this reason, I sketch the functions of polyglossia according to a schema of my own in order to take into account the variety of the texts I analyze.

Rudin differentiates between "mimetic" and "artificial use" of EL, whereby overlaps between those two areas are certainly possible, since the examples for "artificial use," such as satire, parody, irony, or symbolism can be mimetically as well as aesthetically motivated (14, 22). However, I do not agree with Rudin's assessment that "mimesis . . . constitutes the bigger share by far of the uses of secondary languages in Western literature" (14), because the texts I analyze here do not confirm this viewpoint in any way. Nevertheless, using Rudin's broad categorization, we gain a basis of operation from which further categorizations can be carried out. However, I prefer the term poiesis to the term "artificial" and speak of poetic functions according to Roman Jakobson's work, because they include self-reflexiveness as well as outward reference in a semantic or pragmatic sense (on this, see, e.g., Kloepfer, *Poetik* 44), with poetic being defined, according to Arnold Rothe, "as a criterion of description, but not as a designation as genre or a criterion of evaluation" (50). Further, I challenge the contrariness of these two terms, because mimetically motivated code-switching is just as much a part of overall textual strategy as any other poetry-based process. For this reason, mimesis is placed next to all other phenomena as one poetic function in hybrid texts.

We usually talk about mimesis when extra-textual reality is brought into the text, as for instance, when the speech of bilinguals is imitated or songs and poems are cited. This mostly happens in theater plays such as Peter Turrini's *Ich liebe dieses Land*: the Polish cleaning lady Janina speaks her own German interspersed with Polish insertions and a Polish syntax and with Beni she at times speaks foreigner talk such as "I Poland. You?" (19), while Beni the refugee from Nigeria speaks English and on one occasion a Nigerian language (19). A Polish lullaby, as well as the gospel "Glory, Glory, Hallelujah" are also put to use in the text (30, 43). The non-German or broken German portions of the text form a stark contrast to the standard German spoken by the officials on the stage and lend the play authenticity, so that the readers or audience likely arrive at an almost automatic solidarity with the two foreigners who are physically and emotionally abused by the German bureaucratic system. Their languages make them appear "genuine," and exactly therein lies the meaning of polyglossia used here: beyond their individual fate, they refer to the collective, Beni to the tragedy of the asylum seekers who are being turned away and Janina to the unsuccessful integration of the immigrants (particularly so in Germany), who have left a repressive homeland behind them, only to find a new, similarly hostile one, albeit in a different way, where they are exploited and disdained.

Bringing authenticity to the stage is also the concern of Herrera in the play *Jaguar Hotel* in the book *Mayan Drifter*, where on the one hand he describes his journey in the Mexican region Chiapas, searching for traces of the Mayan tribe Lacandón, and on the other hand publishes the draft of the play *Jaguar Hotel* and a poem with the title "Anahuak Vortex," with Mexico City as its central theme. One of the women characters of the play—described as the "Chicana activist Margarita"—expresses herself in view of the assembling of a local partisan movement in the poor Chiapas region as follows: "We want this thing to work out smooth. Tú sabes, it's about the proceso. Not the producto. We want this whole onda to shine and buzz like hot salsa on huevos rancheros. No more pedos. Or fat-ass excuses by the políticos, the new governor of Chiapas, Ponce de Leon, the bobazo presidente Gortari in Boston drinking cranberry juice, eating pie á la mode in Amsterdam, the Sinaloa cartel cabrones eating our tortillas. If there's going to be any kind of new movimiento here, la cosa's gotta be solid—solid like us Indian women (*touches her heart*), like an

Indian heart" (202). The mixed speech style of a Spanish-English bilingual is mimicked here in order to lend the character authenticity: second language interferences almost always refer to ideologically laden key terms, such as *movimiento*. *Onda* (wave) is likewise a synonym for a political movement, *la cosa* (thing) is often used in connection with the Chicano/a movement, and *políticos* or the *bobazo presidente* (the idiot president) are terms which express the disdain for the office-holding politicians. Beyond that, bilingualism also characterizes Margarita as a person who, as a self-proclaimed Chicana, unites both the US and Mexico within herself and as consequence uses both languages.

An example of how the mimetic use of multilingualism also functions in prose texts is found in Zaimoglu's *Abschaum*, which is written throughout in Kanak Sprak, a colloquial speech style including scatological and argot elements, mostly paratactically linked main clauses, numerous hedges, such as *na ja* ("well"), *weißt du* ("you know") in phatic functions, elliptical clauses, and the like. The whole is written in an ML tinctured with a northern German dialect with numerous Turkish intra- and intersentential references, which mostly do not contain any additional information, but paraphrase and comment on the information given in German. For example, in the beginning of the "Messerstecher-Story" ("Knife-stabbing-story") is written: "Ethem's a drug addict gipsy from Turkey, Türk çingenesi, Kasımpaşa, belalı, and Fatih from Konya's my friend. They both go clear out vending machines sometimes" (98). In his study on "Kanakstan," Klaus-Michael Bogdal suggests that "the narrator in *Abschaum* speaks Turkish (in life-like speech) when Turkish had been spoken in the situation that he narrates or when he wants to emphatically highlight what he is narrating" (239). In his opinion, Zaimoglu's Kanak Sprak is not to be always rated as authentic "because it does not point back to a homogenous language community, but to individuals, whose identity is fragile and whose language competence is very different from one another" (238). Rather "Kanak Sprak [is] an aesthetic construct . . . for which real language use only provides raw material. As a poetic event it requires participation in the culture of Germany, which changes a little at the same time of its appearance" (240). This assessment can be verified in all the texts of my corpus, as it becomes evident that the style of oral speech is always only purportedly mimetic and that it is always subordinate to the overall poetic strategy and with its orality serves stereotypical ideas of non-Western narrative traditions of African or Arabian provenance. This occurs in that an allegedly deficient language style develops into an aesthetic form, and the usual evaluation of the superior Western writing culture versus the inferior southern, Indigenous, African, or other oral culture is put into perspective. By opting for noncanonized language registers, as for instance in *Brick Lane,* with Asian English used in the letters of Nazneen's sister from Dhaka, alterity becomes a poetic style and represents a place, a person, or a language variety and at the same time places the noncanonized language as an equal next to the German, English, or any other European language's standard register. Bogdal, in accepting the "foreign image" of the "Kanak" (the Turkish immigrant worker), rightly sees the decisive difference from the "immigrant worker literature of the 1970s and 80s that wrote against the foreign image and solicited sympathy for the foreigners" (242). This observation can expand to all NWL texts analyzed here. Beyond "writing back," this new literature has reached a self-awareness that allows it to have a playful way with different languages and varieties. Therefore, it would be inadequate to interpret colloquialism as pure mimesis. Of course, the form of address of the lyric "I" to a *gringo* or *gringuito*—permeating the entire volume *Vater unser in Lima*—is adapted from actual language use, but at the same time this kind of mimesis transports topographical, ideological, and other connotations. In this respect, mimesis is far from being the opposite of poiesis. Rather, it represents one part of the reception-guiding structures incorporated in the text. Another is the function of spatial substitution.

Strutz and Zima suggest that "the foreign word in the poem, the novelette, or the novel stands quasi metonymically or by synecdoche as a substitute of a foreign world, which exists only as a connotated one" (*Literarische* 7)—provided that the reader is monolingual I might add—because the bilingual reader can follow the code-switching and understand the "foreign word" or might not even perceive it as such, so that foreignness does not necessarily arise. Any interference from an EL disturbs the textual coherence of the ML and carries into the text the world linked to the EL, so that the disturbance of textual coherence is effectuated deliberately as a poetic strategy. In this manner, the alterity effect augments—the more explicitly the secondary language makes its presence shown—either through quantity or through quality. Examples of a quantitatively massive presence of the EL would be in *Trini*, the theatrical play *Ich liebe dieses Land*, *Augenblick der Liebe*, and *Abschaum*. In all these texts the reader frequently comes across passages in a foreign language which are partly of considerable length and bring intensively the foreign world into the text. In principle, this already happens with any single-word interference, since any name of an Indian dish or an Arabic piece of clothing, for instance, evokes the cultural area that goes with them, as I have suggested.

The same effect is achieved—this time qualitatively—by placing the foreign word in a prominent position such as the title. Rothe underlines the signaling effect of foreign-language titles and names a few standardized properties of these conspicuous headers (from a Western and European perspective): "Latin titles usually suggest a cultural and particularly religious commitment, Spanish and Italian ones suggest a Mediterranean exoticism, English ones modernity or, in the case of a mystery story, such as *Irish Coffee*, authenticity and doing the genre justice" (67). The ostensible effort for authenticity might provide us with an explanation for chapter headers, such as "Sarath" in *Anil's Ghost* or "D. F. sur-real," "circunvalación," "Fuente Vaqueros danach," or "Beyoğlou, istiklâl cad" in the poetry volume *fernlautmetz*. Still, the phatic function of the title, the establishment of contact, is in these cases not necessarily a given, because few readers will identify Sarath as a proper name and many will not necessarily understand the first poem's title's reference to Mexico City, the second one's to García Lorca's birthplace, or the third one's to Istanbul's main shopping street, particularly as the connection between title and text is not necessarily verifiable in the poems that follow. Thus the risk of "a partial or complete [social] communication failure" (Rothe 85) is factored in the text. This definitely affects the monolingual, possibly even the multilingual reader, because, while in the case of Chicano/a literature's English-Spanish bilingualism the readers/recipients are also often bilingual. Oliver, for instance, in *fernlautmetz* asks of the reader much more knowledge of language and places.

A further method of world building can be carried out with proper names. Thus, it is no coincidence that in Djebar's *Les Nuits de Strasbourg,* the Algerian Thelja's French lover is called François, the only German is called Hans, and Thelja's Jewish Moroccan friend is called Eve: their stories, personalities, and they themselves act inside the textual structure in the sense of an *aliquis stat pro aliquo*, standing in for their people and their countries or regions. Every foreign name in the text, be it Hindi in an English text, Turkish in a German, or Náhuatl in a Spanish, refers beyond itself to a spatial dimension that is not identical with the language of ML, so that a tension between two worlds is built into the text that can range from peaceful coexistence to hate-filled conflict and all stages in between. In this respect, a built-in dialogicity can be observed, but only if we also grant the practice of dialog a dissonant component in contrast to general language use. According to Rolf Kloepfer (following Mukařovksý), dialogicity arises when "the mutual intersection of two different worlds (of perception)" is given (88), in this case exceeding Bakhtin's polyphony. For Amodeo, dialogicity develops already through tension between the German-language text and the "author's foreign name, so that, next to the predominant language in the text, another language is present in the background and dialogues with the German" (121). This occurs, however, only to some extent in postcolonial relationships or traditional immigration countries, like Canada and the US, because what is really a "typical" US-American name? Thus we have to ascertain that polyglossia in hybrid texts creates zones of contact, where nonidentical spaces—such as different regions, countries, or urban agglomerations—interact with one another and where single names or words, as well as text passages in EL, evoke these worlds of alterity and bring them into ML. In this sense, the secondary language performs a function of substitution, which, owing to tension with ML, also has an effect on it and creates reciprocal relationships that allow us to speak about a dialogicity inscribed in the text. However, dialogicity does not limit itself to the spatial dimension, but can also occur on a temporal axis.

In connection with "immigrant worker literature," scholarship suggests that its texts orchestrate the loss of the home country and at the same time the not-having-arrived-yet at the host country. Provided that we are in fact dealing with processes of (im)migration, this view might theoretically apply. In NWL, however, we are often dealing with texts in which this form of chronological succession is not described, because the protagonists unite within them or even reject classification or because a fictional historiography is carried out that can be fit into languages, images, and spaces within the framework of selection. This brings up the question of the connection between interference and its historicity on the one hand, and its historical dimension in the context of ML on the other. While examining French deconstruction, Wolfgang Ernst establishes "a separation of history and alternative memories," because "the state's and the nation's historiography cannot represent the collective memory anymore" (9). Instead, "nothing else remains than an archi(ve)textural network—configurations and memorization techniques of a past which no longer develop into phatic history" (Ernst 9). It need not be emphasized that these archives born out of disorder and separation anxiety are contingent to the greatest degree and, as a rule, represent an individual attempt to anchor the subject somewhere between or beyond national literary canons, that is, the question is always a "new interpretation and reconfiguration of already existing material" (Ernst 46). This subjective recourse to a multitude of history/ies is mostly staged in the language of the respective spatial context or by narration on a metatextual level.

The references to García Lorca in the poetic work of Oliver offer an example of this. As a paradigmatic victim of the fascist Falange (who murdered García Lorca in 1936), Oliver shows the parallelisms between Franco's terror and the racist attacks by neo-nazi groups in Germany in the 1990s. In this manner, violence against García Lorca's Otherness (he was homosexual) is placed as a *tertium comparationis* with the violence against other ethnic groups, so that the references to García Lorca bring his history in the contemporary Spanish context, and in a further configuration are applied to German conditions of the present. In a similar manner, Anzaldúa invokes in *Borderlands/La frontera* the world of Aztec gods to stage the double rape of the Mexican peoples: first by the Spanish conqueror, represented allegorically by Hernán Cortéz's Indian interpreter Malinche-Marina (on this, see, e.g., Dröscher and Rincón), later by the US, which annexed large areas of northern Mexico in the nineteenth century and made the resident population there into second-class people. The same historical dimension is addressed when in *Trini* the female protagonist is equated to the earth goddess Tonantzín (74, 149) or in *Border-crosser with a Lamborghini Dream* the cycle of poems carries the titles "Blood on the Wheel" and "Broadway Indian," where the former refers to Aztec sacrificial rites and the latter includes so much vocabulary of the Huichol language that Herrera thought a glossary of the most important expressions was necessary.

In other texts, from the Caribbean for example, it is *Créole* interferences which are suggestive of the African past, while in Maryse Condé's texts historical and ethnographic annotations supplement the glossary and footnotes to bring a little closer to the reader the numerous African tribes appearing in the texts along with their languages and traditions. Özdamar, in her novel *Mutterzunge*, places the search for her mother's lost language, Turkish, at the center and this search leads the woman protagonist to her grandfather, who spoke and wrote Arabic, which she attempts to learn. In the text there are loan words from Arabic into Turkish (29, 39, 46) and "philological" discussions (41). As if in a memory spiral, Turkish words in the

German text provoke the Arabic one, the same as in Anzaldúa's text, where Spanish words evoke the pre-Colombian era, or in Djebar's text, where Arabic words evoke the Berber. All these interferences refer both to spaces and to times: they express the omnipresence of places and the simultaneity of different temporal stages. Thus, words in other languages function as an accumulator of places, spaces, times, and cultural references of alterity that are brought into new contexts and are thus reconfigured. By means of this spatial and temporal archaeology of histories, already existing archives are expanded and supplemented as data storage, so that as a result hybridity arises, which distinguishes such texts of globalization—that is, NWL—from previous ones. In principle, the interference of another language is always a marked element in the linguistic sense, since it stands out noticeably from the linguistic environment of ML. Already Adorno condoned the shocking effect of the foreign word as enlightening and even subversive, because "the foreign word resists—and in that it is a model for the poetic word par excellence—the frictionless, seemingly self-evident use, the thoughtless use, even abuse. But where friction arises in the first place, understanding seems . . . possible after all" (qtd. in Schmitz-Emans, *Dichtung* 96). Particularly because of its markedness, the foreign element thematizes and referentializes the text in itself and through deviation from the code steers our attention to the norm of said code of the ML by exposing the textual structure by means of its policy of deviation. This phenomenon is comparable to transtextuality, one that allows us a certain transfer of theory from this area onto multilingual texts (see Broich and Pfister 54). This is because, as in transtextuality, the disturbance of textual coherence has as a result a complication of meaning on the one hand, and a diffusion of meaning on the other (Lachmann, *Gedächtnis* 122). However, it produces a syncretistic style, as Renate Lachmann suggests: "the dialogical principle and intertextuality" as a "linking with the respectively corresponding cultural models" on the basis of Dostoyevsky, Belyj, and Mayakovsky. She defines style as "an ensemble of strategies of exclusion and homogenization [acting] with regard to genre, language, and culture that attempts to totalize the named areas. Syncretism, on the other hand, appears as a detotalizing approach turning itself against style, in entering the areas affected by the exclusion and in the transgression of the boundaries of homogenisation" (*Gedächtnis* 200). In this manner, the "heterogeneous [is designed] as its own quality" (201) and the foreign sign turns out to be polyvalent: it performs not only spatial and temporal functions of substitution, but at the same time it focalizes the arbitrariness of the relation between *signifiant* and *signifié* (Schmitz-Emans, *Dichtung* 90) by confronting the singularity and immobility of the signified with the multiplicity of the signifiers. In that moment, however, when more options of signifying are open for every signified, the contingency of standardized national languages as the only permissible medium for literature becomes clear.

Lachmann argues that a complication of meaning arises here for the bilingual readers, since they identify the foreign word with its connotations and integrate it into the fabric of the text, but at the same time also call up unnamed options, in keeping with the observation that a deviation from the code always conjures up the code itself in its normal form. For monolingual readers a diffusion of meaning sets in, whose degree depends on the extent to which the interference's meaning is elucidated by the textual strategy by translation, for instance, or a paraphrasing explanation. If, however, the meaning remains unexplained, a—temporary—interruption of the realization of the text occurs and this shifts concentration from the content to the expression of the linguistic sign and lays bare the materiality of this sign, so that the self-referential level of the text temporarily overrides the referential one. By concentrating on the material side of the multilingual textual fabric, poeticity as "the making aware of the motivational relationship between sound and meaning" (Lachmann, *Dialogizität* 35) is demarcated from the proseity of everyday language: the text's linguistic signs lose the implicitness and distinctiveness of their existence, because the interference makes clear that a foreign word can stand at any place in the text. Transferred on language as a cultural medium per se, this results in a relativization of the cultural term itself, a subversive effect that is supported by the transtextual processing of literature in another language.

A frequent motivation for recourse to "other" literatures appears to lie in the endeavor to be deliberately placed outside a canonized national literature and to present other options, which, under aesthetic points of view, are established as equals next to those of ML. In this manner the texts practice a transgression of the hegemonial discourse: the national, the unambiguous is sacrificed in favor of the transnational and heterogeneity, whereby at the same time an emancipatory vector is provided, because through transtextual pluralism the restrictedness of a nationally oriented understanding of literature is laid bare and attacked. Furthermore, many transtextual references stand in by synecdoche for other societal models, historical eras, or political ideologies, which are then mutually reflected in the text. Thus, for example, the allusion to Pablo Neruda in Oliver's work, which evokes a whole bundle of connotations, ranging from the US's imperialist politics toward Latin America to the not yet overcome consequences of the Pinochet coup in 1974. In Rushdie's or Schami's texts, on the other hand, parodist features stand in the foreground, which ultimately also have a decanonizing effect in both directions. It seems to me that it is exactly here where the paradigm shift lies in comparison to German-speaking immigrant literature of the 1970s and partly of the 1980s, because authors do not write any more against something; they borrow from multiple cultures and process these into a poetic formation that cannot be narrated otherwise. In this manner the texts generate a third space, which can afford to make eclectic use of national literatures without necessarily displaying a preference or solidarity toward either of them. In this, an expansion of the transtextual space over the whole world takes place. However, the question concerns to what extent such narration is followed by readers, and this brings us to the question of reading multilingual texts.

In order to discuss the reception aesthetic side of multilingual texts at least to some extent, I reflect upon a few fundamental considerations. Wolfgang Iser held the tenet with regard to fiction as being a structure of communication, that is, not as to what it means, but what its effects would be, and that is what one ought to focus on (*Wirklichkeit* 278). In *The Act of Reading*, Iser worked with the term of "textual coherence," which is interrupted in the text by blank spaces, so that on the one hand the deautomatization of the fictional text takes place and on the other hand the readers, especially in texts with numerous blank spaces, such as *Finnegan's Wake*, are forced to acquiesce to "irritation." Umberto Eco developed Iser's approach further and suggested the concept of the "model reader," who the writer has in mind for the text and who is supposedly able to deal with the expressions in the same way as the writer deals with them since communication depends on a structuring of codes the reader is able to decipher (*The Role* 17). Therefore, "every type of text selects explicitly a general model of possible reader through the choice a) of a specific linguistic code, b) of a certain literary style, and c) of specific specialisation indices" (*The Role* 17), which could be specialized knowledge, for instance. Such models offer gain for the concept of NWL only to some extent, since they start from the assumption—although it is unspoken—of a more or less monolingual situation and isoglossia between reader and text. However, even in multilingual texts a basic monocultural context builds the operative basis for considerations regarding the reader.

On the basis of Eco's model reader—here applied to hybrid texts—it is helpful to behold a different textual strategy, one that ideally brings out a reader whose linguistic and possibly even transtextual competences are approximately identical to those of the writer. This can happen, for example, in Djebar's texts when the interference is discussed quasi philologically at a metamultilingual level and any doubts regarding its meaning and use are clarified in the primary language, so that the text itself offers an encyclopedic competence (Eco) necessary for the understanding of the text. This, however, is an isolated case connected to the general thematization of complex language relationships (French-Arabic-Berber) in Djebar's texts.

Rudin, in his study on Chicano/a novels, arrives at the result that the vast majority of interferences consist of only one word and 95% of those are nouns (110). In case of doubt, they can easily be looked up in a dictionary. Many of the words are either loan words, such as *papaya*, *rancho*, *plaza*, or *tequila*, words which are in use in English (mainly in the south of the US) or designate cliché perceptions regarding the Hispanic world and are therefore also accessible, such as *adiós*, *muchacho*, *siesta*, or the swear-word *caramba*, or they are cognates, such as *veterano* or *miserable*. Only few words are actually "hermetic Spanish," that is, interferences which are really not accessible to the non-Spanish-speaking reader, whereby this applies mostly to longer passages (Rudin 116–20). With regard to the integration of these interferences in the text, Rudin notices that a translation is offered in all novels he examined, be it in parentheses, as an attributive expression, in footnotes, as a paraphrase, or even explicatively (124). A typical example is "Your *abuelito* is dead, Papa says early one morning in my room. *Está muerto*, and then as if he just heard the news himself, crumples like a coat and cries, my brave Papa cries" (Cisneros

56). Here, the interferences immediately draw the readers' attention to themselves because they are italicized, and every monolingual reader can deduce the facts (the grandfather is dead) from the following sentences. The bi- or multilingual reader, on the other hand, has to put up with the redundant narrative style, because such bilingual text passages are always overdetermined by additional explanations and translations, which under the circumstances can be at the expense of suspense in the text. Thus, Rudin arrives at the following: "the foreign language may disorient monolingual readers and make them feel excluded; they may even deplore the fact that they don't know Spanish. But their disorientation functions as an element in creating suspense; if they knew Spanish, the text would not be half as intriguing" (226). In Rudin's opinion, the primary goal of Chicano/a authors writing in English is to produce a "proper English . . . as if they, as 'Hispanics' and as 'minority writers,' had to prove to the 'mainstream public' that they are capable of writing a competent English prose," while it was reserved for the "native speakers" among the authors, such as James Joyce, to undermine the English literary discourse through bold linguistic innovations (229). Following Rudin, the Spanish interferences are not blank spaces—which would force the reader to participate in the shaping of the text—and do not result in communication failure for the monolingual recipient. This could also apply to some of the texts I analyze, but by no means can they be applied to texts such as the poetry volumes by Herrera or Oliver, because the code-switching there is conducted without any explanation or paraphrases. Even where understanding is made easier for the monolingual reader with glossaries or notes, the question arises as to what extent a French-speaking reader of Condé's novel *Ségou*, for instance, is able to learn and is prepared to follow the novel's multilingualism based on African idioms without getting lost in the thicket of the numerous references. The additional information in the text is effectively against a readership that is nonmultilingual and not familiar with African cultures. Christopher L. Miller describes this phenomenon as "anthropological rhetoric" and sees it as a characteristic of African Francophone literature (234).

A similar case is Zaimoglu's texts with their "Kanak Sprak": "the Turkish immigrants at first suspect whether they are being ridiculed for their deficient language; German readers feel excluded. Both groups usually overlook the fact that Kanak Sprak is an aesthetic construct that draws its raw materials from real language use" (Bogdal 239). Here, blank spaces are created by the Turkish insertions, which the German-speaking reader cannot fill in. Still, as a nontranslation they constitute a "mode of interaction that is implicit, context-shaped, laced with innuendos and allusions" (Boback 78). Peter Boback interprets this conscious denial of communication system theoretically as a "mode of exclusion of cultural self-reference" and thus ultimately as a "message of identity" of "strategic importance" that refers to the nonnegotiable, difference, and particularity (79, 83–84). In this respect, it constitutes a component of a specific textual strategy to the same extent as the above-shown tactics of the Id-s comprehension, which creates its readers for itself—readers, who are thrown back to their own (linguistic) boundaries and have to content themselves with that. Nevertheless, Iser's maxim can certainly also be applied here, namely, that an excess of blank spaces ultimately leads to abandonment of the act of reading, just as a prevalence of explanations and references deprives the text of its manageability because the flow of the text is interrupted much too often.

The plethora of interferences from Indian languages in English-language texts, for example, particularly in the field of food or clothing, indicates that much vocabulary from Indian languages has been borrowed in English everyday language, just as with terms in German from Turkish, for example, "Döner Kebab" or "Kaftan," and this does not impede understanding in English or German. In the US the strong presence of Spanish is taken into account by many radio stations or in advertisements, banks, and telephone prompts. In 2005 France admitted Djebar, a writer whose first language is not French, into the pantheon of the *Académie Française*, which is a symptom of the large presence of the Maghreb and other Arabic cultures in French everyday life. In general, not only can we observe a qualitative and quantitative rise of different forms of multilingualism in literature, but there also exists an audience that increasingly accepts and appreciates these texts, the more so as the publishing industry makes a great effort to market this literature. Therefore I venture to make the prognosis that the presence of polyglossia in literature is in the future going to be an even more widespread phenomenon than it already is. And in publishing the sales figures of books by authors such as Schami, Djebar, or Rushdie speak for themselves.

As I suggested a number of times with various examples, multilingualism and transtextuality in literature are not new, and contemporary hybrid texts represent only a wider spread of such tradition-rich multilingual text production. Comparable to their present position as counterdiscourse to established literary discourse types, multilingual texts have always played a subversive role in the literary system, be it as burlesque from the sixteenth to the eighteenth century or be it as surrealist or Dadaist experiments in the twentieth century. In this state of affairs the critical question arises as to where the paradigm shift lies, and what actually differentiates a Joyce novel from a Rushdie one, for instance. In sum,

> 1) The quantity of multilingual literature has reached unprecedented dimensions. Contemporary marketing and distribution possibilities have brought forth multilingual literature from the niche of the special for either a highly educated or particularly interested readership. In Germany, for example, each time the latest novel by Schami is published, it reaches bestseller status. The same is the case with Djebar's novels in France, and Rushdie has reached such a degree of global fame, thanks to the *Fatwa* of the Iranian mullah, that his texts almost need no advertisement, because they become best sellers from Mumbai to Los Angeles anyway. This is happening regardless of the fact that most of the texts by these authors offer the monolingual reader a considerable chal-

lenge owing to their linguistic and thematic complexity. Apparently, the reading public is prepared to accept a certain degree of multilingualism, for which the increasing presence of polyglot relations in everyday life might be responsible. Even in Europe, the last purported stronghold of national monolingualism, it has become unlikely even in remote areas to pass any given day without any foreign language. In the big cities numerous ethnic groups and languages are omnipresent anyhow, be it Turkish in Frankfurt, Arabic in Paris, Ukrainian in Madrid, or Tamil in London. On the African continent, in both of the Americas, or in countries such as China, India, or Russia, multilingualism has always been the norm. Thus it is not surprising that not only more multilingual texts are produced than ever before, but that they are also increasingly read and appreciated. The apparent acceptance of this paradigm shift is also reflected in the fact that distinctly "national" authors without any background of (im)migration, such as Walser or Muñoz Molina, have written multilingual novels with parts in English.

2) The variety of the foreign language interferences attests to a shifting of the threshold of tolerance for such impositions to unprecedented levels. With hybrid texts the reader is confronted with new forms of expression and such texts convey the impression that in the last three decades almost all thinkable polyglossia possibilities were tried out: intrasentential or intersentential code-switching, interferences of a lexical, phonetic, morphological, or grammatical kind, transfer of metaphors or proverbs, transtextuality and metamultilingualism, foreign language insertions ranging in length from that of a single word to entire passages, translated in footnotes, paraphrased in the text, enumerated in word lists, and metanarratives, and so on. This manifoldness on the side of literary production corresponds to the variety of reception options: textual strategies range from the explanation of almost every foreign element to ostentatious alterity and thus extreme hermeticism for the monolingual reader. With this wealth of forms NWL texts have undoubtedly left far behind them the conventionality of earlier multilingual literature.

3) The functionality of multilingualism surpasses in its complexity that of older texts. Admittedly, macaronic poetry, for instance, also placed language mixture at the service of a subversive counterdiscourse. Multilingual works around the turn of the last century—characterized by deep language skepticism—also undermined the imperialist ideologies of the European nation-states—but contemporary hybrid language constructs transport all that and more. That they question everything national and homogeneous through the mere fact of their linguistic heterogeneity places them at the forefront of current literary production. The fact that hybrid literature leads national literature *ad absurdum* by

means of their authors' globally laid out transtextuality—by referring to other cultural models beyond national, linguistic, and cultural boundaries, and by incorporating them in the matrix language at a level of equal value—is a recent phenomenon which can be compared with a decanonization of the institution of the national literary canon and the entire establishment of prizes and honors attached to it. Intratextually, the foreign word functions for the characterization of people and places or the illustration of situations or conditions and thus is one of the foundations of the textual strategy that in monolingual texts has to find recourse to other literary means of world creation. In hybrid texts coherence is suspended, whereby the reading habits which were taken for granted are broken up and attention is directed toward the text's materiality. Moreover, the arbitrariness of the *signifiant-signifié* relationship is laid bare, where, however, more signifiers come into question for a single signified, any sign becomes contingent and polyvalent. This ultimately results in the dissolution of cultural boundaries thought to be stable.

4) Finally, it is necessary to verify the shift of reception behavior by readers. The ideal case of bilingual or multilingual text-reader isoglossia is certainly not rare. However, apparently there is an increasing number of more or less monolingual readers who are prepared to get involved with texts in another language and with texts that have hybrid narration. The reason for this is to be found, first, in the poetic discourse of multilingual texts, which is based on techniques (translation, annotation, paraphrase, etc.) that render interferences intelligible. This leads, on the side of isogloss reception, to a pleonastic and overdetermined text structure. Second, hybrid texts often contain redundant information that is not absolutely necessary for understanding the text, because they merely refer back to the utterances expressed in an explicative, expressive, or summarizing manner. And third, it has been shown that even with foreign-language insertions narrated as hermetic, communication is established with readers even if it entails only manoeuvring the reader into an inferior position—which is comparable to that of an immigrant, colonized person, or foreigner—so that asymmetrical power relations are exposed and reinterpreted. Thus, alterity is experienceable by readers quasi "firsthand" during the reading process, because they do not read about experiences of alterity, but they read alterity directly and without any intermediaries.

Chapter Six

Nomadic Biographies in New World Literature

In the previous chapter I describe how polyglossia represents a morphological and structural characteristic of NWL. In this chapter I elaborate on the content and thematic aspects of hybrid literatures. Although in my opinion the discourse of globalization is no more than epistemic positioning—in Peter Sloterdijk's words a "philosophically inspired grand narrative" (11)—narratives of globalization are indispensable to "shed light on the situation" even at the risk of generating new mythologizations exactly there, where they should be uncovered as such (11). After all, we can retreat with Sloterdijk to the lowest common denominator of globalization according to which narratives are characterized "always by operations with effects in the distance" (19). There is agreement that the mechanisms of globalization do not unilaterally proceed in any way in the direction of homogenization—the much-invoked "McDonaldization"—but that a stronger emphasis on regional or local differentiations can be assigned to them as a complement. Thus Reingard Nethersole detects three interrelated movements in/of globalization:

> First, enormous technological achievements, particularly in the areas of telecommunication by means of microchip and development of semi-conductors, air traffic, and maritime transportation, have interlinked the world in terms of communications and transportations, which can be assessed to be technical globalization. Alongside it stands financial globalization in the form of a historical maximum in liberalization of traffic of gold and capital. And both contribute to cultural globalization. . . . Under the leadership of multinational corporations and under the sign of a Coca-Cola and McDonalds culture reaching from the Cape to Cairo and from Berlin to Beijing, the world may superficially look similar everywhere, but differentiating moments stand opposed to the homogenizing globalization processes, which reveal themselves worldwide as a search for individual, ethnic, and national identity. . . . In combination with and fostered by the other two globalization processes, cultural globalization brings about an increasing worldwide networking, availability, and amalgamation of the most different particular or local characteristics beyond cultural and linguistic boundaries. (51)

As I elaborate in previous chapters and as Nethersole suggests, the global and the local are not in opposition to each other, but "the local . . . [represents] not only a constitutive part of the global," but "often [develops] in it first" and in this manner "global structures that promote diversity" are being built (Breidenbach and Zukrigl 93). Thus the crux of the matter is that "single groups [become] different in a very similar manner, because the dimensions, along which they vary, have become more limited and therefore mutually more intelligible. They have become quasi compatible to each other" (Breidenbach and Zukrigl 93). According to Nassehi, global is "the horizon, where the localities meet and become aware of their structural epistemological similarity exactly because they are aware of their diversity" (*Geschlossenheit* 198). Those processes are analyzed in the humanities and the social sciences which on the one hand work to "expose" culture as "behavior-relevant interpretation inventory" and its "signification systems" which function in their respective context and thereby "make circumstances comparable, by uncovering their different cultural codification," but on the other hand reveal exactly through this process of classification "every culture as another culture of another culture" and that "things can also be different and can be observed differently" (Breidenbach and Zukrigl 235).

The above paradox underlines my analyses, because even when we work with supposedly stable "English" or "Mexican" cultural patterns as observation schemata, this always takes place while being aware of the contingency of the said paradox. On the other hand, a closed system is necessary as an operational basis in order to even get the comparison of these elements going as a process. I emphasize that it cannot be a question of dividing portions of national cultures in the sense of percentages to the container paradigm in order to subsequently decide based on it whether a text is more "British" or more "Turkish." Rather, we use such national designations only to the extent that it is unavoidable for the description of fundamental text constituents and in order to work out the relation between the different cultural contexts as the third space is generated exactly by this dynamic interplay, where something new, unprecedented, emerges. Therefore, it has to be demonstrated with which discursive strategies this amalgamation of elements foreign to one another takes place and whether an overarching structure is identifiable in the genesis of cultural compatibility.

Bhabha emphasizes the point that "alternative histories of the excluded" do not stand in the foreground, because "the currency of critical comparativism, of aesthetic judgment, is no longer the sovereignty of the national culture"; rather, the question concerns "a radical revision in the concept of human community" and "what this geopolitical space may be, as a local or transnational reality" (*The Location* 6). Moreover, it is inevitable, that "the Western metropole must confront its postcolonial history, told by its influx of postwar migrants and refugees, as an indigenous or native narrative internal to its national identity" (Bhabha 6). This claim—made from the perspective of postcolonialism in the 1990s—has not lost any of its raison d'être, but needs to be broadened and modified, because postcoloniality does not only flow from the periphery toward the center: instead, it is more insightful to concede to the hybrid constructs their own space. The one does not exclude the other. For example, in the case of an author of Turkish origin such as Zafer Şenocak—who writes on mostly Turkish German themes and narrative style—it might be correct to classify his texts as components of German-language literature. However, other texts, for example Oliver's or Özdamar's, would be designated inadequately, obviously, as German-language literature. Because such hybrid forms of literature emerge under conditions of postnationality and are characterized by "deterritorialization" and "displacement" by means of transfers, mixtures, and shifts of local experiences, new forms of multilayered ethnic and social identities are created.

In a quasi postnational global situation characterized by migration, exile, and diaspora, the rigid concept of nation that was underlying the discussion about world literature and at the same time was considered as the "repository of world literatures also becomes questionable" (Bachmann-Medick, "Multikultur" 270). Thus, we find ourselves before "the cross-border manifestation of a collective imagination of ethnic groups scattered the world over who have their decisive connection and communication media exactly in the form of literature, texts, books, newspapers, and films" and therefore it is high time to "reconsider the [traditional] processes of cultural comparison" (Bachmann-Medick, "Multikultur" 271). Arjun Appadurai differentiates between five aspects of globalization: 1) "ethnoscapes," under which he summarizes those who have left their ancestral cultural space—as tourists, immigrants, refugees, exiles, or guestworkers; 2) "technoscapes," the highly qualified executives of multinational corporations or globally operating institutions; 3) "finanscapes," who constantly jump across cultural and national borders in their workplace as bankers or stock exchange traders; 4) "mediascapes," who are responsible for and produce repertoires of stereotypes and images and information which flow like an unending current through newspapers, magazines, movies, television, and the internet, and propagate in the heads of diversely socialized and enculturated people all over the word; and 5) "ideoscapes" which has to do with scenarios of violence and counterviolence and of power and conflict.

Since the standard categorization and classification of concepts have become obsolete under globalization, it is now necessary to create new theoretical configurations in order to understand the hybrid literature of (im)migration, exile, and diaspora in its dynamic between globalization and localism. In the preface to *Literatur im Zeitalter der Globalisierung*, Schmeling, Schmitz-Emans, and Walstra write that "regarding literary production, factors of globalization are observable on at least three levels: 1) at the level of text distribution and circulation; 2) at the level of literary structure; and 3) at the level of literary thematization" (8). I agree to this as a fundamental deliberation and thus through the representation of the conflict of the individual philologies with "their" respective minority discourse it turns out that meanwhile an awareness of the transnational existence of literature in general and of hybrid forms in particular prevails. Structure and thematization are of a decisive importance for NWL and it seems to me that this is where the need for action lies. In this respect, I go one step beyond global literature, because I apply it as a *tertium comparationis* to a heterogeneous text group with polymorphous hybridity and undercut it at the same time since monocultural (if there even are any) and monolingual texts are not factored in. Of relevance is the exposure of transnationally used strategies for the creation of fictional realities and the analysis of the common narrative mechanisms despite the cultural, thematic, and ideological heterogeneity of the texts.

The analysis of the large number of hybrid texts available in many languages allows me to construct a complex system of key differences. At first I make a distinction between three different text-constituting components which pertain to protagonists in the texts, their spaces, and time constructs. These three groups are in turn broken down to subgroups: 1) "personnel" includes phenomena under conditions of globalization such as exile, work- or education-related (im)migration, marriage migration, and the second generation of immigrants, while at the level of localism it includes religious, local, or regional customs, rites, mores, dress regulations, or regional languages and oral traditions; 2) "place/space" at a global level, where the metropolises play an important role in NWL texts, but also amorphous nonplaces such as airports or hotels without distinctive identities; to these are added borders as zones of contact or transnational areas of contact of a larger extent (such as the Caribbean or the Alemannic triangle Black Forest-Alsace-Northwest Switzerland; in contrast to these, on the local side stands, for example, the concretely defined place of the village or the town or even a specific natural landscape that cannot be thought of as exchangeable); and 3) "temporal layers," where the global-local dichotomy is not adhered to, since it is mostly about the simultaneity of the nonsimultaneous which at times are not compatible with one another but are mixed in a new simultaneity.

Beck cites as one of the "cosmopolitan practices" of the present the "extensive mobility" of people, who, to an unprecedented extent, "have the right to 'travel' corporeally, imaginatively, and virtually" (*The Cosmopolitan* 42), where this "traveling" can be triggered for the most different reasons and can take place hidden under the cargo area of a lorry or in the cabin of a luxury cruise liner. The fact is that never before have so many people moved from one place to another. Toro names the consequences of this mobility: "In many of our societies we are experiencing radical reorganization related to the diasporic and migratory movements, which are changing and profoundly altering the shape that these societies are currently taking. I am referring to such places as Canada, Australia, New Zealand, the U.S.A., and, in a certain way, Western Europe. This has led an ever-increasing number of academics to start paying attention to these new emergent cultural practices, reorganisations, and voices" (60). Gert Mattenklott ties a new interpretation of Goethean world literature to the migration processes by pointing out "that 'world literature,' this supposedly noblest export article of classical humanism, receives its strongest impulses from external and increasingly internal wars: world literature as a symptom, if not product of strife" (613). As examples he mentions Ondaatje's *The English Patient*, Rushdie's *From Shame*, and Walcott's *Omeros*, all of which thematize fates of (im)migration and tell stories of people who had to leave their environment due to circumstances of violence and now attempt to find their way in a new topography or await death in a destroyed no-man's land, like the "English patient." Often enough, these are stories of losses, and the term world literature, according to Mattenklott, is perhaps "too tightly associated with the history of mental colonisation" for it to be brought in to the discussion without prejudice (615). In fact, the attempts of literary studies to grant a "universal" validity to the "emergent," "young," or "minority" literatures attest to an unbroken respect for the great names of the Western-dominated history of literature, which stems from a deeply ingrained "mental colonization" in the sense of Mattenklott.

An area that is seldom thematized in literary studies is marriage migration. In English-language literature, Ali places this subject at the center of her novel *Brick Lane*: eighteen-year-old Nazneen from Bangladesh is married off to a supposedly good party, an older, educated Bengali man, who has made it in London as a "civil servant" and constantly collects more diplomas. Speaking only two words of English, she arrives in London and slowly expands her activity radius. This process of years of obtaining mental and material independence culminates in a love affair with Karim, the leader of the "Bengal Tigers" activist group (240), but whose marriage proposal she still refuses, although her husband Chanu has returned to Dhaka and she decides to stay in England at first and turn her long-standing home work as a seamstress into a profession. Nazneen's story in London is contrasted to that of her beautiful and active sister in Bangladesh, who is abused by her first husband, then works as a factory worker in Dhaka after leaving him, becomes unemployed because of her "indecent behavior" and almost slips into prostitution, but is saved from this low point by working as a housemaid and nanny for a rich Bengali family in "Bollywood" conditions. Nazneen's path is symbolized by "ice skating": while this word seems to be her biggest stumbling block with the English language immediately after her arrival (36–37), when she sees the sport on television for the first time, she dreams herself away from her monotonous life while watching a figure skating scene—the figure skater, who frees herself from her partner's secure grip and glides over the ice, alone, at an intoxicating speed, is rewarded at the end with the applause of an invisible audience (93), which seems for Nazneen to illustrate the epitome of the independent woman. At the end of the novel, it is ice skating wherein lies something like a happy ending: her daughters and Razia take her to an ice skating rink as a surprise: "Nazneen turned round. To get on the ice physically—it hardly seemed to matter. In her mind she was already there. She said, 'But you can't skate in a sari.' Razia was already lacing her boots. 'This is England,' she said. 'You can do whatever you like'" (492). These optimistic final sentences of the novel resonate and, after all the stories unfurled in the text of physically and emotionally abused women, express a hope for better living conditions and that even the smallest resistance against— mainly, but not exclusively—male repression ultimately pays off. *Brick Lane* is a text on migration-related customs and dislocations in different social environments, namely, in the society of the country of origin—Bangladesh in this case—as well as that of the host country. Almost all fixed culture-specific patterns of perception are debunked: the behavioral codices of the one environment are not valid in the other or in the setting of another generation and even seemingly ideal conditions quickly turn out to be repressive or at least debilitating for the individual. So, Nazneen notes that her husband Chanu with his degree in English literature can indeed recite Shakespeare, but cannot cope with the demands of the English labor market and never concretely puts any intention into action: "He can see, thought Nazneen. He can comment. But he cannot act" (92). He is a typical loser, who, in the course of the novel, undergoes a steep fall from academic grace through unemployment to being a taxi driver, cushioned only by Nazneen's sewing at home, regarding which, however, he only knows to take on the role of the mightier once more: "He performed a kind of rudimentary quality control, tugging at zips, and twiddling collars while probing his cheeks with his tongue. Chanu totted up the earnings and collected them. He was the middleman, a role which he viewed as Official and in which he exerted himself. . . . 'We're making good money this week. . . . Don't worry. I'll take care of everything.' For two whole months she did not even know how much she earned" (207–08). He usurps her work and her income, albeit only temporarily, since soon thereafter he announces with a great gesture his hiring as an "employee at Kempton Kars, driver number one-six-one-nine, and the Home Fund will prosper" (209). Then, Karim, "a new middleman" and soon Nazneen's lover, comes into play. The figure of Chanu transports the cultural gap between Bengali and English behavioral patterns, which seem even more comical, because he describes himself as progressive and Westernized: "I don't stop you from doing anything. I am westernized now. It is lucky for you that you married an educated man" (45). And then with the same breath he goes on to forbid her to go out alone, since she would not have done that in Bangladesh and he would provide her with anything she would ask of him; besides, people would talk about him, were she to go alone out on the street "and I will look like a fool," so that ultimately other people's ignorance is the reason for this prohibition (45).

On a different side, in the character of Dr. Azad's wife appears in a decided counterposition to that of Chanu, exposing his pseudoliberal attitude as a blatant delusion. After a discussion in the physician's home that almost degenerates into a fight because the physician's daughter in a mini-skirt vigorously demands money to go out, Chanu lectures about "the tragedy of immigrant lives" and the "clash of cultures" between assimilation and preservation of the cultural legacy of one's own, surviving in a "society where racism is prevalent" (113). This is followed by what could almost be called a keynote address, in which the unwillingness of Bengali immigrant women to at least adapt to a small degree to the English behavioral norms is fiercely criticized:

> "Why do you make it so complicated?" said the doctor's wife. Assimilation this, alienation that! Let me tell you a few simple facts. Fact: we live in a Western society. Fact: our children will act more and more like Westerners. Fact: that's no bad thing. My daughter is free to come and go. Do I wish I had enjoyed myself like her when I was young? Yes! . . . Listen, when I'm in Bangladesh I put on a sari and cover my head and all that. But here I go out

to work. I work with white girls and I'm just one of them. If I want to come home and eat curry, that's my business. Some women spend ten, twenty years here and they sit in the kitchen grinding spices all day and learn only two words of English. . . . They go around covered from head to toe, in their little walking prisons, and when someone calls to them in the street they are upset. The society is racist. The society is all wrong. Everything should change for them. They don't have to change one thing. That, she said, stabbing the air, is the tragedy. (114)

The novel, however, leaves no room for doubt that this persistence of the brought-along tradition on the part of the women is not to be attributed to their lack of will, but as a rule is the result of men's pressure to accept alternative life concepts only for themselves, but by no means for the female members of their families. For this reason the text arrives at a dramatic climax when the older daughter Shahana runs away from home in order to escape the imminent return to Dhaka. In this, the narration is about the fight of the second generation. On the other hand, Nazneen's story demonstrates how even seemingly hopeless conditions can be transformed into positive ones by means of the resistance and energy of the persons concerned. Still, no Manichaeistic world view with clear solutions is built, especially as a result of the simultaneous unfurling of her sister Hasina's situation in Bangladesh through her letters. She does live—from a Western viewpoint—in a backward society dominated by Qur'an law, but she takes her fate in her own hands much earlier than Nazneen does and has her own income as a worker, again much earlier than Nazneen, although the obstacles she has to overcome are bigger than they would have been in England. Nazneen, on the other hand, makes her revolution rather in the form of passive resistance at first; only after a longer process of finding herself does she give in to Karim (288) and only at the end does she refuse to follow her husband, by staying behind in London alone with her two girls, depending solely upon her own self and her own income (478, 481). Through the behavior of the protagonists in *Brick Lane* in dealing with everyday problems, positive or negative stereotypical beliefs about English or Bengali culture are put into perspective, and instead of absolute solutions there can only be momentary negotiations, whose longer-term consequences are uncertain. At the same time it is made clear that these negotiations of constantly new positions in the societal structure change people: Nazneen at the end is not the "girl from the village: totally unspoilt" nor "a good worker: cleaning and cooking and all that" anymore (23), as her husband once described her in a telephone conversation, nor is it certain whether she is going to find her place in London. The optimistic ending of the book merely implies such a possibility, but at the same time allows for more options such as a visit to Dhaka (forever?), a career as a designer, or other developments altogether.

A parody of marriage migration is offered in Kureishi's *The Buddha of Suburbia*: the protagonist's uncle and aunt want to tame their unruly daughter Jamila by having her marry a man from India and, further, to have a capable son-in-law take over the grocery store so as to unburden them after many years of work. But instead of a strict Indian husband, it is Changez who comes to London, with a maimed arm, grown up in a rich home with servants, who does not care about the store in the least, but wants immediately to go to a bookstore to buy English literary classics (83–85). Jamila at first fights tooth and nail against her father's marriage plans for her, but agrees when her father threatens to commit suicide. She avenges herself in her own manner in that she bans her husband right after the wedding into a room of their apartment and does not let him near her. He is financially supported by Jamila, some-times Karim, and his family in India—"which was unusual, because it should have been the other way round as Changez made his way in the affluent West" (98)—and a Japanese prostitute in a red kimono helps him overcome his forced sexual abstinence (98). At the end he does share an apartment with his wife, but Jamila has a relation-ship with another man and has a child, whom Changez affectionately takes care of (279). This marriage arrangement unfurls all thinkable transgressions and upends all traditional roles: not only is it the man who is "imported," but he is inferior to his wife in every respect and comes to terms with a more or less parasitic existence as a "girl Friday." As in *Brick Lane,* the marriage migrant finds a different situation than expected and inevitably has to modify his life concepts in order to survive, where the understanding of his role and the behavioral patterns brought along are of little use and the host society does not offer any new ones which he can adopt (for further examples of marriage migration, see, e.g., Shyam Selvadurai's *Cinnamon Gardens,* Nuruddin Farah's *A Naked Needle,* and Schami's *Die Sehnsucht der Schwalbe*).

Forced migration in the form of escape from war or persecution for political or ideological reasons can be demonstrated with multiple examples in the novels. The expatriate's existence gives the occasion for the novel *Bait* by Albahari, where not only the story of the first-person narrator is unfurled, but also fifty years of the Balkans' bloody history by means of the tape recordings of his late mother, which he listens to in his Canadian exile. The protagonist swims "on the surface of life" (75) without simply living it, he pokes at it "like a child who slowly picks through its plate and removes the tendons from the white meat of a chicken" (76). His condi-tion is one of radical disorientation: "I'm sitting infinitely far from everything that once made me what I am, or what I could have been, or what I was. And that chaos of grammatical tenses confirms to what extent I find myself outside life, in which only the present tense exists and there is no grammar" (76). Grammatical rules are for the first-person narrator a symbol for an anchoring in space and time, which he has lost in Canada. Writing is for him an attempt to cope with this loss and to gradu-ally gain new ground beneath his feet. Narratively, this process takes place over the manuscript with the mother's story that the first-person narrator writes and gives his Canadian friend Donald to discuss and proofread: writing is "a search for a proper measure of the relation between the real and the unreal" as Donald formulates it (12). He is friend and enemy at the same time, he is the surface which the first-person narrator can rub against and get excited about, until he lets go of him at the end, by slamming the door in his face, making him feel solid material with all his body for the first time (157–58).

The protagonist almost defiantly declares coping with the new living situation as being exclusively his own matter and says he reserves the right to his own methods, which also include the backward-orientated examination of his own past, as it is represented by writing about his mother's life, which in Donald's opinion only leads to a situation where "all of those who arrive are only marching in place instead of moving forward" (84). The first-person narrator's efforts are directed against this negative assessment, because he exacts for himself the shaping of a future-orientated life concept under the new conditions, but without banning from his memory the parts of his previous life in Belgrade and Zagreb that he brought with him. Thus, the book ultimately is a testimony of the struggle for the genesis of a reasonably stabilized patchwork identity, where the jumbled elements find new relations to one another and take new positions in the coordinate system of the structure of personality.

The asylum seeker Beni from Nigeria in Turrini's play *Ich liebe dieses Land* is not even given the possibility of *Bait*'s protagonist in the first place, because his path leads him from custody pending deportation over a short, apparently safe stay in the home of the Polish cleaning lady Janina directly into the German penal system. After torture and imprisonment in Nigeria he stows away on board a ship following the advice of a German sailor, because it will be simple to overcome the language barrier: "If anyone wants something from you, you simply say "Ich liebe dieses Land" ["I love this country"] and they will also love you. He had been away from Germany twenty years" (57). The Germany Beni encounters does not love him; all its representatives are corrupt, cynical, and cruel and the only human character in the play is Janina whose song of praise for the "German paradise" (40) on the one hand stems from her bad experiences in socialist Poland and on the other is taken *ad absurdum* in every scene with Germans. The sentence that prompts Beni at the end to a last happy "I love this country" in his cell is Janina's news that Mr Clean is now thirty cents cheaper in the super market Aldi. Their communication is based on their absolute speechlessness with each other and readers know that Beni's sentence is not going to protect him from deportation. Thus the play shows a failed attempt at immigration and describes the inhumanity of state mechanisms.

The (im)migrant or asylum seeker is often narrated from the viewpoint of the foreigner who makes the familiar and his or her own as foreign. This also happens in the story "Orbiting" in Bharati Mukherjee's volume *The Middleman and Other Stories*, where Rindy, a US-American of Italian origin, introduces her friend Ro from Afghanistan to her family on the occasion of Thanksgiving Day. Ro is always occupied with family matters such as preventing the deportation of a cousin who is in the US illegally and the like. Rindy comments on that with a foreignization: "When I'm with Ro I feel I am looking at America through the wrong end of a telescope. He makes it sound like a police state, with sudden raids, papers, detention centers, deportations, and torture and death waiting in the wings" (66). Moreover, this immigrant resists the cliché of the tattered, starving inhabitant of the Third World and presents himself to Rindy's family as a well-dressed, attractive young man from a good family, who surprizes Rindy's mother with a bunch of flowers and politely ignores Rindy's father's tactless utterances (69). In this manner, Mukherjee reassesses the center-periphery relation, because the US-Americans are exposed by their ignorance and arrogance: "He [Rindy's brother-in-law] thought only Americans had informed political opinion—other people staged coups out of spite and misery" (74).

If we consider these narratives and their protagonists, whose migration takes place due to political or ethnic motives, we reach the conclusion that the dichotomous division of the world in the sense of the wealthy US versus poor Africa or ignorant Third World versus the educated First World is in this dimension even less accurate than in other types of migration narratives. Rather, this Western notion is effectively and systematically dismantled in the texts. This is directly dependent on the fictional characters, who, exactly because of their level of education, analyze and criticize political and ideological relationships and are therefore persecuted: the condescending and discriminating behavior on the part of the authorities or the residents of the host country insults them even more, since they are as a rule in no way worse off—financially or in terms of education—than the "hosts." By laying bare these mechanisms, the writers of these narratives represent a case for an unbiased opening toward the foreign and relativize supposedly fixed hegemonial relation systems. Migration for reasons of education or work is undoubtedly the most common of those described in the texts and they could be separately analyzed as related to education or the search for work. Still, the examples I discuss can be brought about both for exclusively education-specific migration and mere work-related migration.

In order to upgrade his studies in medicine, Juan Zamora, the protagonist in one of the stories in Carlos Fuentes's *The Crystal Frontier,* goes to Cornell University. His first confrontation with the liberal US-American bourgeoisie happens with the Wingate family, who, like other wealthy families around campus, traditionally take in students from rich Latin American families and offer them an environment equally comfortable to their own home. *Pater familias* Tarleton Wingate proves to be a fervent Reagan supporter and has made his money by dealing arms, especially selling arms to the Salvadorian military to fight the "communist threat." So, it fits well into the family's worldview, which has been shaped by fear of communism, when the television broadcasts pertinent images in the evenings: "When the Wingates all sit down to watch television, they kindly invite Juan to join them. He doesn't understand if they are pained when terrible pictures of the war in El Salvador appear—nuns murdered along the roadside, rebels murdered by paramilitary death squads, an entire village machine-gunned by the army as the people flee across a river" (*The Crystal* 34). The narrative strategy is careful and the ideological and emotional gap between Juan and his hosts is established with half sentences whose deeper meaning is only deduced in the course of the story. Despite the high pressure to adapt, to which Juan opportunistically gives in by ensuring the Wingates that he also is a member of a rich family and thus a communist hater and that he is a Reagan supporter, he stands out because of his vastly better manners compared to his fellow students, who do not stop short of eating spaghetti with their hands (50). The conflict with his hosts only arises in the moment when Juan's love affair to a blond student, a classic representative of a WASP (White Anglo-Saxon Protestants) US-American, going by the moniker "Lord Jim" comes out. The idyll between the two young men, who are opposite to each other even in appearance, does not last long, because the past soon comes between them, when Juan talks about the old Medical School in Mexico City: "It was a very beautiful colonial building that had housed the offices of the Inquisition. Lord Jim responded with a nervous laugh: it was the first time Juan had left him for a time that was not only remote but even forbidden and detested by the Anglo-Saxon soul . . . Jim's nervous laugh was a small break in the tension or the distance (were they the same thing?) which that simple reference to the Holy Inquisition had introduced into the way they were together, the first irruption of a past into a relationship that the two boys lived only for the present" (42).

The building of the Inquisition symbolizes the Catholic Spain of the *leyenda negra*, the clerical repression with torture and imprisonment during the reign of Philip II. In short, everything the Protestant-enlightened England and later that the Anglo-Americans fought against from Jim's view stands for alterity par excellence. However, it is not only the past that separates Juan and Jim, but also the future, because it is fixed that Jim will have to be married despite the unrealistic idea in the text that a homosexual adventure is accepted as part of "a gentleman's education" (49), but not as a perspective for life. So, Juan leaves the place, that—as he admits—is not meant for him and takes with him the memory of the moment when Jim gets irritated by the hypocrisy of Wingate, the arms dealer and defrauder, and performs a change of sides toward Juan's perspective. The title of the story, "La pena" is made explicit in the beginning exactly with its Mexican use: only in Mexican Spanish does *pena* (pain) mean the same as *vergüenza* (shame) (29), because that is exactly what makes Juan turn his head away when he tells his story. The text gives clues as to this shame by means of its ironic narrative distance of the protagonists toward US-Americans: it is the shame of his cowardice in the face of Wingate's cynicism. Shame, because he does not fight for the love of his life, shame that he was ashamed of his poor family and has kept it hidden from the wealthy US-Americans, although his father as an attorney could have become rich if he had been only a little corrupt. In the end it is shame that remains, but it is characterized by pity and compassion, for himself and the others. In the last story we see him again, fourteen years later, as a physician who treats illegal immigrants from Mexico in the slums on the other side of the border in the US who do not dare to go to a hospital. Thus the circle is closed: "Juan Zamora learned not to complain. Silently, Juan Zamora learned to act" (245) and his transgressions in any direction have become an accepted part of his identity.

In this respect Fuentes's story can be read as an appeal at first, that immigrants should not disown themselves by assimilation and acculturation and to remain true to themselves and their values, even if the host society appears to be superior and progressive (see his *The Crystal* and *This I Believe*). However, by exposing the dubious basis of their prosperity, Juan (as well as his noncorruptible father) turns out to be morally superior. US-American society with its cynicism and its corruptness has temporarily offered Juan a model, but when he realizes that he is out of place in this environment because of his origin and his history, he returns and manages to find a place for himself in the Mexican world and to live his homosexuality, as well as his professional ambitions, something which would not have been possible in the supposedly tolerant and achievement-oriented US. While Juan needs the detour over education-related migration in order to reconcile with his country of origin, Anil Tissera, the protagonist in Ondaatje's novel *Anil's Ghost*, at the end hastily leaves the island of Sri Lanka, where she was born and raised, in order to save herself from her persecutors. After she completes her undergraduate and post-graduate studies in Great Britain and the US, she returns to Colombo as a specialist in forensic anthropology at the behest of an international human rights organization in order to help the local authorities solve some unexplained murders which are apparently the work of a well-organized terrorist group. She does not have any family in Colombo any more, as her family is spread all over the world. Her friend Cullis—with whom she has a relationship—because he is married attempts at one time to imagine her childhood in Colombo, because, as he laments, "you are a complete stranger to me" (33). She will not have herself defined over Colombo and at first does not want to return there ever again, since she has been acculturated in the Anglophone world: she feels herself to be a citizen of the world in the truest meaning of the word: "In her years abroad, during her European and North American education, Anil had courted foreignness, was at ease whether on the Bakerloo line or the highways around Santa Fe. She felt completed abroad. (Even now her brain held the area codes of Denver and Portland.) And she had come to expect clearly marked roads to the source of most mysteries. Information could always be clarified and acted upon. But here, on this island, she realized she was moving with only one arm of language among uncertain laws and a fear that was everywhere" (54; further on Ondaatje, see, e.g., Tötösy de Zepetnek, *Comparative Cultural Studies and Michael Ondaatje's*).

In the course of her investigations, which she conducts with the archaeologist Sarath, the involvement of the government in political assassinations becomes clearer and clearer. The skeleton "sailor," through which Anil would have been able to prove her allegations against the army and police units, disappears before the critical hearing and she has to present her evidence and argumentation without the corpse and thus is outmaneuvered by the officers and at the end is openly threatened. When she expounds her findings from the forensic investigation coolly and with certainty, she identifies herself with Sri Lanka's population for the first time: "It was a lawyer's argument and, more important, a citizen's evidence; she was no longer just a foreign authority. Then he heard her say, 'I think you murdered hundreds of us.' *Hundreds of us.* Sarath thought to himself. Fifteen years away she is finally *us*" (272). At this point, Anil represents the citizens of Sri Lanka who denounce the government's dirty

war in the name of the fight against terrorism and she becomes one of those who up
to that point had embodied alterity per se for her. This is by no means to be read as
a romantic "back to the roots." To the contrary, because she has to fear for her life,
the confrontation with the century-old Sri Lankan culture and the present of the half-
official civil war shaped by repression and persecution has brought to the surface
a buried part of her personality, the existence of which she herself was not aware.
Anil's Ghost is a text about identity construction beyond gender, nation, and culture
and in the case of Anil lead to a "third phase of interdependency . . . when she returns
to Sri Lanka developing a multicultural perspective that is transnational rather than
global or universal in its construction" (Cook 6).

The stereotypical idea that (im)migrants exchange their poor but nevertheless southern idyllic environment for a materially more advantageous but therefore emotionally underdeveloped existence in a wealthy northern country is not
realized, at least not in the texts analyzed here. To begin with, we encounter a
surprising number of protagonists who come from a relatively well-off social environment and who frequently change residence for reasons of their profession:
one of them is the first-person narrator and literature lecturer Claudio in Antonio
Muñoz Molina's *Carlota Fainberg* and another is Ondaatje's forensic pathologist
Anil. One more is the seismologist Beltrán Soler Niemeyer in Alberto Fuguet's
Las películas de mi vida who grows up in Los Angeles, moves at the age of ten to
Santiago de Chile, completes his undergraduate studies there and obtains his doctoral degree in Paris, and ultimately practices disaster tourism all over the world
as the director of the Centre for Earthquake Research in Santiago. His family is
spread over the Americas and an aunt lives in Genève. His maternal grandfather
as a seismologist had already led a similarly cosmopolitan existence. His paternal
grandfather, however, is an example of the conflicts entailed in a change of country
at the age of 54. Here, the blatant breaks and dissents appear as an inevitable condition of transnational biographies, but do not inevitably lead the people affected to
professional or material failure.

Comparable successful life concepts are presented in a series of novels. Özdamar narrates in *Seltsame Sterne starren zur Erde* instructive and fruitful years of
apprenticeship as a theater assistant at East Berlin People's Theater in the 1970s,
crowned with a proposal for a doctoral degree in Paris and the possibility of becoming an assistant director there. She is in a kind of exile in Germany because of the
military dictatorship in Turkey, but her motives for emigration are first and foremost
of a professional nature. The first-person narrator in Özakin's *Die blaue Maske,* who
travels in Switzerland and Germany in search of traces of her deceased childhood
friend Dina, feels uncomfortable in the society of Turkish immigrants. The first-
person narrator in the *Blaue Maske* reports that she suddenly started crying during
a Turkish concert "not only because of homesickness, but also because I felt myself
foreign here. I was separated as if by a wall of time from the melodies and the crowd
that awoke my memories and senses. I had left them behind in my childhood" (186).
These words express an existential feeling of foreignness that ultimately leads to a

dehierarchized transculturality set beyond countries and places: "Back where?" asks the narrator at the end of the novel, "To Istanbul or Berlin? At the moment I simply cannot decide that" (195).

Asian immigrants in the UK, Canada, or the US, for example, in Jhumpa Lahiri's *Interpreter of Maladies*, in Mukherjee's *The Middleman and Other Stories*, in Ali's *Brick Lane*, or in Khureishi's *The Buddha of Suburbia* are also as a rule educated and often work at universities or large corporations. These novel characters travel by plane, know the world of airports and international hotels, and can find their way almost everywhere due to their education. I should like to mention that this, too, is a marked departure from immigration narratives produced in the nineteenth and up to the mid-twentieth century in Canada, Australia, and the US, where such narratives were, as a rule, about mostly European lower-class immigrants and their successes and failures, and in these narratives there is scant description about negative aspects of the host country.

Identity construction thus turns out to be a purely individual, flexible, and provisory matter, subject to negotiations depending on place and time and adjusted anew on a case-by-case basis. When writers thematize dissent, it often enough does not ignite as a cultural conflict between the native culture and the foreign in the new environment, but the protagonists appear as crushed between two different systems of culturally specific perceptions which are useless for their transnational and hybrid way of life. Instead of dissent, there is often a self-adjustment to living conditions. In this respect, problems of identity play a relatively small role in the texts and identity appears as a dynamic process, whose new adjustments are not necessarily free of conflict but proceed without existence-threatening complications. Apart from this upper- and middle-class migration, the texts also describe migrations of poorer population strata, who leave their place of origin out of need and are in search of better living standards for themselves and their children. The typical case of such migration are Mexican immigrants to the US, who cross the border both legally and illegally and usually perform low-paid work. Portillo Trambley's novel *Trini* places in the titular heroine such a character at the center; the same happens in some of the short stories in Fuentes's *The Crystal Fontier*, as for example the character Chávez, who is flown by a rich Mexican entrepreneur along with others to New York to clean the glass fronts of skyscrapers, because Mexican workers are cheaper than those from a US-American cleaning company. A somewhat broader setting is created in the episodes in Cisneros's *The House on Mango Street,* where immigrants from Mexico live in the neighborhood but other Latin American nations are also represented. The individual episodes, narrated by Esperanza, tell of discrimination and violence against women, of the bitter fight for survival, and of a vague nostalgia for Mexico. Cisneros describes a forced code-switching that could only be gradually transformed into a positive experience by means of an escape forward, into a neutral third sphere: "In English my name means hope. In Spanish it means too many letters. It means sadness, it means waiting . . . At school they say my name funny as if the syllables were made out of tin hurt the roof of your mouth. But in Spanish my name is made out of a softer something, like silver, not quite as thick as sister's name—Magdalena—which is uglier than mine. Magdalena who at least can come home and become Nenny. But I am always Esperanza. I would like to baptize myself under a new name, a name more like the real me, the one nobody sees. Esperanza as Lisandra or Maritza or Zeze the X. Yes. Something like Zeze the X will do" (11).

In *The House on Mango Street* the first-person narrator expresses her aversion toward both identity options—the Spanish Mexican and the US-American—although she valuates positively her Mexican name that carries negative connotations for her in the face of her fellow students' mockery. Still, she feels a prisoner of her name, since she cannot turn it into an inconspicuous version, more common for the US-American mainstream, as she depicts "Nenny" to be. Her wish to become a "nobody," to be invisible with an absolutely neutral name that does not refer to anything and that does not trigger anything expresses a radical uneasiness with her existence. And this can be interpreted as a migration-related loss of rootedness. It is that case of not-belonging-anymore and not-having-arrived-yet which keeps the immigrant in an unstable condition in a grid of coordinates with constantly shifting points and where identity is experienced in a painful manner as an incomplete process and not as a practicable way of life. Immersion in the crowd and disappearing in the masses therefore presents itself for the adolescent Esperanza as the most desirable goal in order to—at least temporarily—evade the difficult process of indentity construction. The search for identity is a classic subject of stories which thematize becoming an adult and it is only natural that the problem of identity is frequently found in novels which place the second generation of immigrants at the center of events.

Kureishi uses the form of the bildungsroman in *The Buddha of Suburbia*, which tells us of the protagonist Karim, the son of an Indo-English family from the South London suburbs, and his path from an underachieving student with divorced parents to a celebrated star of avant-garde West End theatrical productions: "on stage alone with the full glare of the lights, with four hundred white English people looking at [him]" (228) is Karim's biggest triumph. His success sets in, when he accepts his alterity—his Indian origin—and deploys it as a differentiating quality. The first sentences of the novel confront the reader with the uncompromising self-awareness of a seventeen-year-old who purports to know exactly who he is, but in the same breath hints at all the doubts which are going to chase him from one station to another, always in search of new experiences: "My name is Karim Amir, and I am an Englishman born and bred, almost. I am often considered to be a funny kind of Englishman, a new breed as it were, having emerged from two old histories. But I don't care—Englishman I am (although not proud of it), from the South London suburbs and going somewhere. Perhaps it is the odd mixture of continents and blood, of here and there, of belonging and not, that makes me restless and easily bored" (3). Karim is situated in a transnational space and a hybrid existence between continents and histories, but at the same time insists on his Englishness, albeit a "funny" or even "odd" one. Karim's career is shaped by permanent negotiations with his environment and with himself, where both the Indian and the English parts of his identity are cause for conflict: he acquires practice as an actor in personal as well as in professional circles and adapts his behavior according to the situation at hand, even running the risk of entering in disagreement with his family, friends, or employers. In doing that, the problem of "authenticity" arises, exacted of him by his environment. The British want the Indian exotic in him, but he himself emphasizes his "Englishness" which is expected of him most of all by his father, who had dreamt of good grades in school and a physician's career for his son. Maneuvering between these two extremes is the theme of the novel at the end of which Karim has learned "to locate" himself and hopes that "perhaps in the future [he] would live more deeply" (284). In other words, he has evolved into a resident of a third space, whose outlines are flexible and form themselves anew depending on the context.

Zaimoglu narrates in *Abschaum* different social circumstances, because, although it is also concerned with the second generation, in this case Turks in Germany, he presents a biography diametrically opposite to Karim's success story: the protagonist Ertan Ongun stylizes himself as a "Kanak," a "lowlife" Turk, because he cannot find something like a home, neither in "the run-of-the-mill society" Germany nor in Turkey with his parents, who have only taught him "aggression" and from whom he received "beatings" (180). Thus, a huge emptiness remains for him where he cannot "develop any feelings anymore, man, my feelings are dead, I know only money anymore, because I know, money is the only thing, with which one can make a place for himself in this shitty society, and I cannot come to terms with that, it makes me sick" (180–81). The text presents a second generation immigrant, who, in contrast to many others, has failed and who at the end cannot even be defined as a criminal, a junkie, or sick person (181), but one who changes back and forth like a zombie between the "shitty dictaphone" and "drugs" (182). Nonacceptance and incomprehension, which he has experienced as an adolescent both on the part of the German and the Turkish society, turn into self-destructive tendencies and outward aggression, without the text being able to offer an escape from this vicious circle. The epilogue points to the representativeness of this biography that stands by synecdoche for numerous other "immigrant children" who now are "the Kanaks, of whom you Germans have always warned" (183). A third space is also created here in a certain sense, but an uninhabitable one that only exists as a negative space, because Ertan's rejection occurs in both directions: "Now I sit here and try to shock our intellectuals, I try to scare our assimilated, to scare certain people here: fascination by means of the criminal subject, fascination by means of the wild Other" (180). The protagonist is alterity personified; unlike Karim, he makes no concessions.

Ralf Dahrendorf detects the existence of a "massive counter-tendency" to globalization whereby it "consists in a decisive turn to spaces smaller than the nation-states of the nineteenth and twentieth century. Their protagonists do not want Canada, but Québec, not Great Britain, but Scotland, not Italy, but Padania. . . . Moreover, this new regionalism is only a symptom of the counter-movement to

globalization. There is also a new localism, a new search for community in all possible forms, a new religiousness, and most of all a new fundamentalism (22). Thus,
while terms like regionalism and localism bring most of all spatial dimensions into
focus, I am interested in the cultural practices of these spaces which are used for the
creation of symbolic identity discourses. Relevant in this respect is Dahrendorf's
reference to the aspirations of collective experiences which are expressed primarily
in the gatherings of people with the same (im)migration background on the most
different of occasions, be it religious or folk celebrations, rituals, or customs which
have been brought along from the homeland to experience unforeseen appreciation
in the new surroundings.

Beck-Gernsheim describes this as a process where many (im)migrants "start
a path of re-traditionalization, re-ethnization. Idiosyncratic forms of 'exile religion'
or 'exile nationalism'" occur in order to strengthen and defend the identity perceived
as their own against potential attacks on the part of the culture of the majority: "The
more inhospitable and dismissive the new environment presents itself and the more
discrimination it holds, the sooner can a return to the group of the same origin and
their symbols set in" (23). Thus these symbols and the identity linked to them can
be created anew, as Beck-Gernsheim demonstrates with the example of Caribbean
immigrants to Great Britain, whose British citizenship and upbringing were worth-
less and who, as a reaction against discrimination, created an African Caribbean
culture for themselves "with its own celebrations and festivals, with masks, music,
and dances" (24), a "symbolic ethnicity" maintained by the following generation that
barely have any connection to the country of their parents' or grandparents' origin,
but use the exoticism of this origin to stand out from the masses of the majority society: "ethnicity, then, as a leisure article, a hobby, a life décor" (27). That traditions
are an invention of approximately the past two hundred years anyway, is suggested
by Giddens with the example of the Scottish kilts, which originated in the Victorian
era or the Indian uniforms under British rule with turbans and sashes, so that the
soldiers would look "authentic" (37–38). For Giddens, traditions were always re-
invented by the ruling classes "to suit themselves and to legitimise their rule" (40).
It is not duration that is decisive for the establishment and surviving of traditions,
but "ritual and repetition" (40). In contrast to individual habits, traditions are always
"properties of groups, communities, or collectivities" which "define a kind of truth"
and thus "provide a framework for action that can go largely unquestioned" and be-
stow power on the custodians of these traditions (42).

In literature, these phenomena are found in numerous variants of which I
examine selected aspects here as they are relevant for the positioning of fictional
persons in regional or local identity markers such as clothing and food or religious
practices. In the chapter on multilingualism we have already seen that language also
plays an important role as an identity-generating element. Here local or dialectical varieties, such as the Berber (e.g., Djebar), the Alemmanic (e.g., Oliver) or the
Créole (e.g., Condé; Lahens), aim at a level separate from the national. With regard
to multilingualism, I argue that with single-word interferences—which make up a

high percentage of the interferences in general—numerous references to clothing and food occur, and I present a few particularly interesting cases.

In texts about immigrants from Asian Indian cultures to Anglophone cultures, such terms as *dal*, *kebab*, *chapati*, or *sari* are not explained, since these words have become components of English. Neither would anyone think it necessary to translate jeans or pizza to German, as these terms have become part of everyday German vocabulary. Mexican tacos or frijoles belong to the same category and their intelligibility can be taken for granted in US-American and Candian English. Still, these terms often function at a different level than pure synecdoche: they mark individual points of reference in the grid of identity construction. For example, in *The Buddha of Suburbia* Kureishi uses British and occasionally US-American English, as well as Indian cultural markers, behavioral patterns, and societal conventions, with an ironic distance, whereby all matters cultural are exoticized through exaggeration and parody. Thus, cultural parameters are made relative, one is arbitrarily interchangeable with the other, and Britons are not any less exotic in their behavior than immigrants from India. Exoticism sells: Karim's father becomes the "Buddha of Suburbia" because he passes on yoga and some profusely banal maxims (words of wisdom) to White, frustrated English people; Eva, who later becomes his partner, exclaims happily when she meets Karim for the first time: "Karim Amir, you are so exotic, so original! It's such a contribution! It's so you!" (9), while his mother refuses to accompany her husband to one of his yoga sessions at Eva's, since it is her husband Eva wants to see and not her: "I'm not Indian enough for her. I'm only English" (5). To her husband's suggestion to wear a sari she does not react, because it is not part of her strategy for survival to be, at all costs, "authentic" according to other people's notions, notions based largely on external factors, such as skin color or clothing. In contrast to Karim or his mother, Eva's son Charlie shows no inhibition in using his Cockney accent to sell the rock star from Great Britain to US-Americans: "He was selling Englishness, and getting a lot of money for it" (247); he realized earlier than Karim that he could gain tangible advantages by corresponding to other people's idea of "authenticity." Karim's father, on the other hand, has learned to use his seemingly naïve and lost Indianness profitably to flirt with women (7) and offers no objections when Eva tries to squeeze him into a "Nehru jacket," so that "the waiters would think he was an ambassador or a prince, or something" (282).

Characters, such as Karim's father, Eva, or Charlie, are the winners of "competition" because they are flexible enough to fit into other people's cultural stereotypes when they can profit from it. The novel's theme is character development, in the course of which Karim, with his increasing life experience, acquires exactly this ability of continuously negotiating and playing off cultural clichés. Setting his acting career in motion is a result of this learning process that allows him to overcome himself and bring to the stage that very cliché of the Indian that he—as well as his entire family—had always refused and makes this daily, even hourly, role-switching into his profession. Identity breakdown or personal failure are experienced in the text only by people such as Anwar, Jamila's father, who cannot adapt and wants to

prolong his Indian life in London, while his wife Jeeta, although a Muslim, gradually modernizes the store and even endeavors to get a liquor license (172). It is when
Anwar dies that Karim feels an Indian for the first time: "But I did feel, looking at
these strange creatures now—the Indians—that in some way these were my people,
and that I'd spent my life denying or avoiding that fact" (212). He blames, partly,
his father, who never hid the fact that he preferred England to the heat and chaos of
Mumbai and who never fetishized his Indian past "as some liberals and Asian radi-
cals liked to do" (213). Therefore, Karim realizes that he has to create his existence
as an Indian by himself: "So if I wanted the additional personality bonus of an Indian
past, I would have to create it" (213). Multiculturalism is understood and practiced
by Karim as positive and desirable, because he became aware that it can be—meta-
phorically and financially—converted into capital. Thus, culture is a question of vo-
lition, of free choice, and not something one is born with and then has to live with it;
rather, it is something that can be changed, like clothing, daily, even hourly.

Similar processes of development are at the center of the plot in Ali's *Brick
Lane*, where Bangladeshi Nazneen at the end adds facets to her identity which would
be unimaginable in her home country; she ends up being a completely different
person than she was at the beginning. As with Karim and the other characters in *The
Buddha of Suburbia*, this change manifests itself in Nazneen not only in her behavior
but also in large part in her clothing as an expression of societal norms and positions. In the novel's thirteenth chapter—whose main event is the start of her sexual
relationship with Karim, the Bengal Tigers' young leader—the coming violation of
conventions is preempted at the start. Nazneen puts on a particularly conspicuous
silk sari that first emboldens her to dance but then suddenly weighs like tons on her
body: "The sari, which seconds ago had felt light as air, became heavy chains" (277).
In a daydream she goes through the possibilities that would open for her if she were
dressed differently: "if she changed her clothes her entire life would change as well.
If she wore a skirt and a jacket and a pair of high heels then what else would she do
but walk around the glass palaces on Bishopsgate, and talk into a slim phone and
eat lunch out of a paper bag? If she wore trousers and underwear . . . then she would
roam the streets fearless and proud. And if she had a tiny skirt with knickers to match
and a tight bright top, then she would—how could she not?—skate through life
with a sparkling smile and a handsome man who took her hand and made her spin,
spin, spin" (278). Western clothing represents a life style that seems—at first—to
be unreachable for Nazneen and at this point she has become aware of its existence
and starts to compare the Western lifestyle to her Asian one and dares to take steps
into the direction of the heretofore radical Other. At the end, her excursion to the
ice rink implies the option of coexistence of the two worlds, since she is learning to
skate wearing a sari. Thus she adopts Western patterns of behavior through her self-
employment and through her decision to stay in London alone with her daughters.
Since Ali tells the story from Nazneen's perspective throughout, readers become
witnesses to an increasing opening toward new norms and conventions in Nazneen's
social environment. Dr. Azad's Westernized wife and daughter—both of whom wear

short skirts and converse in English—are at first presented as a chilling example of a family broken by the diametrically opposed behavioral norms of the West and the South East, but even here Nazneen already feels that her own misfortune is even bigger than that of Dr. Azad, only she cannot name it yet.

Cultural contrast is manifested also by Shahana, who wants to be English, despite—or perhaps because of—the massive emotional and physical pressure exerted on her by her father: she does not want to listen to Bengali classical music; her written Bengali is deficient; she wants to wear jeans; she hates her kameez and spoils her entire wardrobe by pouring paint on it; if she can choose between baked beans and dal, there is no contest; when Bangladesh is mentioned she pulls a face; she does not know and would not learn that Tagore was more than a poet and Nobel laureate, and no less than the true father of her nation. Shahana does not want to go back home. When the imminent return to Dhaka seems to become reality, she runs away and prompts a dramatic search operation by her mother. This panic reaction contributes to their decision against remigration. Shahana decides in favor of England's culture and becomes a typical representative of the second generation who, among the many conceivable options, can chose a mixed identity adequate for her, even against her parents opposition. The other extreme is represented by the young militant Islam followers at the Bengal Tigers meetings, who are at first described as "small black tents" and then turn out to be "the girls who attended the last meeting, who wore hijab, [and] had upgraded to burkhas" (279). The choice of words ("tents," "upgrade") makes it easy to read the irony toward this kind of fundamentalism, whereby this text passage is characteristic of the careful textual strategy regarding judgments: direct evaluating utterances pro or contra the behavior of others are rarely spoken by Nazneen, but through the descriptions of her actions and reactions she always reveals a clear opinion, as, for instance, when she tries to protect Shahana from her father's beatings (180–01, 200). Using the example of Nazneen and her daughter, Ali represents two different paths to the acquisition of a hybridity based culture, whereas their environment offers numerous others.

Both clothing and food mark points of culture in Muñoz Molina's *Carlota Fainberg*. Marcelo Abengoa, a realtor from Spain and continuously traveling cosmopolitan, demonstrates in the neutral airport concourse in Pittsburgh, through his clothing alone, an *españolidad* that is self-sufficient. Abengoa stands out from a sea of t-shirts and running shoes through his clothes *de corte europeo* (50) and does so with a solid naturalness, which Claudio—the first-person narrator and professor of literature who is always worried about assimilation and political correctness—envies, although he pretends to feel superior. Abengoa is the embodiment of lived authenticity, not in the sense of provinciality, but as a person who adapts and makes concessions. Claudio, on the other hand, with his downright panicked attempts at acculturation to the US-American way of life and the US universities' norms of behavior—who only drinks diet Pepsi and eats organic food (35, 70), who cannot speak Spanish without English insertions anymore, and who at the end does not succeed in a career as an acedmic—turns out to be a more and more deplorable and at the same time comical character. His lecture in Buenos Aires ends as a fiasco, but his stay there provides him with "authentic" pleasure, for the first time in a while, in the form of a good lunch with steak, red wine, dessert, and a strong espresso (146–48), a lunch that would be impossible for him in his US environment. Yet, in this key scene, he experiences himself as a split personality, and after the lunch sleeps in the hotel through the entire afternoon and the rest of the lectures. At the end of the story it remains unclear whether Claudio will continue to alter his acquired US-American patterns of behavior or whether he will venture a new beginning in Spain (190–01). He is the prototype of the immigrant who does not succeed to generate for himself an individual third space in which to live, "trapped between two worlds, without the feeling of belonging at all to the one or the other" (Senís Fernández 118; see also Sturm-Trigonakis, "True Cosmopolitanism").

The physical appearance and what people add to it plays an important role in texts of NWL, because cultural differentiations are thus symbolized and made narratively tangible (see Schroer 88). Clothing and food often refer to a country of origin because when they are transported to a new environment, they can create a feeling of emotional security in the host culture. However, like the burkhas of the women in *Brick Lane*, they can also lead to confrontation. At the individual level they signal successful identities or split personalities. Even when they can be transnationally functional, they always produce a placing in space and time that is located apart from the parameters of the national, so that clothing and nutritional habits are employed in the texts as cultural practices that either complement or contrast. Religious practices, the same as cultural practices, represent an "identity anchor," since for (im)migrants "it [becomes] something special that sets them apart from the surrounding society" especially when it is highly secularized (Beck-Gernsheim 32). Religion is capable, in the moment when it is not a matter of course and ordinary, on the one hand of marking "group-membership and identity" and on the other of offering "support, protection, and a safe haven, particularly in the face of the turbulences in a foreign and unfamiliar environment" (Beck-Gernsheim 33). Thus, religion is not to be thought of as a fixed component of a specific identity, but is exposed depending on environmental influences to processes of transformation and syncretism.

In NWL texts religiousness often provides the occasion for conflicts between (im)migrants and the host society or between the different generations of immigrants. On the other hand, many NWL texts register with a downright seismographic sensibility the strengthening of religious fundamentalisms in the Islamic communities of the diaspora, as well as the protestant branches in the US. In the corpus examined here, it is apparent that religion plays a certain role in all Anglo-Asian texts, that Islam always occurs in dichotomy with other religions, and that we can detect a certain presence of religious practices which do not stand on the fundaments of world religions, but represent regional phenomena. In the texts of Kureishi, Ali, or Rushdie many references to religions of India or Islam can be found, but, as a rule, they express more critical distance than belief. This happens in an exemplary manner in *The Satanic Verses,* which not only spreads a real pandemonium regarding the three religions but also retells the Qur'an and Mohammed's story in a new context. Rushdie's stories "The Prophet's Hair" and "The Harmony of the Spheres" (*East, West*) are also about religion and the contact with it. The first story is about the theft of a strand of hair of the prophet and gives occasion for exercizing criticism of the Qur'an's fundamentalist interpretations, while the second story is about the Indian khan seeking spiritual help from the Welsh Eliot, where both men plunge into a peculiar tangle of religions and philosophies. However, the story does not end with the fulfilment of the ironic title and a spiritual synthesis of East and West, but ends with the Welshman's suicide and with khan's failed relationship with Mala, a physician from Mauritius. Even the hybrid identities that are feasible in England apparently do not necessarily offer an escape from alienation and disorientation.

In *Brick Lane* the representation of religious practices—here Islamic—also aims at an ambivalent attitude toward religion, not only because the meetings of the Bengal Tigers with their inflammatory speeches provoke criticism, but also because their leader violates Sharia law in entering a relationship with Nazneen. Just as there are no simple truths in Rushdie's texts, neither are there any in Ali's, and the otherwise tradition-conscious Chanu does not send his daughters to the newly established Madrasa—the Qur'an school in his neighborhood—because he does not agree with the traditional learning of Arabic and therefore unintelligible texts from the Qur'an and because the Buddhist and Hindu past of Bangladesh would be neglected: "'Don't forget', he tells Nazeen, 'Bengal was Hindu long before it was Muslim, and before that Buddhist, and that was after the first Hindu period. We are only Muslims because of the Moguls. Don't forget'" (197). Islam for Chanu is a result of an exercise of power that should not cover older cultural history. Such religious contingency is also strengthened by the character of the Afro-Briton, who seeks to be admitted into the ranks of the Bengal Tigers in order to finally find a home in an authentic and determined group: "'I tried Pentecostal, Baptist, Churcha Englan', Cat'olic, Seventh Day, Churcha Christ, Healin', Churcha Christ, Jehovah Witness, Evangelical, Angelical, and the Miracle Church of our Saviour'. . . . 'All loose'n lax like anything. Loose *and* lax'" (279). The Muslim Bengal Tigers, he hopes, will satisfy his need for hardcore religion. Religions' potential for violence also leads to the tragic death of the US-American Priscilla Hart by a Muslim whose wife Priscilla helped get an abortion for her eighth pregnancy and is a main theme in Shashi Tharoor's *Riot*. Here religion and the exercise of power (mainly by men) attached to it invariably represent a specific regional setting that is brought along to the host culture. As with other cultural practices, under the influence of religions emerges a pluralism of religious customs and hybridizations that makes it impossible to make unequivocal evaluative judgments; thus religion should be classified as equally relative and processual as food or clothing or other behavioral norms.

A further example of the function of religion in NWL texts is Naipaul's *A House for Mr Biswas*: Biswas's wife's family, the Tulsis, understand themselves to be Hindus and also have a son-in-law, Hari, who reads the holy scriptures and takes on the role of the priest in every ceremony. At the same time he is also mocked

as a constant eater and as a constant latrine user because of his chronic constipa-
tion (103). And Mrs Tulsi has no inhibitions to procure for her sons the bases for
a promising career by sending them to a Catholic school, which Mr Biswas makes
extensively fun of, since the sons—whom he calls "gods" because of their privileges—wear crucifixes as "exotic and desirable charms" (113) and before exams are
subjected to all kinds of magical rites which would ensure good performance: a bath
in lavender water, a glass of Guinness beer, holy coins and lemons in every pocket
(113). The aggressive reactions on the part of the Tulsi clan to Mr Biswas's derisive
"You call yourself Hindus?" speak for themselves. Still, Mrs Tulsi's daughter Chinta
does not shrink from conducting an investigation for her missing eighty dollars by
invoking the Saints Peter and Paul, which confirms Mr Biswas suspicion once again
that Mrs Tulsi and her daughters are in reality "old Roman cats" (381). He in turn
also sends his two older children, Anand and Savi, to Sunday School and lets them
warble away church songs at home, which makes Mrs Tulsi takes for a new start of
religious confrontation (307). Naipaul demonstrates that the syncretistic religiousness of Indian immigrants of higher castes to Trinidad divides the group because
of its pluralistic forms instead of creating a group identities and thus the religion
brought along does not contribute to the creation of a reasonably stable identity, but
a deficient one instead.

    That religiousness can also function in a positive manner as a catalyst on the
path to an individual identity can be illustrated with Lahens's *Dans la maison du
père*. The novel is set in Haiti, where the protagonist Alice Bienaimé finds her way
to an identity schema adequate for her, through the Vodou dances from Africa. Her
upbringing is at first Roman Catholic—as for all children of families of the Haitian
middle class—and all that is connected to Africa is frowned upon and disdained
(54). The Mademoiselles Védin run their school with a brutal regimen and their goal
is to "make out of the young negresses that we were colored girls of France" (41),
but Alice quickly realizes that this only leads to a "lesser life . . . an awkward copy"
(41) from which the African part is banned. However, magical rites are present in
everyday life although forced to the social margin as matters of the lower classes.
Thus the house's servant, Man Bo, at the death of the grandmother "whitewashed
all the mirrors with starch paste to prevent grandmother Lucie from giving up her
journey towards the dead in order to return to watch us quietly and disrupt the activities of the living," but Alice's mother prevents her from placing a magical scapular
on her bed (55–56). The groundbreaking experience for Alice is her participation in
a (at the time of the novel in the 1940s forbidden) Vodou ceremony, which evokes
in her fear and fascination at the same time and which she interprets as an "act
of self-discovery" that will also contribute to the development of her identity (99).
Through classical ballet she turns to other forms of dance and discovers worship for
African dances (84, 94). At the end, after an ecstatic dance performance, she realizes that Haiti is too small for her and that she has to flee from this world of "first
communions, weddings and baptisms, all these second-hand opaque rituals of the
petty bourgeoisie of the tropics who always pretend but never show it" (143). In this

respect, both forms of religious practice in Lahens's text have a catalyzing effect: Catholicism, because it proves to be dishonest and forced and Vaudou, because with its help Alice discovers her vocation, dance, and frees herself from everything phoney of the imported French culture.

The world of pre-Colombian gods functions in a similar manner in the texts of Anzaldúa and Portillo Trambley as an identity anchor. For example, for the women characters in *Trini* it is Tonantzín, the Earthmother, with whom Trini identifies against her Catholic upbringing on the part of her aunt Pancha. In accordance with Native American religions, nature is presented as having a soul: "This was the place where the rainbow lived. After baptizing the sky with rain, the rainbow would pour himself into the rocks and rest there until the next rain storm" says Trini in one instance (Portillo Trambley 12). Such descriptions pull the reader into a Native American perspective where everyday dealings can be interrupted by magical occurrences and where humans are one with nature. A component of this magical world is El Enano, a dwarf-like apparition that always materializes for Trini in times of crisis, that is, after her mother's death in a difficult financial situation (223). When the family on its way north and stops in a village in the area of the Tarahumara Indios, they are invited to a worship service: the Virgin Mary and the four-breasted goddess Tonantzín stand peacefully next to one another on the altar and the service soon leaves its Catholic rite and ends—to the indignation of Pancha—with a wild Native American dance, which then leads to communion with *chichi* (brandy made of corn) and *pinole* (toasted Indian meal). This syncretistic ceremony has for Trini a similar liberating effect as the Vodou mass for Alice: she knows at once that she—although a *mestiza*—will stay true to her Native American origins: "she said nothing, but leaned against the rock and looked down at Tonio sitting slightly below her. She handed him the bowl and knew it for a fact: 'I am Tonantzín'" (75). Tonio is the one who calls her that for the first time, her future husband, and who is going to leave her again and again in difficult situations, but who recognizes her bond with the earth and knows that she will remain Native American, *descalza*, even in the city "in spite of the lipstick and high heels" (148). Being Tonantzín means for her having a kind of home everywhere, a sphere that belongs to her and gives her the independence to not belong to anybody—"I belong to myself, Tonio—people don't belong to others" (149) is how she rejects Tonio's new advances. Thus the text suggests that only old religiousness and spirituality are able to offer true help to people stricken by poverty and blows of fate such as Trini: Catholicism cannot afford this because it is foreign and exhausts itself in empty formulas without any connection to nature.

If Portillo Trambley emphasizes the Native American side and narrates stereotypical identities, Anzaldúa breaks these fixations and pleads for the coagulation of the binary to something higher and for the acceptance of ambivalence: "*Coatlicue* is a rupture in our everyday world. . . . Simultaneously, depending on the person, she represents: duality in life, a synthesis of duality, and a third perspective—something more than mere duality or a synthesis of duality" (46). This state can degenerate into helplessness, can lead to a permanent inner rapture of cultures, languages, and role

models, from which Anzaldúa can only take out flexibility and "tolerance for ambiguity . . . she learns to be an Indian in Mexican culture, to be Mexican from an Anglo
point of view. . . . Not only does she sustain the contradictions, she turns the ambivalence into something else" (78). This something else, the third, that makes up the
existence of the Chicana, in it is her power, and from it her multiple identity develops.

In sum, I submit that in NWL texts a broad spectrum of fictional representatives of worldwide nomadism can be perceived. Toro calls "nomadicities" one of the
salient characteristics of literature of the postimperial period, whereby it always tells
of "displacement . . . that is, it presents a literature that is inscribed by the fracture
and the wound of displacement" (92). This "displaced" literature performs fictional
existences in the third space and as context depending identity formation. On the one
hand it generates a new culture of the in-between, "a culture that is neither here nor
there, a culture that resists a binary placing, a culture that for many is threatening
since it is a culture/cultures which results from displacement, and therefore assumes
multiple geographies and cartographies, and multiple identities" (Toro 93) and on
the other hand it tells of multiple identities tailored for the individual. Identity formation particularly under conditions of displacement cannot be defined from origin
and/or nationality anymore (Toro 95), especially since the question for identity is not
"Who am I?" but "Who am I in relation to others, who are the others in relation to
me?" and thus it is always a relational matter and therefore implies alterity (Zybok
207). Identity is constructed through "others' anticipated expectations and the individual's desire" whereby behavioral security occurs when the subjects find a balance
between social integration and the ability for interactions on the one hand and their
being themselves on the other hand (Zybok 207).

The multiple nature of identity formation underlines texts of NWL where plu-
riculturalism makes the starting configuration more complex than under conditions
of monocultural situations and where the subject is confronted with a greater number
of demands for roles but also with options and possibilities. No matter whether the
texts concern themselves with (im)migration with regard to marriage for financial
reasons or for education, NWL texts almost always treat the manner in which the
fictional characters find their way through the identity tangle, or not. According to
Beck, it is a favorite pastime of "inhabitants of cosmopolitan modernity" to overturn
established categories and he emphasizes that "the mixing to which this leads is not
a sign of failure, the failure of integration, but of just the kind of individuality which
determines identity and integration in cosmopolitan society. In this way, individuality arises through overlapping and conflict with other identities. . . . Conflict is the
driving force for integration. Cosmopolitan society arises to the extent that national
societies are split and 'disintegrate'" (*The Cosmopolitan* 76–77). Destructive elements of identity formation are narrated in NWL texts often and this is delineated by
constructively reinterpreting the potential for conflict inherent in (im)migration processes. For the completion of multiple identity constructs, however, I note another
important parameter and this is that cosmopolitans and (im)migrants are narrated in
local and regional frames of reference and that this occurs in both complementary

and contrary valuation. As is clear in my analyses, frames of references often represent a counterweight to globalization on the one hand and they are also subject to it on the other. Thus the references are modified in a syncretistic and eclectic direction, so that for example in religious cultural practices both differentiation and homogenization occurs. This vindicates the dictum that globalization cannot exist without regionalization and that, by implication, unification processes provoke measures for differentiation.

Chapter Seven

Transnational Spaces, Places, and Layers of Time

Global cities and borders/borderlands as transnational spaces

Spaces are, just as time, real patterns of categorization which appear in literature as symbolic representations and inscribe fictional characters in space and time constellations. Comparable to identity, perceptions of space as "surface morphology" and surface as a designation for "unnamed and uncircumscribed geographical extension" are always to be considered "culturally determined," because "space and surface only take on a meaning within the dynamic of the social situation (interaction, identity, and time), in which boundaries are drawn around the blank surface extension and the thus enclosed area is defined. Cultures express themselves inside the space they use (e.g., through cultivation methods, forms of settlement)" (Haller 243). Space, thus, is not naturally given, but is constructed. According to Markus Schroer, space cannot be examined in "its effect on the social, on individuals, and society"; rather "spaces [have to] be built first . . . in order to obtain a meaning for social processes" (29). In contrast to this mental construct, "locality" is to be understood as "a named, marked—that is, localizable—geographical extension with names and borders" and designates a locality that is the "field of interaction of a social group" and can by all means also exist in imaginary form. A further quantity is "territory" as a "place which is occupied or for which a claim of ownership is raised (e.g., nation-states) (Schroer 29). Borders between territories are always the expression of legal, political, and cultural conventions, since their validity is orientated at being clearly separated by boundaries from the groups separated from each other" (Haller 243).

Imaginary territories often refer to a real or mythical past or an anticipated future, as Dieter Haller describes with regard to Jerusalem in Jewish and Christian tradition or Constantinople as a center of Hellenism (29) and such references are indicators of culture dependence. Texts of NWL include a multitude of other, imaginary, but also real boundary lines which transverse fixed ones and thus emphasizes the relevance of "both the spatial and the temporal dimensions" which result in the "trans-local, local-global, trans-national, national-global, and global-global" (Beck, *The Cosmopolitan* 76–77). Thereby "the cosmopolitan project contains the national project and at the same time extends it. From the perspective of transnational domains of experience and action it becomes possible to test and combine options and shifts in perspective which are excluded by frontiers. . . . The cosmopolitan outlook has its home in amazement and in the expanding the in-between in which seemingly eternal certainties, borders, and differentiations become blurred and effaced" (Beck, *The Cosmopolitan* 77). It is exactly these in-between spaces that NWL narrates and expands. On the other hand, the acceptance of expanded global spaces confronts us with the paradox that their existence is subjected to a tightening of space and that is experienced by their most extreme form, where with an almost simultaneity by means of the internet or satellites the most disparate spaces of our planet can be brought together. The answer lies therein that the global, exactly because of its inconceivability—in the maximal, as well as the minimal—can only be explored at the local: "it is impossible to even think about globalization without referring to specific places and locations" (*The Cosmopolitan* 88). The global space is therefore a "pattern of observation" for the "disparity of regional and spatial perspectives" and a "horizon, where localities meet and become aware of their structural epistemological similarity just as they perceive their difference (Nassehi, *Geschlossenheit* 219).

It is this structural similarity in the respective local literary processing of global phenomena I illustrate here. First, I discuss with metropolises as the places where hierarchies are rescinded and hegemonial center-periphery relations change in mutual reciprocity of influences (see, e.g., Toro 36, 46) and second, I thematize the border as a zone of contact as an imaginary line that separates and connects defined units and yet at the same time allows the outlines of these units to become blurred. The latter constitutes the point from which "something begins its presencing" (Bhabha 5). Since the global cannot be configured without the local, Bhabha's notion foregoes a separation between the phenomena of the globalization and localizm sphere, since such phenomena appear in literary representations and are about a hermaphroditic, "glocalized" discourse system. It is the dynamic of this interdependency between local and global that should stand in the foreground of scholarship, because the processes of translation and transfer take place as "cultural experience[s]" which are converted into an "inner experience[s]" (Schwab 62).

Cities are now sold in many instances on the idea of hybridities (on this, see, e.g., Lisiak). One cannot spend a week in Paris without being reminded of the value of hybridity and the message does not obey the logic of ethnically defined individuals side by side. Rather, it aspires to go beyond that logic offering a representation of a global world in which demarcations—of race, nation, class—are no longer divisive (see Vergès 356). Françoise Vergès expresses this observation on the occasion of an issue of *Vibes* magazine, in which the Parisian eighteenth *arrondissement* is celebrated as a vibrating "ghetto" with the best couscous and the most exciting "beur princesses" and "African Queens" (356). Ever since Georg Simmel, the Chicago School of Sociology, and Luis Mumford, the big city has been described as a point of intersection of many ethnic groups and cultures. However, in the age of globalization this classic characteristic has experienced an unforeseen quantitative expansion on many more cities than in Simmel's time and it has moved away from multiculturalism as the coexistence of distinguishable cultures toward the direction of hybrid forms. Manuel Castells has observed the evolution of the big city since the 1970s and describes the contemporary metropolis as a "process by which centers of production and consumption of advanced services, and their ancillary local societies, are connected in a global network, while simultaneously downplaying the linkages with their hinterlands, on the basis of information flows" (1: 417). The significance of global cities lies in that they represent a hub for the forwarding or redirecting of the multiple flows characteristic of a globalized network society whereby flows are defined as "purposeful, repetitive, programmable sequences of exchange and inter-action between physically disjointed positions held by social actors in the economic, political and symbolic structures of society" (Castells, 1: 442; see also Barabás; Tap-scott).

Distances or time differences do not play any role in this network anymore and cultural differences also tend to be leveled by the omnipresent hybridity of the megalopolis, so that Rushdie can claim to be a Bombayite and afterwards a London-er and that this means "to fall in love with the metropolis" (*Imaginary* 404). It is no coincidence that *The Satanic Verses* is of the quintessential examples of London city novel of the 1990s, where all kinds of mixtures are celebrated. Mumbai and London offer a homeland in equal measure, because these two cities resemble each other in structure and function. Sociological investigations demonstrate that young Turkish immigrants move in an urban identification network between Frankfurt or Berlin, Istanbul or New York and contrary to common perceptions, there can be no ques-tion of "cultural conflict, disjointedness, identity crisis," but there arises a "multiple integration . . . with relevance to both local and transnational space; an integration, admittedly, that the German majority population is not aware of, because they lack the sensorium for it" (Beck-Gernsheim 94–95).

Many (im)migrants live in a "polygamy of place" as Beck formulates this (*The Cosmopolitan* 43) by which he means that the functions and meanings of individual places change depending on the situation and intermingle and the center-periphery is being replaced by a de-hierarchized network of places, in which, ranging from polycentrism to placelessness, there exists a rich palette of different possibilities for individual locations in space. For this reason it would have been pointless to want to search for the global and the local separately in the texts, because one can only be explored within the other and the same place functions sometimes as a global me-tropolis, sometimes as a confined, identification making locality, so that literature is always about "glocalization" processes and structures. Even when the narration dif-fers depending on the plot, the texts have a common thread laying bare the integrat-edness of local circumstances in global contexts. This happens in the two London novels in which suburbs are confronted with the center: in Kureishi's novel the move of the protagonist Karim and his family from the South London suburb Beckenham to Kensington and posh West End symbolizes the escape from the limited immigrant environment and the conquest of the center: "So this was London at last, and nothing gave me more pleasure than strolling around my new possession all day. London seemed like a house with five thousand rooms, all different; the kick was to work out how they connected, and eventually to walk through all of them" (126). London's center is the point where all threads converge and from which all options are open and connections can be made to other similar metropolises, in this case New York. The conquest of the center along with the spatial dimension has a social one, because for Karim the move is tantamount to a challenge: he claims a place in the affluent and predominantly white London center of power and at the end he triumphs as an actor on stage before a white audience. Not only since Pierre Bourdieu do we know that power relations are expressed in the control of power: having a "good address" gives social prestige and symbolizes a specific social status. In Kureishi's novel the success story is not only expressed in the plot by telling how a young man predestined to be an outsider from an immigrant environment, in the end makes his career by employing his alterity: his social ascent is also symbolized by the location and thus the ideal as an indispensable prerequisite for success is exposed as invalid, because Karim achieves his goal not through adaptation to the system of social norms—good grades in school, a steady job, well-ordered family environment, and the like—but achieves success when he throws overboard his attempts of acculturation regarding the white English middle class. However, the text makes it clear that the adaptation demanded of him by the intellectual and supposedly unbiased theater people—this time the cliché of the "typical" Indian—is at first equally degrading. In this respect, the text relativizes the fixed perceptions of stable cultural values and norms systems. In Kureishi's novel the workman, Ted—as a representative of the not overly educated middle class—is at the end more cosmopolitan and tolerant than the leftist among Karim's actor colleagues and the morally corrupt directors. Only in a metropolis can all these contrasting groups interact and find their niches for survival and only a city offers such a broad spectrum of social role models.

Another version of the suburb-center relation can be found in Ali's text, because the estate, the immediate environment of young Nazneen, is the foreign world which she has to walk through arduously and with small steps and whereby by means of the strict personal perspective through Nazneen's impressions the foreign view is always maintained: a revolving door on the ground-floor of a tall building presents itself as a "glass fan, rotating slowly, sucking people in, wafting others out" (56) and a mobile phone is described as a "radio" that "appeared to speak back" (59). Nazneen feels foreign and at the mercy of this city, just like her sister Hasina in Dhaka feels lost. By means of this parallelism it becomes obvious that the feeling of foreignness is not bound culturally or place-wise, but is a result of specific social circumstances. And, as in Kureishi, Ali's novel also fathoms the relationship between the suburb and the center: an excursion to Buckingham Palace is conducted by Nazneen's husband with military precision and accoutrements worthy of an expedition. Her possibilities for space appropriation remain limited to her immediate environment, which, however, is an enormous feat for Nazneen considering her adverse starting position as a stranger. The title already suggests that Brick Lane, the street of Nazneen's apartment, means "world" and a world in the sense of a microcosm in which Nazneen's gradual evolution to mental and financial independence takes place and and at the same time a macrocosm, where different nations, other distant places, and diverse events are present simultaneously so that the local and the global pierce through and the one influences the other.

A house of their own as a piece of homeland, as a place where to settle down is at the core of the novels by Cisneros and Naipaul, where the house is again set in relation to the larger whole of the surrounding city. In *The House on Mango Street*, the protagonist with the aptomyn Esperanza dreams of a better house than the shabby one of her parents on Mango Street, which they in fact own, but "it's not the house we'd thought we'd get" (3). The text thus creates a typical fringe group situation: if the ownership of financial, cultural, and social capital makes possible a power of control over space (Bourdieu), then the absence of these forms of capital means for the people involved that "they are kept away from desired goods and persons. Because of a lacking control over space they are subject to the occupation by others, have to suffer the noise of the neighbours as much as the view out the window obstructed by the nearest high-rise building" (Schroer 96). From this perspective of underprivilege, the center does not play a role—since it is at an unreachable distance as it is—and consequently, the city where Mango Street is, is not described, not even named, although it reaches with its social structure into Mango Street, for instance by forcing the "better people" in view of the influx of Mexican immigrants to search for a new place to stay (Cisneros 13). The house on Mango Street stands in for the unrealized hopes of Mexican and Puerto Rican immigrants, who behave as if they were still living in their homelands and therefore for Esperanza only remains the chance to leave the "sad red house, the house I belong but do not belong to" (110), that is, to do the same as the immigrants in order to escape the suffocating social structure surrounding them and to relocate and then possibly return from a strengthened position.

Mr Biswas does live in numerous places in numerous houses, but none offer him a place of home because they belong to his wife's hated Tulsi clan, who always show him only his status of being tolerated. Contrast to the overcrowded, chaotic living conditions of the Tulsis represents for Mr Biswas Trinidad's capital, Port-of-Spain: "The organization of the city fascinated Mr Biswas; the street lamps going on at the same time, the streets swept in the middle of the night, the rubbish collected by the scavenging carts early in the morning" (Naipaul 281). So, he finally finds a house and thus peace and quiet for himself and his family, even when the house at the time of his death is still burdened with a three-thousand dollar debt: "how terrible it would have been, at this time, to be without it; to have died among the Tulsis, amid the squalor of that large, disintegrating and indifferent family; to have left Shama and the children among them, in one room; worse, to have lived without even attempting to lay claim to one's portion of the earth; to have lived and died as one had been born, unnecessary and unaccommodated" (13). In the order of the big city, Mr Biswas does not only find a meaningful job (as a reporter), but also in general a place in life that up to then had only pushed him around: his place in life is symbolized by his own house, which finally gives him power of control over space and thus a position in the social space as well.

As a metropolis that bundles up all powers and to which the people refer to anew—voluntarily or not—appears Condé's Africa epic, which depicts the French invasion of West African territories along the Senegal River in the second half of the nineteenth century. Segu is the polycentric city of the hybrid in an African dimension. In an era, when belonging to a tribe still represents the decisive identification marker, a generation grows up in Segu that identifies itself with this powerful city, loves it like Omar (321) or longs for it like Samuel, who fled to Jamaica, in order to find freedom there (265). That an African identity is gradually formed beyond ancient ethnic solidarities is on the one hand an influence of the French invaders for whom Africa's inhabitants regardless of their tribe appear all the same while on the other hand this kind of African transnationality is lived as an example and made a reality in Segu. Condé creates in her novel a situation where the metropolis Segu represents the incarnation of mixtures which seldom come about in a peaceful manner, but are mostly the result of war. In metropolises, the local manifests itself in the shape of specific neighborhoods and the global in the meeting of different ethnic groups, religions, and lifestyles at the same time: the city is self-sufficient and simultaneously part of a rhizomatic construct by being networked with other urban agglomerations. *Brick Lane*, for example, introduces Bangladesh's capital into Nazneen's London surroundings: events reflect each other where common perceptions of the "bad" life there and the "good" life here are revealed to be clichés in the West. Nazneen has achieved neither financial security nor personal freedom of action through her dream wedding to an educated Bengali man in London: her daily house work, her shopping with her husband, and her complete dependence on him, her claustrophobic existence between the four walls of her small and overcrowded apartment makes this clear. In contrast to this, her sister in Dhaka works in a textile factory and is financially independent, although the strict religious norms are her doom. At first, however, apparently more possibilities are open to her than to Nazneen in London. Ali emphasizes that both women in their respective environments have to fight hard to first mentally create their personal lives and then to also make them a reality and that the social conditions of these fights for survival are different. Transnational comparisons are not made within a more or less unified cultural space, but they connect contrary poles. Thus, Nazneen finds Buckingham Palace "extraordinary only in its size" but otherwise "very plain" (Ali 291) and would, if she were a queen, build something really "elegant and spirited, with minarets and spires, domes and mosaics . . . something like the Taj Mahal" (292). As Nazneen sets the reference system in South East Asia, traditional paramaters of valuation are turned upside down and the former incline between motherland and colony is reversed. What is applied positively at the level of art also functions in a negative sense, when the Indian Changez in a shabby part of London feels reminded of Kolkata (Kureishi 224) or the young Indian student's husband visiting New York sees as many fraudsters at work as in Mumbai (Mukherjee 40).

Both in Özdamar's and Özakin's texts the impressions, which the female protagonists experience, evoke associations in relation to Istanbul and Berlin, respectively, where certainly further places can come into play: the plot in *Die blaue Maske* is set in Zürich and from this starting point creates reminiscences of the German and the Turkish metropolis, while in Özdamar's stories along with Istanbul more places, such as Paris, Amsterdam, or New York, are brought to the fore. Özdamar's first-person narrators have a "personal street map" of each of these cities of significant places, such as a book store or a butcher's, people, or a homeless man (*Der Hof* 17–18) or an African American beggar (86), or such banal items as the chairs in a café (85). The mirror is the leitmotif of the texts. Beyond the topographic anchoring, the *conditio humana* is the same for all people. In the autobiographical story from Özdamar's time as an assistant director at the people's theater in East Berlin there is similar motif, when her husband gives her this certainty at her departure for Berlin: a random street scene in East Berlin with families on a Saturday evening reminds the narrator of a Saturday in Istanbul when she is separated from her husband and sits in the evening on a bank next to a road sweeper (99) or when the First of May Parade in East Berlin evokes the news of the dead in Istanbul during the First of May demonstration there. The female protagonist in Özakin's *Blaue Maske* similarly commutes back and forth between Istanbul, Berlin, and Zürich in search of the traces of her friend Dina and at the end of her search in Zurich cannot decide, which place she will "return" to.

The people in these texts live in conditions of the polygamy of place and, consequently, in conditions of placelessness. Wherever they momentarily are every one of their whereabouts simultaneously contains the others where they had been at sometime in their lives. According to Sloterdijk, a characteristic of contemporary globalized society is a loosening the "attachment to places" as "large populations adopt an unprecedented mobility" and the increasing of the number of transit places, to which "no residence relationship is possible for the people who frequent them" (238). NWL reflect this view of Sloterdijk's in a multifaceted manner: the polygamy of place characterizes immigrant life in the metropolises and the polygamy of place and life in transit. For example, in Oliver's *fernlautmetz* the writer processes the sounds of yonder and shapes them as the stone mason does his hard working materials. The titles of the individual poems reveal a tireless cosmopolitan: from Innsbruck over Kufstein we go to Paul Celan in Riga, Cannes stand next to García Lorca and Fuente Vaqueros, and Bogotá evokes La Paz, Mexico City, and La Havana. The texts do not seem to be able to anchor themselves anywhere; the images of one city already conjure up those of the next one almost before the reader can decipher the setting. Oliver is also the poet of the Black Forest, who in the volume *nachtrandspuren*, for instance, erects a poetic monument to his home-village Hausach and puts winter flowers on the windowsills (110, 111) or sets the scene for a snowstorm with a nursery rhyme (*Austernfischer* 86, 89).

A similar restless wanderer between worlds and metropolises is also the narrator in Walcott's poetry cycle *Midsummer*, where an alter ego of the author first arrives at his Caribbean home island St. Lucia, spends the summer there, leaves again in autumn and travels to Boston, his city of exile, Chicago, and England. At each of these opposite places every other is mentally present: "summer is one-dimensional / as lust, and boredom like a whetstone grinds a knife / or a pen. Above the flat, starlit roofs, ambition / is vertical. You miss the other city's blazing towers, / passing repeated hedges of hibiscus allamanda, croton" (26). In the boredom of the tropical heat and the exuberance of tropical plant life, the lyrical he longs for are the towers of the "other" city, while the Caribbean island fades away in the mixture of diesel exhaust, snowfall, and a fishmonger in Boston: "a trawler groping from the Port of Boston, / snow, mixed with steam, blurring the thought of islands" (72). A disappearing of distances, a hopping from point to point from metropolis to metropolis, an omnipresence in all places simultaneously, and yet at the same time existence in a nowhere and in-between a passing pause at a concrete place is what characterizes how many NWL texts handle spaces and places. The existential way of being is being on the road, is the journey: "I only sat in a taxi that brought me from the airport to the city centre. I was on the road, as always, nothing more" (Tawada, *Überseezungen* 73) and condenses in this short sentence the leitmotif of an entire literary genre where being on the road has become an existential way of living and arriving is only of secondary importance or is not even an issue at all.

The atopical existence of numerous fictional NWL characters cannot be better illustraded than in an airport that appears in numerous texts, sometimes at the margins, sometimes as occasion for more detailed observations such as in Muñoz Molina's text, when his protagonist gets out of a taxi in front of a random airport and goes through the automatic glass doors (95–97). Airports are concrete, identifiable localities and yet at the same time non-places: they are as a rule tied to a big city, that is, located in the empirical space, and yet their users find themselves already in an amorphous nowhere they have not yet left, but neither have they arrived at yet. They resemble each other almost up to interchangeability, because their function is identical everywhere and they resemble each other in many features ranging from architectural and interior design through air-conditioning, background noises, and temperature to even the passengers: "when literature reacts to the challenges of globalization process with a mythologization of places, then the airport . . . undoubtedly assumes a prominent, even the first position" of "in-between space," a "threshold space" open to all directions and a "peculiar pattern of categorization of global space" (Schmitz-Emans, *Reaktionen* 305). The airport is where a part of the compression of global space takes place.

"Dissolution of boundaries and virtualization" (Schmitz-Emans, *Reaktionen* 285) of space can be proven in the text corpus examined here by referring to globally applicable computer-aided communication technology. In this context, a character as Walser's Gottlieb Zürn in *Der Augenblick der Liebe* who writes letters to his adored Beate in the US, is almost anachronistic: this long-winded process is compensated with frequent phone calls, because "if something arose between him and her, then it was telephonically. Telephonically. . . . Of all the words coined by the authorities, it was the most beautiful one" (133). In contrast, Tawada in *Überseezungen* makes detailed observations on the difficulties of writing Japanese and German on the computer and reaches the conclusion that "the computer company has lured a woman by means of a forbidden fruit into a trap and locked her into the computer case" (15–17). The blank spots in the e-mails, on the other hand, can be ascribed to the fact, that, for instance, "German umlauts on the way to America often fall into the Atlantic and there disappear. The oceans are probably already overflowing with umlauts and ideogrammes" (107–08). In Tawada's text the management of complexities is conducted by means of a superficial simplification, yet whose comic and surrealism do not leave any doubt that technological advances indeed hold pitfalls for the individual user. In *French Dream* by Mohamed Hmoudane on the other hand, internet cafés belong naturally to Paris's city image and are frequented by Maghreb youngsters as a meeting point and for chatting: "City of Salé. District of *Hay Essalam*. Six or seven Internet cafés in a very limited perimeter. Broadband connection provided. Even though nothing is urgent here. The boys surf on the gigantic waves of illusion. Real time jabbering" (79). And after that comes superficial correspondence in a chat room that culminates in the insight that "We don't exist" (80). In *Carlota Fainberg*, the narrator is aware of the unreality and artificiality of his environment characteristic of the place transformed into an atopia that forms a virtual point in a virtual network beyond the empirically measurable localizations, expansions, distances, or speeds. Thus, in the texts the priority falls to being on the road, be it from one metropolis to another, be it from an airport or an e-mail address to another; arriving has become secondary. Because arriving would bring with it a statement and a standstill at the same time, the decision in favor of *one* place, *one* way of life, *one* identity; but most texts are about restlessness, commuting between cities, places, worlds, and this is probably not done anywhere as blatantly as in those texts, which we could call "literature of zones of contact" (see Pratt; Riese).

Ette recognizes in the borderlands between Mexico and the US one of the most important theoretical points of departure because on the one hand the separation between the two Americas is concretized in this space as a visible border and on the other hand because it is also exactly there that the separated worlds permeate each other and become innovative in the hybrid again and again and generate what has not existed before. With regard to Latin American literature, Ette filters out six different cultural poles which range from classical Iberian culture reaching to antiquity the long marginalized Native American cultures and the regionally different peoples' cultures of the Iberian conquerors, through African cultures and mixed cultures of the *Créole* upper classes right up to the phenomena of mass culture of industrialization (318). Such multipolar cultural models do not allow the drawing up of borders between the foreign and the self; rather, they provoke dynamic processes of culture mixing (Ette 318). For the Caribbean space Rex Nettleford detects a comparable zone of contact based on a "process of cross-fertilization following on the encounters between the old civilizations of Europe, Africa, and Asia on foreign soil and they, in turn, with the old Amerindian civilization" (202). These theoretical configurations developed on US-American conditions are worth considering for other hybrid constellations as well. In all these processes of exchange and fluctuation it is of decisive importance that they happen in both directions, regardless of whether a financial imbalance is in play or not, even if it is blatant as in the case of Mexico and the US. Beck observes an "Americanization of Asia, Europe and Latin America," but also detects the "Asianization and Latin Americanization of the United States" to equal measure and "new categories of fusion and interdependence" arise in view of which the national and the transnational cannot be thought of as mutually exclusive orders, but as paradigms which "also complement and combine with each other in a variety of ways. Behind the façade of enduring nationality, processes of transnationalization are taking place everywhere" (*The Cosmopolitan* 64).

Writers sensible to the phonenemena of hybridization observe a Creolization of the Western world. Against this background a space such as the Caribbean offers almost ideal conditions of an "intercultural laboratory" where on the one hand the "intercultural experiences, often conflicting and painful, of the first era of globalization which was initiated by the colonial expansion of European powers" can be studied and on the other hand a development can be anticipated: "it seems to herald the cross-cultural constellations of the future which would respond rather to a dynamic of multicultural fragmentation and Creolization than to a movement of uniformity due to a process of financial and communicational globalization" (Lüsebrink 234). What is common practice since the last third of the twentieth century in border towns, such as Tijuana, that is, a daily crossing of the borders in both directions, a self-definition as inhabitants of a liminal zone that has something of both countries, an awareness of the fact of always having alternatives to contemporary way of life, decision making, attitude, and the like)—all that has been reinforced and accentuated by movements of (im)migration accompanying globalization, so that we have to admit that García Canclini is right in his assessment that borders represent a laboratory of the global. Despite the enthusiasm over the apparently efficient key concept of the borderline as a zone of contact, "the concept of the border remains diffuse both in certain diplomatic rhetoric, as well as in a great part of the social essays and cultural studies" and a distinction between "physical, territorial borders" and "cultural, symbolic borders" (Grimson 91) might at first seem commonplace, but is set as a premise as such only in few cases. Hence I point out that in the following I discuss primarily territorial borderlands but which at a second level could mark cultural and symbolic borders. At the same time, I cannot also thematize cultural zones of contact in general, because then I would have to bring to the fore almost all global spaces and areas with "pure" in the sense of unmixed culture and its practices.

A literature of the zones of contact would thus barely represent anything else than an "ethnographic act" and a "performance of alterity" (Herlinghaus and Riese 8), where cultural translation processes can be performed or refused. A substantial importance corresponds thus to language, because therein any translation materializes front and center and generates the third space of hybridity. This is why Anzaldúa announces in the preface to her *Borderlands/La Frontera* that the switching of "codes" in her book—from English to Castillian Spanish to the North Mexican dialect to Tex-Mex to a sprinkling of Náhuatl to a mixture of all these—reflects the language of the Borderlands. In language mixture—that naturally does not always turn out as decidedly as in Anzaldúa—undoubtedly lies the most visible enactment of alterity including fictional spaces, the people settled in them and, of course, the plot of the respective texts. By using the interplay of these elements Djebar's *Les Nuits de Strasbourg* outlines the Alsatian city as a zone of contact of peoples, history(ies), and languages as I discuss above. France and Germany are categories whose outlines cannot be fixed: François works in Rhein-Freihafen and one Sunday morning takes Thelja along for a ride over the Pont de l'Europe Bridge to the German side. On the way there, Thelja is thinking about the two queens who where led over the Rhine in order to be wed. After crossing the bridge, Thelja wonders about the absence of any customs or police checkpoint and about the fact that as an Algerian citizen she would have actually needed a visa for Germany while this is for François no cause for anxiety. The passage reveals the drawing of borders as illusory where the respective Other is still always present in the "own" territory, so there can be no talk of state sovereignty: the abolition of the border in its material form of barriers and passport controls is an external expression of the awareness of this illusion.

Cities like Strasbourg—which in the course of history have changed hands multiple times—symbolize the contingency of the drawing of borders. Thelja, the Berber, influenced by Algerian hatred toward the French colonizers but still in a relationship with a Frenchman; her lover François whose father had fought for Alsace autonomy and who learnt German and French from his grandfather; Hans, the German husband of Jewish Eve from Algeria and Morocco who is learning French and Arabic at the same time to be able to communicate with his wife; Eve, who after many stations has landed in Strasbourg and now is expecting a child with Hans and has sworn to never speak a word in German; Irma, whom her Jewish parents had hidden from the Germans in a foster family and whose mother, a recognized heroine of the *Résistance*, wants nothing to do with her; her friend Karl, who was born in Algeria and ended up in Strasbourg with his parents because of the Algerian war; Jaqueline, who produces the play *Antigone* with teenage Beurs, the children of Maghreb immigrants and is shot by her jealous Algerian friend Ali: Strasbourg is for all of them a city of transition. Strasbourg has no borders for them and even the river Rhine connects, rather than separates because the various memories of wars and conflicts links them together and can be overcome in a synthesis: it is a city of flowing borders and a zone of contact par excellence.

The Mexican-US border on the other hand is a bulwark of the rich First World against the "invasion" from the poor Third World. Herrera narrates the brutality of this border in his poem "Your Throat Burns, Red" (*Giraffe*) about an illegal border crossing at night. In choppy, short sentences which suggest the breathlessness of the running group, gloomy images in black and red are created:

> You spin off toward different horizons
> Kneeling, seated, lying down, crouching
> You drive the iron—lift them weights,
> Invisible
> You write on the wall
> Where there ain't no wall
> The universe
> The fat wall, girl—falling up.
> A vertical ocean.
> You be in the black box. Now. Your hands
> Scratch your face. You walk. You run
> Full speed—on the double. With the eyes turned up
> Frantic speed. Possibly blind. (4)

The poem continues in this style where onomatopoeic expressions, argot, and redundancies are used. The border wall is gigantic in scale and the surrounding territory is like a "black box" where the border crossers stray confused, disoriented, and helpless in the dark, full of fear of meeting the "fat guard," the "men machines. Women machines" (6). When the refugees have already gotten over the wall, they encounter a patrol of rangers, who open fire on "the hungry. The rot, the heroes, the courageous, the stutterers" (10). With their machine gun salvos they kill all but one, who bends over a shot girl and mourns her and thus at the end conjures up the bloody scene once again (14). The border in this text is a death trap for the poor, who go into a fight against machines and that is condemned to failure from the start. So, only one person remains at the end, whose task it is to mourn for the dead and to convey this terrible news to the others. In this grim scenario there is no room for zones of contact or cultural translation. Herrera's text retains a constant ambivalence where irony turns to cynicism. As in Herrera's poem, the border functions as a separation line between two different worlds in Portillo Trambley's *Trini*: "tomorrow she would be in a strange world" (187) and beyond any Aztlán romanticism, the novel makes clear that Trini finds land for the seeds she brought with her beyond the Río Grande into the US and can feed her family including her father and aunt, but the manner in which she inherits this land and how she lives on it hint at Mexico and her Native American roots. Her grinding poverty in the US has ameliorated, but on the other hand her children alienate themselves from her more and more because of the new lifestyle, so that at the end it is only consistent that she wants to return with her son to the Mexican Indian territory. In her new environment she remains a foreign body that can adapt only superficially to certain circumstances. In this respect the text propagates that, even in zones of contact, cultural translation takes place under circumstances to a reduced degree, especially for the first immigrant generation. The characterization of the border zone as a "war zone" remains today and this border is still interpreted as a bulwark of the "free" and "neo-liberal" First World against the Third World: "investments in space, in spatial barriers, in borders, and the like, are in this respect to be always perceived as investments in security, clarity, stability, and lucidity of social relations" (Schroer 69) and this is how attempts by US to leave the border to Mexico visible and tangible can be explained.

The diverse aspects of the US-Mexican border from the Mexican point of view are thematized by Fuentes in his *The Crystal Frontier* in order to underline the coherence of the individual fates on both sides of the border. That, which in Herrera is dealt with in only one sentence ("a wall where there ain't no wall"), the border forms in Fuentes's texts the pivotal point of the narrative events. For Fuentes, it is "the illusory crystal divider, the glass membrane between Mexico and the United States" (*The Crystal* 27) which raises the question for the people at the border: "What country? What memory? What blood?" (*The Crystal* 111). The border is an illusion, because many people belong to both sides, like the Chicano poet José Francisco, who collects and writes down the stories from either side, "the quantity of unburied stories that refused to die, that wandered about like ghosts from California to Texas waiting for someone to tell them, someone to write them" (*Crystal* 251). The stories of the space cannot be clearly appropriated, "but where is here and where is there? Isn't the Mexican side his own here and there? Isn't it the same in the gringo side? Doesn't every land have its invisible double, its alien shadow that walks at our side the same way each of us walks accompanied by a second 'I' we don't know?" (*The Crystal* 250). The other side of the coin, the other side of the I, the person's shadow: these are the metaphors the writer uses to express the obligatory reciprocity in the relationships between the here and there, the one cannot exist without the other. For the people from this borderland there seem to be no materialized benchmarks; the US-American investor's modern factory on the Mexican side where cheap Mexican workers assemble color television sets, is "a mirage of glass and shining steel, like a bubble of crystalline air" (*The Crystal* 119) while in New York, where again a cheap Mexican work force is flown to in order to clean buildings, the skyscrapers are also described as "illusion" (*The Crystal* 179) as "a building completely made of glass became visible, with nothing in it that wasn't transparent: an immense music box made of mirrors, unified by its own chrome-covered, nickel-plated glass, a palace like a crystal deck of cards, a toy of quicksilver labyrinths . . . a Teotihuacán made of glass" (*The Crystal* 179).

Such descriptive passages do not offer anything concrete, no orientation; rather, they evoke images from fairy-tales, from fantasies which compose themselves and dissolve like hazy images and then form again and dissolve again. It is a dreamscape, where Fuentes places his characters and thus it is not surprising that magical things happen, such as young Lisandro's kiss on the office window, which is returned by Audrey, a US-American and for a second suspends both from their loneliness and foreignness. Another such poetic moment takes place when the ranger Mario Islas catches a young Mexican illegally crossing the border, who claims that he was baptized by the former and the question arises why this miracle they both accept the lie and why Mario lets the young Mexican go instead of arresting him and deporting him, "why two complete strangers had lived a moment like that together"

(*The Crystal* 243). The border in Fuentes's text is an ambivalent zone of contact, which, besides the exploitation of cheap labor and all kinds of tragedies also creates moments of fairy-tale poetry when reality gets lost in the border's ambiguity. The individual episodes show a migration to both sides and score against clichés: rich industrialist Don Leonard Barroso constantly crosses the border seeking pleasure with his daughter-in-law and lover Michelina,and in order to multiply his wealth; others seek their luck in the US as students and fail; others open up exquisite Mexican restaurants and become rich and reputable. Fuentes demonstrates a broad range of possibilities that the zone of contact around the border offers and he does this from the Mexican perspective and devaluates the common clichés of the starving, uneducated Mexican. His characters are self-confident even when they are poor. In all metaphorization and mythification of the US-Mexican border, however, we should not forget that "the borders are conceivable as a point of contact only because there exists a limit that separates two entities that, in some way and for some reason, continue to see themselves as different to one another" (Grimson 93).

In sum, narratives of privileging space as a traditional category of classification in the sense of national space and enclosed by defined borders suggest the problematics for the placing of fictional characters in a fictional setting. The principle of the hierarchy of arranging space from the continent to the village where the larger always includes the smaller has apparently become largely obsolete for texts of NWL and been replaced by other patterns of classification. In the texts analyzed, the "compression of space" (Sloterdijk 392) is staged, for instance, as places being side by side without hierarchy when in reality they are far apart. The topos of the big city, small town, village, or landscape is unhinged from its anchoring in traditionally conceived concepts by means of the nation-state and thus located in a new context: "deterritorialization is . . . not simply the dissolution of territoriality, but the necessary other side of a topical order, that expands into the atopic, without ever ceasing to be topology" (Willke, *Heterotopia* 8). This new contextualization can be found, for example, in the literary staging of the metropolises. Contrary to the notion of the "crisis of the city" (Heitmayer, Dollase, Backes; Schroer; Siebel), big cities in NWL play a prominent role by either invalidating or reversing the notion of center-periphery dichotomy as polycentric constructions. If, for example in Kureishi's *The Buddha of Suburbia*, the conquest of the London city center by Indian immigrants is narrated, Ali devaluates in *Brick Lane* the attractiveness of the city center and valorizes a small suburb as a global intersection of commodities, cultures, and information. By this process the power of control over space correlates with social, cultural, and financial capital. That this process apparently represents an important literary theme can be read in the frequency with which the texts thematize the conquest of the power of control over space, be it a prestigious flat in an old building in London or a small home of one's own in Port of Spain. Metropolises in NWL are conceptualized as pivotal points for the flow of commodities, capital, and information, yet they are not configured as self-sufficient or independent entities anymore. In the majority of the texts analyzed one place always brings to mind one or multiple others and not thought of as a diachronic succession as in (im)migration, but simultaneously. The disappearing of distances, the digital flow of information and images lift the inevitability of being able to stay only in one place. The homogenization of activities, demand, and supply leads to the devaluation of specific places' exclusivity. In that moment, however, when the option exists to live somewhere else—because the job description is the same, because we speak the other language well, because we have family members there, or because being illegal we are persecuted anyway—something contingent adheres to the decision in favor of one particular place and that exacerbates a more in-depth identification with only one place. This results in a polygamy of place that makes a permanent locating in one place not seem worthwhile, but when the places become interchangeable life evolves itself into a hybrid existence.

This existence in permanent temporariness has led NWL writers to a mythification of the airport as a representative place of passage and transition par excellence. In the space of the rhizome of individual points without any hierarchy in a global grid of coordinates, the airport forms a mythical threshold to nowhere, a frequent abode for transnational individuals on the way from point A to point B. While here we are still concerned with the spatial transport of concrete bodies, laptops, iPads, and the internet mark an exclusively virtual space. Literary references to these tools of global communication make their presence increasingly felt in the texts and create a virtual parallel world that exists temporarily and does not exist anymore only by means of a few small hand movements, which increases their contingency manifold. The loss of clarity and lucidity with regard to the literary performance of urban spaces also extends to the border that is configured both as an element of separation between people, cultures, and states, as well as a connecting zone of contact. We can search for unambiguities in vain: "how a border is perceived decisively depends on what situation we are in and which status we hold: if we face the border as a migrant, a refugee, an ambassador, or a tourist—that makes all the difference" (Schroer 224). In the age of global mass migrations it is no coincidence that the border is thus popular as a literary theme. NWL texts offer a bandwidth of border-crossers of all kinds from the privileged scientist to the illegal immigrant, all of whom are in search of a new social and virtual space for themselves. NWL texts narrate the symbolic appropriation of space and are differentiated from traditional literature by creating de-hierarchized, transnational, and atopic patterns.

The deplacement of national history

Adnan's *In the Heart of the Heart of Another Country* is about boundedness to spaces and environments. The protagonist's revisiting of places is to conjure up past times, jumping back and forth between different times which is incompatible with traditional cyclical or linear concepts of time. This feature is characteristic of texts of NWL. In order to frame my analyses in this chapter, I turn to Reinhart Koselleck's concept of "temporal layers," in which he takes into account that any "historical sequence includes both linear, as well as recurrent elements" and allows "the analytical separation of different temporal levels on which people move, events play out" (19). In connection to postmodern architecture, Castells goes so far as to speak of "the uprooting of experience, history, and specific culture as the background of meaning . . . [an] end of all systems of meaning" (1: 449). For Castells systems of space belong to systems of time and detects the destruction of this "linear, irreversible, measurable, predictable time" which is tantamount to an in-depth transformation where "it is the mixing of tenses to create a forever universe, not self-expanding but self-maintaining, not cyclical but random, not recursive but incursive: timeless time, using technology to escape the contexts of its existence, and to appropriate selectively any value each context could offer to the ever-present" (464). Along with this comes an acceleration and thus a compression of time, which as a consequence makes "time sequence, and thus time, disappear" (Castells, 1: 464). However, when models of time such as the linear or the circular do not hold anymore, we reach a "simultaneity of the non-simultaneous" which means that qualitatively different stages of development meet one another simultaneously, that is, within quantatively measurable time (1: 464). For Nassehi, the discovery of the so-called New World and the confrontation with cultures which were considered more backward than those of Europe "something like a permanent problem of asynchrony spread even within Europe, which, if nothing else, is conditional upon the higher degree of differentiation and complexity of modernized society" (*Geschlossenheit* 134–35). What I add to this is that societies in the Americas have their own complexities and thus it is no coincidence that Carpentier and Fuentes, for example, have built almost their entire work on the simultaneity of the non-simultaneous or that US-American writers such as Morrison or Erdrich thematize in their novels collective consciousness. Not only in European cities are the traces of the past inscribed in their architecture, but "other" metropolises such as Mexico City, Mumbai, or Hong Kong are not shaped any less by the interlinkings of eras and cultures.

What scholars of globalization detect as a breakdown of patterns of time in many societies occurs also in literary production and especially where (im)migration processes or transnational relationships are central and where the borderline work of culture occurs (Bhabha). For Bhabha through a meeting with "'newness' . . . is not part of the continuum of past and present" and therefore has to be invented anew, specifically "as a contingent 'in-between' space, that innovates and interrupts the performance of the present" (*The Location* 7). This is because of questions such as "how does one encounter the past as an anteriority that continually introduces an otherness or alterity into the present? How does one then narrate the present as a form of contemporaneity that is neither punctual nor synchronous? In what historical time do such configurations of cultural difference assume forms of cultural and political authority?" (157). Here, the point of the observers plays a role that should not be disregarded because the knowledge and cultural baggage in the background define the distribution of events on a scale between the archaic and the contemporary, so that we would inevitably end up with a linearity of historical perception, which is exactly what should be avoided. When, for example, in Shashi Tharoor's novel *Riot*, the US-American protagonist Priscilla Hart is murdered by the husband of an Indian woman who had an abortion at Priscilla's instigation, we could interpret this with a Western reading as a typical simultaneity of non-simultaneous worldviews, because women's right of self-determination—at least in most European countries—is a matter of fact and therefore the murder seems to have happened stemming from specific cultural motives. The text, however, does not include any hints steering its readers in this direction. To the contrary: violent conflicts between Muslims and Hindus are equally possible as the reason for the murder as Priscilla's love affair with the married government official Lakshman. That her death is ultimately connected to her work with an organization that educates Native Indian women on their rights and on contraception is purely a coincidence. As the text offers three alternative possibilities to solve the murder and at the last moment takes a decision in favor of one—and that is officially covered up—Western conceptions of causal relationships are made relative. The murder was not planned and is perhaps to be seen as a result of different cultural norms, but not to be classified as a clash of societal patterns which are set temporally far apart: Priscilla Hart's campaign is equally the Indian present as the repression of women by their husbands and other family members. In this respect, we would foist onto the text Western attitudes were we to interpret the murder case in this manner.

In order to avoid the trap I refer to above, in the following I analyze texts for verifiable temporal layers and their relationship to each to other and thus start from the premise that references to past events induce elements of alterity in the present. This reach of the past as foreignness into the present can be attached to people or places, it can be narrated in the text as real history or it can be constructed as fiction, as a configuration of a more or less mythical past. Examples for the former case are provided by the texts of Djebar, for instance, while the latter can often be found in Chicano/a literature. In both situations a mixing of the global and the local takes place, because local knowledge, local traditions, and local story(ies) are imported into a transnational actuality and how these breaks in time are processed with the result that they are received as a coexistence of non-simultaneities without hierarchy. *Les Nuits de Strasbourg* is a text, where Strasbourg appears as a place where the most different past stories are superimposed and compressed over the novel's characters who live there. Everyone of the characters embodies in his or her nomadic existence a conglomeration of chronologies which are partly space dependent as Thelja's Algerian origin, are partly determined by individual fate as Jacqueline's and her father's story who deserted from the German army in 1944, because he fell in love with an Alsatian woman in Strasbourg, or are component of a collective history, as for example happens with the two Jewish women, Eve and Irma. All these people are influenced again and again by earlier temporal layers even during the most mundane of everyday actions. For example, the love between Jewish Eve and German Hans or Algerian Thelja and French François are stages of overcoming of the past. Even the names of the two men demarcate them as representatives of their entire people, who have inflicted upon the people of their respective partners indescribable suffering: the Germans through the Holocaust and the French through the atrocities in Algeria. Eve and Thelja belong to the group of the former victims, but free themselves from this position of inferiority by becoming, each in her own way, equal rights partners of the men. Eve and Hans agree to a pact for their unborn child, reciting the ancient Oaths of Strassbourg (pledges of allegiance in 842 between Louis the German and his half-brother Charles the Bald), which Eve recites in German and Hans in French, and with this symbolic act they bury the dividing past (238).

Thelja perseveres in her distanced stance and she uses formal to address with her lover almost all the time and does not utter his name. Eve and Hans appropriate consciously the past as alterity and thus remove from it the foreign and the alienating, so that they are able to acquire authority over their actions. With the example of these two couples, Djebar demonstrates how earlier individual and collective temporal layers—which all people carry within them as a component of their personality— give immediate directives for action and can steer the individual's behavior. Thelja's inability for commitment is certainly a personal problem, but behind it stands the Algerian population's collective memory of the long war against the French colonial power. Just as its people, the city of Strasbourg itself has numerous temporal layers which are expounded in detail in the course of the novel and are clearly privileged against the pattern of categorization of space. Thelja searches in Strasbourg for medieval documents of the abbess of the nearby Benedictine monastery, Herrad von Landsberg, whereby the chequered story of this woman's main work evokes Strasbourg's sieges and destruction in the sixteenth and especially the nineteenth century (101–03) and these correlate with the description of the evacuated city during World War II, when its capture by the German Wehrmacht seemed imminent. In this way, a kind of collage image of Strasbourg arises in synchrony and diachrony, where the individual eras do not follow linearly one after the other, but come in short flashes so that a palimpsest is created that is compatible with the identities of the characters and that remains open to and capable of connection with all spatial and temporal sides. Similarly, in Djebar's *Fantasia: An Algerian Cavalcade* different temporal layers are thematized where the childhood memories of a woman during the French colonial regime in Algeria are interwoven with the representation of the First Algerian War. The war reports tell the story from different perspectives. Thus in the text 37 published reports in the course of July 1830 are referred to when the capital Algiers is besieged by the French and ultimately captured and where it is said that only three of those reports come from the side of the besieged and so there can be no talk of a neutral historical narration. The task of the first-person narrator is, therefore, to reveal and reconstruct the events from the Other's point of view to contrast her own version of the higher-ranking French officers (*Fantasia* 44). History as a palimpsest is the theme of this novel: "it is now my turn to tell a tale. To hand on words that were spoken, then written down" (*Fantasia* 165) to release the voices of the past from the prison of their days as the grandmother is able to do in trance. In order to do so in this manner in order to obtain an explanation for the alienation and schizophrenia of

the present, the reduced existence of many other Algerian women results in her contradictory love-hate for French: "for my part, even where I am composing the most
commonplace of sentences, my writing is immediately caught in the snare of the old
war between two peoples. So I swing like a pendulum from images of war (war of
conquest or of liberation, but always in the past) to the expression of a contradictory,
ambiguous love" (*Fantasia* 216).

If in Djebar's it is writing in French, in the language of the enemy, that provokes the controversy with the past, in Lahens's novel *Dans la maison du père* it
is Vodou and its dances which bring to the surface long buried African culture and
leads the protagonist Alice Bienaimé to her vocation as a dancer. The temporal layers referring to Africa are tabooed in the Haitian middle class, have been banished
from the collective memory, and were replaced by the French culture of the colonial
masters and this explains why Alice's father was appalled when the little girl in tears
tells of the horrors of French school: "I stared at my father who in just a few seconds
became an incandescent image like a blurry fire. Silent, he looked at me without
seeing me; his eyes were fixed on other faces that were for a moment called father,
grandfather, great-grandfather and all the ancestors. Education had given him the
feeling that he was out of poverty: his father was a shopkeeper in the country, his
grandfather a farmer and his ancestors had been slaves in the colonial plantations.
It had also given him oblivion, that immense oblivion which always covered them.
All dead without a noise after a whole life of forced silence. And death leading them
back again to definitive oblivion, the one of people of their background. My refusal
was in the eyes of Antenor Bienaimé like the dark and silent grave of the poor" (46).

French education and culture are indispensable prerequisites for advancement
in Alice's society or at least for the preservation of the status quo, so that her rejection
of the French school and the search for her African roots equals to a voluntary social
downgrading. This painful, because the memory of this—in the Western sense—
ahistorical condition is still very much alive. Since Alice admits to her African side
and even stylizes it, she drags this past suppressed through deportation and colonization to contemporaneity and gives it a certain dignity back. Thus the French colonial
masters' claim of superiority is abrogated and the hegemonial discourse devalued.
In this respect, we are dealing with a postcolonial text in the initial sense of the term
that lays bare colonial hegemonic structures and counters them with own value and
norm systems. While for Alice African dance exerts a catalytic effect and lets her become a world-renowned dancer, in Özdamar's *Mutterzunge* it is the loss of the Turkish language that is perceived as tragic and that motivates the protagonist to research
her origins in different stories of the past. In doing so, she moves linearly in reverse,
from the German of her present to the Turkish of her mother's and then the Arabic
of her grandfather's, without, however, keeping to a strict chronological sequence.
Her way to the languages takes her to Istanbul whose repression her brother falls
victim to and to Berlin-Wilmersdorf where she falls in love with her Arabic teacher
and finds out about his seven brothers who died in the fight against the Israelis. The
search for words evokes past and recent events in Turkey, the Near East, and in both

German states in 1970s. Here, too, the reader is confronted with a chaotic flashing of single points in time in a rhizomatic-like time: the text is not concerned with an ordered linear or circular representation, but achieves the authority of the protagonist over past history. In contrast to Djebar's texts, however, where past and present appear in a causal relation, Özdamar's texts are about the individual putting together an identity, which is missing some important pieces. Here the theme is the search and not the arrival.

The reconfiguration of a mythical past is another method of implanting an alteritary temporal layer into the present and to thus explicate it or to gain instructions for the Now: "if in the concept of myth . . . we generally think of something past, jaded, that has to be reconstructed anew in historical memory. Myth, however, is not only the past and archaic depth, but also bright present ... an overhistoric time, an *ur*-time ... which as an everlasting 'always' remains contemporary and preferred there, where the origin event is brought to mind in the present by recitation" (Geyer 7, 17). Of all NWL texts, it is primarily in Chicano/a literature where constructs of the past occur in an always surprising manner. This happens most of all about Aztlán, the legendary homeland of the Mexican people, the place of the life-giving earth goddess Coatlicue, that approximately encompassed today's Southwest of the US and from whence the Mexican people in the ninth century BC were supposed to have migrated to the central highlands of Southern Mexico. Already in the sixteenth century Aztlán is mentioned in Spanish reports as a mythical place of origin and a paradise without disease and hunger. At the beginning of the Chicano/a *movimiento*, the treaty of Guadalupe-Hidalgo 1848 surfaced again, which stated that after the US-American victory over the Mexicans what was then Northern Mexico had to be surrendered to the victors and the Mexicans living in the US-American Southwest were driven out or discriminated against. Further, in the 1960s, the work conditions of the seasonal workers emigrating from Mexico to work on California fields had become thus unbearable and *movimiento* remembered that this country was actually Mexican and following this with the "Plan Espiritual de Aztlán" gathered all socially underprivileged Chicanos/as to fight for fundamental civil rights. The "Plan of Aztlán" aimed at two directions: an economic-political one by turning against the exploitation of Chicano/a workers and their lack of rights and a cultural one by marking differences to the Euro-American society and propagating self-confidence with regard to cultural heritage. In this respect, the Chicano/a movement can certainly be registered in the context of the time of US-American civil rights movements similar to that of the African American population: "Aztlán as a signifier marking the completion or return of the Chicano to a homeland suggests both cultural and social signification. As a representation of place, Aztlán makes claims to a political and economic self-determination not dissimilar to claims asserted by indigenous populations throughout the world. As a symbol of unity, Aztlán asserts a type of cultural discontinuity and rupture that characterize Chicanos in history. Although it evokes a Chicano homeland, Aztlán also foregrounds the difficult relationship Chicanos bear with history—a history, after all, comprised of dispossession and migration" (Pérez-

Torres 61).

The mythical homeland Aztlán and the world of pre-Colombian gods find diverse entryways, so much the more, since contemporary Mexico, shaped by corruption and social unfairness, is all but a country that would invite those Mexicans, who saw themselves forced to migrate due to poverty, to identify with it. Pérez-Torres speaks in relation to this of a "transformation of the pre-Cortesian into fetish" (48), which would obliterate the heterogeneity within the Mexican migrants and would swear all Chicanos to a cultural model that would often enough by no means correspond to the actual cultural heritage of one group or another. Newer studies take into account this heterogeneity: the work by Fox and Rivera-Salgado presents demographic data, which show the great heterogeneity of immigrant Mexicans and at the same time makes clear that *Oaxacalifornia* as a real and mental space is apparently about to inherit the mythical Aztlán (107). Thus, Anzaldúa's text about the borderlands—that has almost already become a myth itself—functionalizes primarily the world of Aztec gods for her sketching of the new *mestiza*, but at the same time she makes clear that the Aztecs were hated as a brutal regime by the people conquered by them and that the governing elite had lost contact to their own population so much that the Spanish under Cortés had an easy job of conquering Tenochtitlán: "the Aztec nation fell not because *Malinali* (*La Chingada*) interpreted for and slept with Cortés, but because the ruling elite had subverted the solidarity between men and women and between noble and commoner" (34). This passage is typical of Anzaldúa's endeavor to deconstruct and reinterpret past temporal layers from a feminist perspective such as rejecting here the "original sin" as the cause of Aztec defeat against a handful of conquistadors and offering a different interpretation of the historical events (34). Here, the "original sin," being Mexico's "ur-betrayal" is seen in the relationship between the conqueror Cortés and the Indigenous Malinche/ Marina. While the mythical past is devalued by other facts, Anzaldúa seizes many other opportunities to establish them first. Thus she tells of the nocturnal apparition of a wraithlike woman in white next to an abandoned church in a village in the Río Grande valley in Southern Texas, who is identified by some Mexican residents there as *La Llorona*, i.e., Mary mourning the death of her son Jesus. But Anzaldúa finds another explanation for this phenomenon: "she was, I think, *Cihuacoatl*, Serpent Woman, ancient Aztec goddess of the earth, of war and birth, patron of midwives, and antecedent of *La Llorona*. Covered with chalk, *Cihuacoatl* wears a white dress with a decoration half red and half black. . . . Like *La Llorona, Cihuacoatl* howls and weeps in the night, screams as if demented" (35). Here, the Catholic explanation of a deeply rooted superstition is interpreted differently with an older layer of history and culture and a mythical past is created with which attitudes and behaviors of the present can be made plausible. Anzaldúa derives this perception of the world from her "consciousness of duality" she only acquired when she overcame the rationality implanted by the Whites and learned to accept the inner world of dreams and the soul, whereby the separation of the spiritual and the real sphere does not exist anymore and by shifting back and forth between the two is for Anzaldúa a fundamental ability of the "*India* and the *mestiza*" (37): Anzaldúa "reworks Aztec mythology and provides an alternate, lesbian, Chicana experience" (Arteaga 41). Anzaldúa lends the Aztec past the status of a reality of its own and of a concrete temporal layer which just as the displacement after 1848 occupies a place in the structure of time as a pattern of classification. Still, we have to underline that this Chicano/a mythic "memory" is clearly a "cultural product" (Pérez-Torres 177): it is symbolic imagery that stages a spiritual and magical counter-discourse to the established poetic and historic discourse of Euro-Americans (Pérez-Torres 201–09).

Herrera also invokes appeals to the Aztec past in numerous of his poetic texts, albeit less concretely than Anzaldúa. In *Border-crosser with a Lamborghini Dream* in a cycle of poems entitled "Blood on the Wheel" Herrera writes about Aztec sacrificial ceremonies:

> Blood on the night soil man en route to the country prison
> Blood on the sullen chair, the one that holds you with its pleasure
> Blood inside the quartz, the beaty watch, the eye of the guard
> Blood in the slope of names & the tattoos hidden
> . . .
> Blood in the tin, in the coffee bean, in the *maquila oración*
> Blood in the language, in the wise text of the market sausage
> Blood in the border web, the penal colony shed, in the bilingual yard
> . . .
> Blood at the age of seventeen
> Blood at the age of one, dumped in a Greyhound bus
> Blood mute & autistic & cauterized & smuggled Mayan
> & burned in border smelter tar
> Could this be yours? Could this item belong to you?
> Could this ticket be what you ordered, could it?
> Blood on the wheel, blood on the reel
> Bronze dead gold & diamond deep. Blood be fast. (10-13)

This Aztec blood shedding provided in the sixteenth century to justify almost any atrocity and repression on the part of the conquerors. That there also existed a counter-discourse in contemporary Europe is shown in the writings of Fray Bartolomé de las Casas or Michel de Montaigne's essay about cannibalism (see Todorov). In the above poem the tables are turned by creating a US-America where there is blood even in the most mundane trivia and where the consequent anaphoric use of the key word "blood" creates a forceful rhetorical pathos and at the same time is reminiscent of ritual incantations. In another text, Herrera again works with anaphoras and deploys an entire host of *braceros*, the mostly under-paid and often illegal crop workers:

> Calling all tomato pickers, the ones wearing death frowns instead of
>   jackets
> Calling all orange & lemon carriers, come down the ladder to this hole

. . .

Calling all apple tossers high up in the heaven of pesticides, stick faced

Calling all onion priests & onion nuns & onion saints killing for rain

Calling all tobacco pullers, thick leaf rollers in the ice burn of North
Carolina

. . .

Calling all watermelon shiners paring the sugary womb in search of
Goddess

Calling all cotton pilots seeding the froth on my mother's grave, rebel-
lious

Calling all strawberry weavers threading your wire mesh heart with
thorns

Calling all tomato pickers, the old ones, wearing frayed radiator masks.
(20)

Despite the surrealist style with its surprising image combinations, the poem clearly tells of people who carry death within them, because they are subjected to inhumane working conditions for example with pesticides or inhospitable weather conditions. The text assigns to the immigrants the role of those who shed other people's blood, but the text demonstrates that it is their blood that is shed here and in this manner the colonial discourse is reevaluated whereby the perpetrators become victims and an alternative view of history is constructed. These two examples are typical of Herrera's work, who draws the material for his images and metaphors from the pre-Colombian era and relates regional and local earlier temporal layers to contemporary life with cultural references of an artistic or culinary kind from around the world. More still than in Anzaldúa are the text passages referring to Aztec mythology interwoven into a lyrical fabric and attuned to sound and rhythm, as well as momentary powerful imagery, so that his poems are often hermetic and do not necessarily allow the reader access. Where Anzaldúa explains and lists numbers and events, Herrera creates snapshots whose association background frequently remains in the dark. What the texts by both authors have in common is that they break up the perception of linear time by re-constructing remote temporal layers and inserting them without any hierarchy into the present. The alterity of another time in the present is suspended by means of the appropriation and the melting of that time with the current one. At the same time, this bringing together of non-simultaneous processes creates a dynamic between the global of now-time and the local or the regional of the past: "those . . . who wish to return to the [Aztec, Mayan, Toltec] pyramid, forget that in the first place, in the present concrete reality which inscribes itself upon us, we have to enter the Cathedral, and dismantle it from within before we can gain access to the pyramid. Furthermore, this pyramid is no longer as it was, but can only be re-constructed as an artifact" (Toro 32).

In sum, I draw again on Schroer's work—who, in his plea for giving the privilege of space over time as a cognitive schema and pattern of classification with regard to the phenomena of globalization—raises the reproach that although sociology has "indeed repeatedly concerned itself with the transition from simple to complex societies, however, it has primarily understood this shift as a temporal one . . . simple society forms still found . . . [and were] considered relics of a past time, whose examination could safely be left to the ethnologists ... Perceptions of social change are shaped by an understanding of space and time deeply anchored in occidental history. While time stands for the mobile, dynamic, and progressive, for change, shift, and history, space stands for immobility, stagnation, and the reactionary, for standstill, rigidity, and stability" (21). In contrast to this traditional sociological reading, in NWL texts I discuss it is exactly the liquefaction of spatial stability in the transnational which occurs. If globalization is defined as a "process of expansion" in space and time (Schroer 125), the question is raised as to what extent we can also apply to the temporal as a paradigm shift comparable to space. That such a one exists is evident if we accept that the "discussion about postmodernism . . . [is] for the time being the last effort to think about societal history in the sense of a temporal sequence" because "the suggestion that there have always been postmodern theories, ways of thinking, etc. refers to the possibility of the temporal coexistence of various, contradictory to each other, temporal tendencies and trends" (Schroer 171). In this manner the innovative characteristics of NWL with regard to the temporal is evident. My analyses of the selected texts shows that the suspension of linearity represents a prominent trait in which—similar to the de-hierchization of spatial relations—different temporal layers are more or less ordered paratactically as equals. The less the fictional characters remain exclusively and lastingly in a specific place, the less they persist in one time. Instead, ever more temporal layers are brought into the present of the narration whose manifestations are exceedingly complex: for example, they refer to the past, to an earlier residence of a/n (im)migrant and thus bring commemorated time into the present one. Or, they pre-empt the future, they narrate myth or historical time anchored in the collective consciousness, or they narrate iterative time that repeats certain events and contextualizes them anew every time.

Conclusion

A new society emerges if and when structural transformation occurs in the relation-ships of production, the relationships of power, and the relationships of experience. These transformations lead to an equally substantial modification of social forms of space and time and thus to the emergence of a new culture. What has been occurring since the 1960s and 1970s through the technical innovations and the economic and political crises of capitalism and in the 1980s by the collapse of the Soviet empire, a new world is emerging that operates with different rules than the world of the twen-tieth century. Castells describes this world as the "network society; a new economy, the informational/global economy; and a new culture, the culture of real virtuality. The logic embedded in this economy, this society, and this culture underlies social action and institutions throughout an interdependent world" (2: 367). An important characteristic of the different networks is the fact that they have a material basis both at local and transnational levels and in principle they can expand without limit: "the power of flows takes precedence over the flows of power" and thus the primacy of transnational activities (2: 500). This does not necessarily imply the frequently invoked death of the nation-state, but its role in the global network has changed to the effect that it acts as a "fiduciary enforcer of globally decided politics" and is involved in this way in transnational political or economic processes (Meyer 67). Asian economies show that nation-states benefit from mechanisms of globalization and at the same time they exercise power over the population with rigorous mea-sures, just as they do over capital flows (see, e.g., Ong). In this respect, it would be wrong to consider the end of the sovereign nation-state. Rather, the question is to modify social topology to the direction of a "flexible political multilevel identity" which "includes the national, the regional, and the global levels" (Meyer 217). We have to bid farewell to the fiction of a homogeneous society, we have to "strip the society concept of its nation-state narrowness" even if the "classical concept of the social is still felt, at least as a ghost pain" (Nassehi, *Diskurs* 432).

However, it is not enough to analyze the emerging complexities of globalized societies through the paradigm shift from national to transnational and to proceed from the demand for oneness to the acceptance of plurality. Instead, what is neces-sary is the analysis of diversity with tools of systemic and contextual frameworks whereby the heterogeneity and complexity of new relations are observable. Knowledge from the social sciences is the foundation for the attempt undertaken here to draw new borders and positionings in the field of literary studies in order to do justice to hybrid texts I discuss in my study. This is because if we understand literature as a symbolic repertoire in the sense of a representative selection from everyday reality, then the sociological look on this everyday reality sharpens the perception of the symbolic data processing, as it is provided, for example, in the form of literary texts as a cultural practice. And here I diagnose a development of symbolic representations in multilingualism, atopia, heterarchy, and polycontexturality: "the new cultural practices seem to have lost their usual localisations in an open process that characterizes both the economic migrant and the intellectual defector. That stabilization of the past, which established an idiom for literary production and national thinking—a great homeland, one and monolingual—is complicated with new habits that include the exodus as one of the possible faces of identity. . . . Between heaven and earth, between borders and official canons, without situating themselves in either, what these unclassifiable texts, even from a linguistic point of view, discuss at the end is the drama of a space for writing itself" (López Parada 377–78).

My objective in this study is to create the space postulated by Esperanza López Parada for the study of "unclassifiable" literatures in order to analyze the complexities of such texts and to disclose their characteristics. In the past hybrid literatures have often been read and categorized as "trivial." In order to overcome this one-sided perception, I imply thought for the social sciences not in order to analyze the texts as to their "verisimilitude" to reality, but in order to bring their alterity and literary specificities into focus. The complexity and diversity in the economy of communication resulting from globalization is correlated with the appearance of linguistically heterogeneous texts, whose symbolic character feeds on more than one cultural environment. This setting can be traced in the NWL and my conclusion corresponds to "what is commonly referred to as culture and identity is a variable and not a constant value for the author" (Pazarkaya 58), since it cannot be the task of a text analysis to trace the biography of an author in his or her text or to verify his or her linguistic competence in the text. Everyday reality of the last quarter of the century—despite all globalization conditioned tendencies of homogenization—is not a world which is moving toward an illusory and perhaps harmful unity, but to a greater degree of differentiation and often to conflicts, as Fuentes emphasizes (*This I Believe* 182–85). For Fuentes any culture exists precisely and exclusively through the exchange with other cultures. In an era when communication on a global scale and with no delay of time has become standard, it would be ironic if literature were to ignore the changes observed everywhere. Of course, literature changes in forms of expression and content and moves from identity to alterity, from reduction to expansion, from expulsion to inclusion, from paralysis to movement, from unity to difference, from noncontradiction to permanent contradiction, from oblivion to memory, and from the inert past to the living past (see Fuentes, *This I Believe*).

In view of this complexity, if we would like to create a range of action, this will not be achieved through the "creation of unity," but only through "the management of heterogeneity" and the "formation of order" (Willke, *Dystopia* 89); in other words, through the creation of a heterotopia of literature as an "ideal-typical category" so as to cope with the "impositions of the hyperbolic contingencies of atopia" and the "symbolic distortions of dystopia" (Willke, *Heterotopia* 11). Having realized this, I establish NWL as a systemic category of literature and culture, which is based on two fundamental differences: 1) multilingualism in the full spectrum of all potential forms of occurrence of one-word interferences to metamultilingualism and 2) the phenomena of globalization and regionalization which are broken down by people, places, spaces, and temporal layers. I present the logic of this systemic view in my discussion of NWL texts. However, because every system must, in principle, be thought of as contingent, its real effectiveness will be put to the test only in the context of other comparable systems such as national literature, (im)migrant and ethnic minority literatures, or postcolonial literatures.

Goethe offered his idea of *Weltliteratur* in opposition to national literatures of various provenance and we must admit that for almost two hundred years we have not escaped the binarism of national literatures versus world literatures. Yet, for all the diminishing of national borders through flows of people, goods, finances, or information, the concept of national literature in literary history—and otherwise—remains a fact and the nation-state is by no means worn out. Critics of globalism such as John Ralston Saul even see the nation-state growing in strength once again, precisely because globalization has not fulfilled its promise for more wealth for all and has led the inadequacy of political governing systems to a power vacuum. In view of this situation, we can assume that national literatures as an umbrella category of literary history is here to stay: "the concept of 'nation' and along that of 'national literature' is becoming more diffuse, but is not disappearing" (Fohrmann 32; see also, e.g., Fürbeth, Krügel, Metzner, Müller). The insistence on the concept of national literature is not the case in European literary study alone, but also with regard to "small" literatures special importance is attached to the genesis of a national literature in one or more national languages, even after having gained independence from a colonial power. The same applies to asymmetric power relations, such as in Catalonia, where writing in the Catalan language denotes an acknowledgment of the Catalan nation and a struggle against the central power in Madrid. In principle, the aversion against the contamination of "their" literature through hybrid forms grows with increasing intensity of the pressures of legitimization while in established, "old" nation-states we attest, as a rule, a certain transparency in dealing with literary hybridization. However, this does not automatically imply equal rights and equivalence with the respective established majority national literature.

NWL as an independent subsystem favors—in contrast to the homogenizing characteristics of national literatures—difference and heterogeneity and privileges hybridization as an aesthetic criterion. Thus NWL has to be thought of as of equal rank to "national literature," because it does not derive its evaluation criteria from national literary specifica, but from its constitution as a transnational, independent system. In this context I would like to note once again that my subject is only texts and not their authors. For example, Muñoz Molina's *Carlota Fainberg* or Walser's *Der Augenblick der Liebe* are classified as NWL, because they meet the formal and contentual requirements for inclusion in the subsystem. At the same time, Muñoz Molina, for example, has written other works such as *Beatus ille* and *El jinete polaco*, which on account of their Castilian language, their subject matter, and their spatial and temporal designs are attributable exclusively to Castilian Spanish literature, and the same applies to Walser with regard to German-language literature. In this respect, then, NWL and national literature are mutually exclusive as subsystems in the systemic understanding of literary history as the main and umbrella concept.

With regard to (im)migration literature we discover intersections between the two categories of NWL and national literature. However, in some instances this type of literature is marginalized, as for example in German-language scholarship where "migrant literature" is understood as "a non-literary category" that "has found an entrance in literary scholarship" and forms "a construct of subject, language, and experience background of the authors" (Blioumi 121). By classifying such texts because of a particular social and historical context of their genesis, nontextual criteria are brought into play, which in my opinion are inadequate and misplaced. Numerous authors of NWL texts narrate processes of (im)migration whose authors have no (im)migrant background, for example, the above referred-to writers Walser and Muñoz Molina. The marginalization of (im)migrant literature as a separate and non-national type of text reduces the complexities of such literature. Nor does "ethnic writing" or "ethnic minority writing" describe the literary activity of a second or third generation of immigrants, because in such cases the culturally conditioned set of symbolic signs are no longer neatly divisible according to parameters of national literature and because the designation of "ethnic literature" implies "that its signified is not an integral or natural part of a land's literary history" (Seyhan 10). A. Robert Lee also raises the question of the meaning of "ethnicity" under the current conditions of globality: "in the fictions of Reed, Vizenor, Castillo, Kinston, and Cha, however, one can look to a different kind of postmodern literary custodianship, that of multi-cultural—ethnic—imagining, and whatever opinion otherwise, that of no one's minority" (232). Thereby the connection to NWL is marked, and the issue is about extracting a group of texts from their minority status as (im)migration literature. Literary texts which thematize (im)migration and its consequences with hybrid linguistic references, as I demonstrate, exist, and more will exist in the future. However, it makes little sense to ascribe them to national literature sas a minority or minor type of texts. As I argue in my book, they are more adequately accommodated in NWL, because their structural and contentual features can be made more transparent than in philological scholarship. In this sense, Mads Rosendahl Thomsen also calls for a separate system for "migrant writing" because "in world literature, migrant writing stands out and forms a constellation of its own, due to the simple fact that the writers have a different relation to languages and book markets than most other writers" with the result that these internationally recognized and received authors "have been able to create a space of their own in world literature, rather than generating a compilation of nationally based literatures that need to be understood within a specific frame of reference" (104; the down side of Rosendahl Thomsen's designation is "migrant" literature with which he abrogates the locus and presence of writers who live permanently in a different country than their country of origin, for example, Turkish German writers; on this, see Tötösy de Zepetnek, "Interculturalism," "Migration").

Just as (im)migration literature overlaps with NWL, there is also an intersection between NWL and postcolonial literature. Some of the texts I discuss are classified as postcolonial (e.g., Ondaatje, Rushdie) but these texts are also located in NWL because they are multilingual and narrate global as well as local elements. However, other postcolonial texts such as by Achebe do not belong to NWL because although their texts deal with colonial and postcolonial issues, they remain in the local or regional. Similarly, some contemporary postcolonial literature overlaps with NWL, namely, those which have overcome the "write back" paradigm and have reached the third phase and are located in the "borderland of different languages, rites of passage, and negotiations between myth and reality, memory and presence, madness and reason, and factual account and revolutionary experimentation in language and style" (Seyhan 107). That ironic, playful, almost relativist dealing with a colonial past requires a certain mental—and perhaps also temporal—distance to the colonial power and a profound reflection on the Self and the Other, which make for something new and generate a third space, but not so in the sense of a peaceful synthesis, but conflict-laden, ambivalent, and always with theoretically open borders.

I note that in some cases examples of NWL cannot be found. For example, the work of Lusophone Angolan author Artur Carlos Maurício Pepetela locates his novels in Angola throughout, often in the capital Luanda, where he focuses on the precolonial past, as well as on the time of the Portuguese colonial regime with the bloody struggle for liberation and subsequent independence. Although many words and expressions from Umbundu, the main African language of Angola, flow in the text, they do not form a multilingual text. Further, the subjects are characterized by Angolan experiences, be it the war against the Portuguese authorities or the daily corruption in modern Luanda. The recovery of the collective memories extinguished by the Portuguese, the ideological and ethnic division of the population left behind by the colonial power, and the problems of postcolonial daily life form a narrative discourse, but without multilingualism as I define the concept. In the younger generation of writers a turn to transnational writing is indicated, such as in the texts of Angolan author José Eduardo Agualusa—who in the form of travel stories expands to ideological, gender, or language transgressions—narrates the loss of fixed borders. The topic and narrative style of his texts would allow it to be classified in NWL, if only it were linguistically doing justice to the transnational and hybrid elements of its action. However, the texts are written in "proper" Portuguese, which consciously avoids any "impurities." At the same time, the example of Angolan literature demonstrates the usefulness of the postcolonial approach as a cognitive schema and theory structure, because the "culture-theoretical aspects treated in postcolonialism basically pertain to any literature, art, or life world that are affected by the dynamic processes as a result of cultural superimpositions or conflicts of occurred 'hybridisations . . . [as an] all-world theme" (Schulte 4). This approach is worth considering when we realize the fact that "the postcolonial situation today already affects the vast majority of people in their everyday lives . . . according to projections, in the year 2050 Europe with the USA, so the 'West,' will make up only about 7 percent of the world's population, of which about 4.7 percent goes to the EU. It is therefore presumptuous to assume that 7 percent of the world's population will shape the fate and the development of international relations in the twenty-first century world-wide" (Guérot 73). Such figures show that the time of the hegemony of the West, even without the "radical questioning of cultural, social, and political paradigms" of postmodernity is near its end including the "supremacy of one culture over another" (Toro 86). It seems to me that the problem lies in the fact that the theory of postcolonialism with its "tyranny of quotationality and citation" (Quayson and Goldberg xvii) despite its commendable incorporation of other discourses such as feminism or gender relationships has led to a loss of applicability with regard to literature. It is not for nothing that compendia such as *Relocation Postcolonialism* (Quayson and Goldberg), *The Cambridge Companion to Postcolonial Literary Studies* (Lazarus), or *The Blackwell Companion to Postcolonial Studies* (Schwarz and Ray) are intended as a relocation and containment of the field.

Therefore, I collate from the above considerations the following: 1) part of the texts characterized as postcolonial literature is identical with NWL, especially recent texts, and 2) the application of postcolonial theories is of some benefit to understanding of NWL as a subsystem of literary history and practice. However, NWL is aimed at global conditions and is less committed to ideological principles than many theorists of postcolonialism practice since it has to do with the inventory and description of a group of texts.

Next, I sum up my view of the "literature of globalization." As paradoxical as it may seem, it is globalization with its tendencies of homogenization that has to be thanked for the fact that cultural representations "insist on regional and local character, in order to thereby enable and obtain identity and identification" (Steinmetz 193). In the final analysis, the result is that the new literature of globalization deploys a regionally and locally rooted repertoire of history against the levelling effect of worldwide popular culture (Steinmetz 200). With example of the novels by US-American John Updike, Steinmetz demonstrates how contemporary texts serve popular and globally circulating images, ideals, and stereotypes in order to reveal them by drawing on regional circumstances. In such texts we can discover a particular "genre of the works explicitly responding to certain aspects of globalization" (Steinmetz 200), whose aesthetics consists of just this, namely, to allow the unifying and the homogenizing element of the global appear contrastive in the use of the different, the local, the particular. However, Helmut Meter suggests that literary discourse is obliged to a "cosmopolitan mentality" for a "diffuse, but also non-specific readership" designed from the outset as easily translatable (272). Meter classifies this type of literature as "cosmopolitan literature" because "the fictional repertoire of such texts—at least in intention—aims at transnational issues and is obligated to an open culture paradigm" (272), where heterogeneity and alterity would not be celebrated but levelled (273). The problem according to Meter is that if literary globalization is achieved by the "establishment of a restricted literary linguistic codes" and "the choice of subject, its thematic concretion, the governing mentality" are highly schematic and "are liberated from the resistance of monolingual conventions," then "a fictional world of local indeterminacy arises" with focus on cinematic storytelling in the style of Hollywood productions (273). Meter rightly doubts that this homogenizing kind of response to globalized conditions that stays on the surface can permanently captivate readers (281).

National literature, (im)migrant literature, intercultural literature, postcolonial literature, and the literatures of globalization as an inflation of literary genres raises the question of whether yet another group exists. So what is the benefit of NWL as a subsystem? How does it differ from already established systems? I submit that the first fundamental innovation of NWL as a category of literary history and its study lies in interdisciplinary methodology. Thus frameworks and methodologies found in sociology, history, cultural anthropology, and so on ought to be applied in literary studies (see, e.g., Pinxten). It is interesting that the cooperation between linguistics and literary studies is, paradoxically, far less common, although both disciplines have, especially for their dealing with hybrid texts, valuable tools of description and analysis with which linguistic hybridity could be systematized and associated with individual philologies. It is apparent that it is exactly the multilingualism of NWL texts which articulate communication strategies of alterity toward the majority literatures, strategies which sometimes accommodate monolingual recipients while at other times seem to confine them to their (linguistic) barriers. Selection, frequency, and length of interferences from the second language allow conclusions about the specific aesthetic of mixtilingual texts. The same applies to the use of transtextuality and metamultilingualism. With conventional, monolingual literary approaches the compilation and evaluation of the formal and structural aspects of hybrid texts is difficult. Thus I make the case for a higher proportion of linguistics in literary studies, especially when it comes to linguistically complex literary structures such as the ones I discuss.

A further innovative aspect of the subsystem of NWL is the postulate to extract the underlying texts out of their minority status in comparison to traditional national literatures and to make visible their specific qualities in comparison with one another. On the content plane, it is evident that it is a literature that stages transnational and transient identities, that tells the story of globalization, while staying rooted in local conditions: a literature where spatial and temporal categories have lost their categorical determination and a literature in which heterogeneity and difference are the subject rather than homogenization and acculturation. Finally, the only system with a wide enough horizon to establish a dialogue between different cultures under hierarchically symmetrical circumstances turns out to be comparative cultural studies. I submit that this theoretical and methodological framework provides the scholar of literature in general and those working on NWL with a non-Eurocentric, holistic approach beyond "rigidly defined disciplinary boundaries" offering an "alternative, as well as a parallel field of study. This inclusion extends to all Other, all marginal, minority, and peripheral entities, and encompasses both form and substance" (Tötösy de Zepetnek, "From Comparative" 259). Consequently, I locate the study of NWL in an application of the tenets of comparative cultural studies because of the framework's postulate that the study of literature "cannot continue to be seen as isolated monads but need to become part of more complex research networks which work both in scholarship, education, as well as in cultural practices in general" (Tötösy de Zepetnek and López-Varela 39).

Works Cited

Abel, Günter. *Zeichen der Wirklichkeit*. Frankfurt: Suhrkamp, 2004.

Ackermann, Irmgard. Afterword. *In zwei Sprachen leben. Berichte, Erzählungen, Gedichte von Ausländern. Patchwork: Dimensionen multikultureller Gesellschaften. Geschichte, Problematik und Chancen*. Ed. Andreas Ackermann and Klaus E. Müller. München: dtv, 1992. 241–51.

Ackermann, Andreas, and Klaus E. Müller, eds. *Patchwork: Dimensionen mulit-kultureller Gesellschaften. Geschichte, Problematik und Chancen*. Bielefeld: Transcript, 2002.

Ackermann, Irmgard, ed. *In zwei Sprachen leben. Berichte, Erzählungen, Gedichte von Ausländern*. München: dtv, 1992.

Adnan, Etel. *In the Heart of the Heart of Another Country*. San Francisco: City Lights, 2005.

Albahari, David. *Bait*. Trans. Peter Agnone. Evanston: Northwestern UP, 2001.

Albert, Christiane, ed. *Francophonie et identités culturelles*. Paris: Karthala, 1999.

Ali, Monica. *Brick Lane*. London: Black Swan, 2004.

Amirsedghi, Nasrin, and Thomas Bleicher, eds. *Literatur der Migration*. Mainz: Kinzelbach, 1997.

Amman, Wilhelm, Georg Mein, and Rolf Parr, eds. *Globalisierung und Gegenwartsliteratur. Konstellationen, Konzepte, Perspektiven*. Heidelberg: Synchron, 2010.

Amodeo, Immacolata. "Die Heimat heißt Babylon." *Zur Literatur ausländischer Autoren in der Bundesrepublik Deutschland*. Opladen: Westdeutscher, 1996.

Anderson, Benedict. *Imagined Communities: Reflections on the Origin and Spread of Nationalism*. London: Verso, 1983.

Andres-Suárez, Irene, ed. *Migración y literatura en el mundo hispánico*. Madrid: Verbum, 2004.

Anzaldúa, Gloria. *Borderlands/La frontera*. San Francisco: Aunt Lute, 1987.

Appadurai, Arjun. *Modernity at Large: Cultural Dimensions of Globalization*. Minneapolis: U of Minnesota P, 1996.

Apter, Emily. *Against World Literature: On the Politics of Untranslatability*. London: Verso, 2013.

Apter, Emily. *The Translation Zone: A New Comparative Literature*. Princeton: Princeton UP, 2006.

Arac, Jonathan. "Anglo-Globalism?" *New Left Review* 16 (2002): 35–45.

Armbruster, Claudius. "Iberische Wurzeln und Rhizome-Postkoloniale und periphere Identitätsbegründungen auf der Iberischen Halbinsel." *Minorisierte Literaturen und Identitätskonzepte in Spanien und Portugal: Sprache-Narrative Entwürfe-Texte.* Ed. Javier Gómez-Montero. Darmstadt: Wissenschaftliche Buchgesellschaft, 2001. 223–46.

Arteaga, Alfred. *Chicano Poetics: HeteroTextes and Hybridities.* Cambridge: Cambridge UP, 1997. <http://dx.doi.org/10.1017/CBO9780511549311>.

Ashcroft, Bill, Gareth Griffiths, and Helen Tiffin, eds. *The Post-Colonial Studies Reader.* London: Routledge, 1995.

Auer, Peter, ed. *Code-switching in Conversation: Language, Interaction and Identity.* London: Routledge, 1998.

Aytaç, Gürsel. "Sprache als Spiegel der Kultur. Zu Emine Sevgi Özdamars Roman *Das Leben ist eine Karawanserei.*" *Interkulturelle Konfigurationen. Zur deutschsprachigen Erzählliteratur von Autoren nichtdeutscher Herkunft.* Ed. Mary Howard. München: iudicium, 1997. 171–78.

Bachmann-Medick, Doris. *Cultural Turns: Neue Orientierungen in den Kulturwissenschaften.* Reinbeck bei Hamburg: Rowohlt, 2006.

Bachmann-Medick, Doris. "Multikultur oder kulturelle Differenzen? Neue Konzepte von Weltliteratur und Übersetzung in postkolonialer Perspektive." *Kultur als Text. Die anthropologische Wende in der Literaturwissenschaft.* Ed. Doris Bachmann-Medick and James Clifford. Frankfurt: Fischer, 1996. 262–95.

Bakhtin, M. M. *The Dialogic Imagination.* Trans. Caryl Emerson and Michael Holquist. Austin: U of Texas P, 1988.

Barabás, Albert-László. *Linked: How Everything is Connected to Everything Else and What it Means for Business, Science, and Everyday Life.* New York: Penguin, 2003.

Baum, Richard. "Lusophonie. Eine neue Dimension der portugiesischen Sprach- und Kulturgemeinschaft." *Lusophonie in Geschichte und Gegenwart.* Ed. Richard Baum and António Dinis. Bonn: Romanistischer, 2003. 93–122.

Beck, Ulrich. *The Cosmopolitan Vision.* Trans. Ciaran Cronin. Cambridge: Polity, 2006.

Beck, Ulrich. *What is Globalization?* Trans. Patrick Camiller. Cambridge: Polity, 2000.

Beck-Gernsheim, Elisabeth. *Wir und die Anderen. Vom Blick der Deutschen auf Migranten und Minderheiten.* Frankfurt: Suhrkamp, 2004.

Benítez-Rojo, Antonio. *The Repeating Island. The Caribbean and the Postmodern Perspective.* Durham: Duke UP, 1992.

Berg, Eberhard, and Martin Fuchs. *Kultur, soziale Praxis, Text. Die Krise der ethnographischen Repräsentation.* Frankfurt: Suhrkamp, 1993.

Bermann, Sandra. "'Mapping the World' and Translation." *Mapping the World, Culture, and Border-Crossing.* Ed. Steven Tötösy de Zepetnek and I–Chun Wang. Kaohsiung: National Sun Yat-sen UP, 2011. 4–16.

Bernabé, Jean, Patrick Chamoiseau, and Raphaël Confiant. *Eloge de la créolité.* Paris: Gallimard, 1989.

Bernheimer, Charles, ed. *Comparative Literature in the Age of Multiculturalism.* Baltimore: The Johns Hopkins UP, 1995.

Bessière, Jean. "Des équivoques de la théorie littéraire. Pour une approche fonctionnaliste de la littérature et quelques justifications de la littérature comparée." *Perspectives comparatistes*. Ed. Jean Bessière, and Daniel-Henri Pageaux. Paris: Honoré Champion, 1999. 289–312.

Bessière, Jean. "Littératures francophones et postcolonialisme. Fictions de l'interdépendance et du réel. En passant par Salman Rushdie, Kateb Yacine, Mohamed Dib, Hampâté Bâ, Ahmadou Kourouma, Raphaël Confiant, Ernest Pépin et d'autres." *Littératures Postcoloniales et Francophonie*. Ed. Jean Bessière and Jean-Marc Moura. Paris: Honoré Champion, 2001. 169–96.

Bessière, Jean, and Jean-Marc Moura, eds. *Littératures Postcoloniales et Francophonie*. Paris: Honoré Champion, 2001.

Bessière, Jean, and Daniel-Henri Pageaux, eds. *Perspectives comparatistes*. Paris: Honoré Champion, 1999.

Bessière, Jean, and Gilles Philippe, eds. *Problématique des genres, problème du roman*. Paris: Honoré Champion, 1999.

Beutler, Bernhard, and Anke Bosse, eds. *Spuren, Signaturen, Spiegelungen. Zur Goethe-Rezeption in Europa*. Köln: Böhlau, 2000.

Bhabha, Homi K. *The Location of Culture*. London: Routledge, 1994.

Bhatia, Tej K., and William C. Ritchie, eds. *The Handbook of Bilingualism*. Malden: Blackwell, 2004.

Bickes, Christine, and Hans Bickes. "Aspekte der Mehrsprachigkeit." *Sprache und Multikulturalität*. Ed. Eleni Butulussi, Evangelia Karagiannidou, and Katerina Zachu. Thessaloniki: University Studio, 2005. 73–80.

Birus, Hendrik. "The Goethean Concept of World Literature and Comparative Literature." *Comparative Literature and Comparative Cultural Studies*. Ed. Steven Tötösy de Zepetnek. West Lafayette: Purdue UP, 2003. 11–22.

Blessin, Stefan. "Goethes *West-östlicher Divan* und die Entstehung der Weltliteratur." *Westöstlicher und nordsüdlicher Divan. Goethe in interkultureller Perspektive*. Ed. Ortrud Gutjahr. Paderborn: Schöningh, 2000. 59–72.

Blioumi, Aglaia. *Interkulturalität als Dynamik. Ein Beitrag zur deutsch-griechischen Migrationsliteratur seit den siebziger Jahren*. Tübingen: Stauffenburg, 2001.

Boback, Peter. "'Übersetzung' und 'Nicht-Übersetzung' als Modus kultureller Selbstreferenz." *Zeitschrift für Literaturwissenschaft und Linguistik* 97 (1995): 73–85.

Boerner, Peter. "Die Deutschen und die anderen. Goethes Bild seiner Landsleute in vergleichender Sicht." *Deutsche Literatur in der Weltliteratur. Kulturnation statt politischer Nation?* Ed. Franz Norbert Mennemeier and Conrad Wiedemann. Tübingen: Niemeyer, 1986. 179–87.

Bogdal, Klaus-Michael. "Wo geht's denn hier nach Kanakstan? Deutsch-türkische Schriftsteller auf der Suche nach Identität." *Literatur und Vielsprachigkeit*. Ed. Monika Schmitz-Emans. Heidelberg: Synchron, 2004. 237–48.

Böhler, Michael. "Deutsche Literatur im kulturellen Spannungsfeld von Eigenem und Fremdem in der Schweiz." *"Das Fremde und das Eigene." Prolegomena zu einer interkulturellen Germanistik*. Ed. Alois Wierlacher. München: iudicium, 1985. 234–61.

Bohnenkamp, Anne. "Rezeption der Rezeption. Goethes Entwurf einer 'Weltliteratur' im Kontext seiner Zeitschrift *Über Kunst und Altertum*." *Spuren, Signaturen,*

Spiegelungen. Zur Goethe-Rezeption in Europa. Ed. Bernhard Beutler and Anke Bosse. Köln: Böhlau, 2000. 187–207.

Bonn, Charles. "Postcolonialisme et reconnaissance littéraire des textes francophones émergents. L'Exemple de la littérature maghrébine et de la littérature issue de l'immigration." *Littératures Postcoloniales et Francophonie.* Ed. Jean Bessière and Jean-Marc Moura. Paris: Honoré Champion, 2001. 27–42.

Boubia, Fawzi. "Goethes Theorie der Alterität und die Idee der Weltliteratur. Ein Beitrag zur neueren Kulturdebatte." *Gegenwart als kulturelles Erbe. Ein Beitrag der Germanistik zur Kulturwissenschaft deutschsprachiger Länder.* Ed. Bernd Thum. München: iudicium, 1985. 269–301.

Boumans, Louis. "Codeswitching and the Organisation of the Mental Lexicon." *Bilingualism and Migration.* Ed. Guus Extra and Ludo Verhoeven. Berlin: de Gruyter, 1999. 281–301. <http://dx.doi.org/10.1515/9783110807820.281>.

Bourdieu, P. *The Rules of the Art: Genesis and Structure of the Literary Field.* 1992. Trans. Susan Emanuel. Stanford: Stanford UP, 1996.

Braunmüller, Kurt. "Zur Ausdrucks-, Appell- und Darstellungsfunktion von Dialekten in der Literatur. Semiotische Untersuchungen anhand skandinavischer Prosatexte." *Dialekte und Fremdsprachen in der Literatur.* Ed. Paul Goetsch. Tübingen: Gunter Narr, 1987. 11–26.

Breidenbach, Joana, and Ina Zukrigl. *Tanz der Kulturen. Kulturelle Identität in einer globalisierten Welt.* Reinbek bei Hamburg: Rowohlt, 2000.

Broich, Ulrich, and Manfred Pfister, eds. *Intertextualität. Formen, Funktionen, anglistische Fallstudien.* Tübingen: Niemeyer, 1985. <http://dx.doi.org/10.1515/9783111712420>.

Bronfen, Elisabeth, and Benjamin Marius. "Hybride Kulturen. Einleitung zur anglo-amerikanischen Multikulturalismusdebatte." *Hybride Kulturen. Beiträge zur anglo-amerikanischen Multikulturalismus-Debatte.* Ed. Elisabeth Bronfen, Benjamin Marius, and Therese Steffen. Tübingen: Stauffenburg, 1997. 1–30.

Brookshaw, David. "Cape Verde." *The Post-Colonial Literature of Lusophone Africa.* Ed. Patrick Chabal. Evanston: Northwestern UP, 1996. 179–233.

Brunkhorst, Martin. "Fugard, Soyinka und die attische Tragödie. Über die Bedingungen der Möglichkeit eines Konzeptes von Weltliteratur." *Weltliteratur heute. Konzepte und Perspektiven.* Ed. Manfred Schmeling. Würzburg: Königshausen & Neumann, 1995. 29–48.

Burke, Peter. *Kultureller Austausch.* Frankfurt: Suhrkamp, 2000.

Callahan, Laura. *Spanish/English Codeswitching in a Written Corpus.* Amsterdam: John Benjamins, 2004.

Candelaria, Cordelia. *Chicano Poetry: A Critical Introduction.* Westport: Greenwood P, 1986.

Canut, Cécile, and Dominique Caubet, eds. *Comment les langues se mélangent. Codeswitching en Francophonie.* Paris: L'Harmattan, 2001.

Carpentier, Alejo. *Obras completas de Alejo Carpentier. Ensayos.* Mexico City: Siglo Veintiuno, 1990.

Carroll, Michael Thomas, ed. *No Small World: Visions and Revisisons of World Literature.* Urbana: National Council of Teachers of English, 1996.

Casanove, Pascale. *The World Republic of Letters. 1999.* Trans. M. B. DeBevoise. Cambridge: Harvard UP, 2004.

Castells, Manuel. *The Information Age: Economy, Society, and Culture*. 3 vols. Oxford: Blackwell, 2000.

Cerquiglini, Bernard, Jean-Claude Corbeil, Jean-Marie Klinkenberg, et al., eds. *Le français dans tous ses états*. Paris: Flammarion, 2000.

Chabal, Patrick, ed. *The Post-Colonial Literature of Lusophone Africa*. Evanston: Northwestern UP, 1996.

Chamoiseau, Patrick. *Ecrire en pays dominé*. Paris: Gallimard, 1997.

Cheesman, Tom. *Novels of German Turkish Settlement: Cosmopolite Fictions*. Rochester: Camden House, 2007.

Chiellino, Carmine. "Interkulturalität und Literaturwissenschaft." *Interkulturelle Literatur in Deutschland. Ein Handbuch*. Ed. Carmine Chiellino. Stuttgart: Metzler, 2000. 387–98.

Chiellino, Carmine, ed. *Interkulturelle Literatur in Deutschland. Ein Handbuch*. Stuttgart: Metzler, 2000.

Chiellino, Gino [Chiellino, Carmine]. "Über die Notwendigkeit, die Sprache, nicht die Inhalte zu lesen." *Muttersprache* 99 (1989): 299–302.

Chow, Rey. *The Age of the World Target: Self-referentiality in War, Theory, and Comparative Work*. Durham: Duke UP, 2006.

Cisneros, Sandra. *The House on Mango Street*. New York: Vintage, 1984.

Condé, Maryse. *Ségou. La Terre en miettes*. Paris: Robert Laffont, 2005.

Conrad, Sebastian, Andreas Eckert, and Ulrike Freitag, eds. *Globalgeschichte. Theorien, Ansätze, Themen*. Frankfurt: Campus, 2007.

Cook, Victoria. "Exploring Transnational Identities in Ondaatje's *Anil's Ghost*." *Comparative Cultural Studies and Michael Ondaatje's Writing*. Ed. Steven Tötösy de Zepetnek. West Lafayette: Purdue UP, 2005. 6–15.

Cruz, Isagani R. "Writing in Two Languages." *Creative Writing in the Asia-Pacific Region*. Ed, Jane Camens and Dominique Wilson. Special Issue TEXT 15.1 (2011): <http://www.textjournal.com.au/speciss/issue10/Cruz.pdf>.

Currle, Edda. *Migration in Europa. Daten und Hintergründe*. Stuttgart: Lucius & Lucius, 2004.

D'Ans, André-Marcel. "Créoles sans langue créole. Les 'Criollos' d'Hispano-Amérique." *Contacts de langues, contacts de cultures, créolisation*. Ed. Marie-Christine Hazaël-Massieux and Didier de Robillard. Paris: L'Harmattan, 1997. 29–50.

Dahrendorf, Ralf. "Anmerkungen zur Globalisierung." *Globalisierung im Alltag*. Ed. Peter Kemper and Ulrich Sonnenschein. Frankfurt: Suhrkamp, 2002. 13–25.

Damrosch, David. *How to Read World Literature*. Chichester: Wiley-Blackwell, 2009.

Damrosch, David. *What is World Literature?* Princeton: Princeton UP, 2003.

Daniel, Ute. *Kompendium Kulturgeschichte. Theorien, Praxis, Schlüsselwörter*. Frankfurt: Suhrkamp, 2001.

De Berg, Henk. "Systemtheoretische Interpretation? Kritische Überlegungen zu Gerhard Plumpes Schlegel-Deutung." *Interpretation 2000. Positionen und Kontroversen*. Ed. Henk De Berg and Matthias Prangel. Heidelberg: C. Winter, 1999. 137–53.

De Berg, Henk, and Matthias Prangel, eds. *Interpretation 2000. Positionen und Kontroversen*. Heidelberg: C. Winter, 1999.

Deleuze, Gilles, and Félix Guattari. *Kafka. Toward a Minor Literature.* Trans. Dana Polan. Minneapolis: U of Minnesota P, 1986.

Deppermann, Arnulf. "Was sprichst du?" *Coolhunters. Jugendkulturen zwischen Medien und Markt.* Ed. Klaus Neumann-Braun and Birgit Richard. Frankfurt: Suhrkamp, 2005. 67–82.

"Die Schale wird zum Kern." *Der Spiegel* 48 (29 November 1993): 232–38.

Dirim, Inci, and Peter Auer. *Türkisch sprechen nicht nur Türken. Über die Unschärfebeziehung zwischen Sprache und Ethnie in Deutschland.* Berlin: de Gruyter, 2004. <http://dx.doi.org/10.1515/9783110919790>.

Djebar, Assia. *Fantasia: An Algerian Cavalcade.* Trans. Dorothy S. Blair. London: Heinemann, 1993.

Djebar, Assia. *L'Amour, la fantasia.* Paris: Albin Michel, 2002.

Djebar, Assia. *Les Nuits de Strasbourg.* Paris: Actes Sud, 2003.

Dollinger, Roland. *'Stolpersteine': Zafer Şenocaks Romane der neunziger Jahre."* *Gegenwartsliteratur. Ein germanistisches Jahrbuch.* Ed. Paul Michael Lützeler and Stephan K. Schindler. Vol. 2. Frankfurt: Suhrkamp, 2003. 1–28.

Drechsel, Paul, Bettina Schmidt, and Bernhard Gölz. *Kultur im Zeitalter der Globalisierung. Von Identität zu Differenzen.* Frankfurt: Interkulturelle Kommunikation, 2000.

Dröscher, Barbara, and Carlos Rincón, eds. *La Malinche. Übersetzung, Interkulturalität und Geschlecht.* Berlin: Walter Frey, 2001.

Durzak, Manfred. "Deutschsprachige interkulturelle Literatur-die Beschreibung eines Phantoms?" *Interkulturelle Begegnungen.* Ed. Manfred Durzak and Nilüfer Kuruyazıcı. Würzburg: Königshausen & Neumann, 2004. 23–36.

Durzak, Manfred, and Nilüfer Kuruyazıcı, eds. *Interkulturelle Begegnungen.* Würzburg: Königshausen & Neumann, 2004.

Eckermann, Johann Peter. *Gespräche mit Goethe in den letzten Jahren seines Lebens.* Wiesbaden: Brockhaus, 1975.

Eco, Umberto. *Im Wald der Fiktionen. Sechs Streifzüge durch die Literatur.* München: dtv, 1999.

Eco, Umberto. *The Role of the Reader: Explorations in the Semiotics of Texts.* Bloomington: Indiana UP, 1995.

Ernst, Wolfgang. *Das Rumoren der Archive. Ordnung aus Unordnung.* Berlin: Merve, 2002.

Ertler, Klaus-Dieter. "Kulturhermeneutische Strategien der Migrantenliteratur. Die Funktion der Lusophonie in *Negão et Doralice* von Sergio Kokis." *Lusophonie in Geschichte und Gegenwart.* Ed. Richard Baum and António Dinis. Bonn: Romanistischer, 2003. 397–410.

Ette, Ottmar. *Literatur in Bewegung. Raum und Dynamik grenzüberschreitenden Schreibens in Europa und Amerika.* Weilerswist: Velbrück Wissenschaft, 2001.

Even-Zohar, Itamar. "Factors and Dependencies of Culture: A Revised Outline for Polysystem Culture Research." *Canadian Review of Comparative Literature / Revue Canadienne de Littérature Comparée* 24.1 (1997): 15–34.

Extra, Guus, and Ludo Verhoeven. "Immigrant Minority Groups and Immigrant Minority Languages in Europe." *Bilingualism and Migration.* Ed. Guus Extra and Ludo Verhoeven. Berlin: de Gruyter, 1999. 3–28. <http://dx.doi.org/10.1515/9783110807820.3>.

Extra, Guus, and Ludo Verhoeven. "Processes of Language Change in a Migrant Context: The Case of the Netherlands." *Bilingualism and Migration*. Ed. Guus Extra and Ludo Verhoeven. Berlin: de Gruyter, 1999. 29–59. <http://dx.doi.org/10.1515/9783110807820.29>.

Fachinger, Petra. "Zur Vergleichbarkeit der deutschen mit der amerikanischen und englischsprachig-kanadischen Migrantenliteratur." *Literatur der Migration*. Ed. Nasrin Amirsedghi and Thomas Bleicher. Mainz: Donata Kinzelbach, 1997. 49–59.

Fanselow, Gisbert, and Sascha W. Felix. *Sprachtheorie. Eine Einführung in die generative Grammatik*. Tübingen: Francke, 1993.

Fendler, Ute. *Interkulturalität in der frankophonen Literatur der Karibik. Der europäisch-afrikanisch-amerikanische Intertext im Romanwerk von Maryse Condé*. Frankfurt: Interkulturelle Kommunikation, 1994.

Firchow, Peter. "Literary Multilingualism and Modernity: The Anglo-American Perspective." *Multilinguale Literatur im 20. Jahrhundert*. Ed. Manfred Schmeling and Monika Schmitz-Emans. Würzburg: Königshausen & Neumann, 2002. 59–68.

Fischer, Sabine, and Moray McGowan, eds. *Denn du tanzt auf einem Seil. Positionen deutschsprachiger MigrantInnenliteratur*. Tübingen: Stauffenburg, 1997.

Fohrmann, Jürgen. "Grenzpolitik. Über den Ort des Nationalen in der Literatur, den Ort der Literatur im Nationalen." *Nationale Literaturen heute-ein Fantom? Die Imagination und Tradition des Schweizerischen als Problem*. Ed. Corina Caduff and Reto Sorg. Zürich: Neue Zürcher Zeitung, 2004. 23–34.

Forster, Leonard. "In dulci jubilo." *The Poet's Tongues: Multilingualism in Literature*. By Leonard Forster. Cambridge: Cambridge UP, 1970. 10.

Fox, Jonathan, and Gaspar Rivera-Salgado. "Building Migrant Civil Society: Indigenous Mexicans in the US." *Iberoamericana* 17 (2005): 101–16.

Fuchs, Gotthard, Bernhard Moltmann, and Walter Prigge, eds. *Mythos Metropole*. Frankfurt: Suhrkamp, 1995.

Fuentes, Carlos. *The Crystal Frontier*. Trans. Alfred McAdam. New York: Farrar, Straus and Giroux, 1997.

Fuentes, Carlos. *This I Believe: An A-Z of a Writer's Life*. Trans. Kristine Cordero. London: Bloomsbury, 2005.

Fuguet, Alberto. *Die Filme meines Lebens*. Frankfurt: Zebu, 2005.

Fürbeth, Frank, Pierre Krügel, Ernst E. Metzner, et al., eds. *Zur Geschichte und Problematik der Nationalphilologien in Europa*. Tübingen: Niemeyer, 1999.

Gálik, Marián. "Interliterariness as a Concept in Comparative Literature." *Comparative Literature and Comparative Cultural Studies*. Ed. Steven Tötösy de Zepetnek. West Lafayette: Purdue UP, 2003. 34–44.

Gallagher, Mary, ed. *World Writing: Poetics, Ethics, Globalization*. Toronto: U of Toronto P, 2008.

García Benito, Nieves. "Por la vía de Tarifa o *La letra con sangre entra*." *Migración y literatura en el mundo hispánico*. Ed. Irene Andres-Suárez. Madrid: Verbum, 2004. 154–92.

García Canclini, Néstor. *Hybrid Cultures: Strategies for Entering and Leaving Modernity*. 1990. Trans. Christopher L. Chiappari and Silvia L. Lopez. Minneapolis: U of Minnesota P, 2005.

Gauvin, Lise. *L'Ecrivain francophone à la croisée des langues*. Paris: Karthala, 1997.

Genette, Gérard. *Palimpsest: Literature in the Second Degree*. Trans. Channa Newman and Claude Doubinsky. Lincoln: U of Nebraska P, 1997.

Georgiev, Nikola. "Die Ehe der Literatur mit der Welt. Weltliteratur zwischen Utopie und Heterotopie." *Weltliteratur heute. Konzepte und Perspektiven*. Ed. Manfred Schmeling. Würzburg: Königshausen & Neumann, 1995. 75–84.

Gewecke, Frauke. "De identidades, territorios y fronteras que se cruzan. La(s) literatura(s) des los Hispanics o Latinos en Estados Unidos (1)." *Iberoamericana* 3 (2001): 205–28.

Gewecke, Frauke. "De identidades, territorios y fronteras que se cruzan La(s) literatura(s) des los Hispanics o Latinos en Estados Unidos (2)." *Iberoamericana* 4 (2001): 179–202.

Geyer, Carl-Friedrich. *Mythos. Formen-Beispiele-Deutungen*. München: Beck, 1996.

Giddens, Anthony. *Runaway World: How Globalisation is Reshaping Our Lives*. London: Profile, 1999.

Giesecke, Michael. *Sinnenwandel, Sprachwandel, Kulturwandel. Studien zur Vorgeschichte der Informationsgesellschaft*. Frankfurt: Suhrkamp, 1998.

Goethe, Johann Wolfgang von. "Epochen geselliger Bildung." *Goethes Werke*. Vol. 1. By Johann Wolfgang von Goethe. München: dtv, 1987. 361–62.

Goethe, Johann Wolfgang von. *Werke*. Ed. Erich Trunz. München: Beck, 1973.

Goethe, Johann Wolfgang von, ed. *Über Kunst und Alterthum in den Rhein- und Maingegenden*. Stuttgart: Cotta'sche Verlagsbuchhandlung, 1816–1832.

Goetsch, Paul, ed. *Dialekte und Fremdsprachen in der Literatur*. Tübingen: Gunter Narr, 1987.

Goldberg, David Theo, and Ato Quayson, eds. *Relocating Postcolonialism*. Oxford: Blackwell, 2002.

Gómez-Montero, Javier. "Ambivalenzen des Eigenen. Identitätsentwürfe in der baskischen, galicischen und katalanischen Gegenwartsliteratur (Einleitende Bemerkungen zu einer kleinen Textauswahl)." *Minorisierte Literaturen und Identitätskonzepte in Spanien und Portugal. Sprache-Narrative Entwürfe-Texte*. Ed. Javier Gómez-Montero. Darmstadt: Wissenschaftliche Buchgesellschaft, 2001. 325–41.

Gómez-Montero, Javier, ed. *Minorisierte Literaturen und Identitätskonzepte in Spanien und Portugal. Sprache-Narrative Entwürfe-Texte*. Darmstadt: Wissenschaftliche Buchgesellschaft, 2001.

González-Millán, Xoán. "Soziale Diskurse und Nationalliteratur: ein paradigmatisches Modell (unter Berücksichtigung der literarischen Diskurse in Galicien)." *Minorisierte Literaturen und Identitätskonzepte in Spanien und Portugal: Sprache-Narrative Entwürfe-Texte*. Ed. Javier Gómez-Montero. Darmstadt: Wissenschaftliche Buchgesellschaft, 2001. 3–42.

Görling, Reinhold. *Heterotopia. Lektüren einer interkulturellen Literaturwissenschaft*. München: Fink, 1997.

Goßens, Peter. *Weltliteratur. Modelle transnationaler Literaturwahrnehmung im 19. Jahrhundert*. Stuttgart: Metzler, 2011.

Graf, Marga. "Lusotropicalismo. Ein portugiesischer Sonderweg? Kolonialpolitik Portugals in Asien, Afrika und Amerika. Politik, Wirtschaft, Kultur." *Lusophonie in Geschichte und Gegenwart*. Ed. Richard Baum and António Dinis. Bonn: Romanistischer, 2003. 59–80.

Gramling, David Jennings, Anton Kaes, Andreas Langenohl, et al., eds. *Transit Deutschland: Debatten zu Nation und Migration*. Konstanz: Konstanz UP, 2011.

Grimson, Alejandro. "Fronteras e identificaciones nacionales. Diálogos desde el Cono Sur." *Iberoamericana* 17 (2005): 91–100.

Grünbein, Durs. *Warum schriftlos leben. Aufsätze*. Frankfurt: Suhrkamp, 2003.

Grutman, Rainier. "Refraction and Recognition: Literary Multilingualism in Translation." *Target: International Journal of Translation Studies* 18.1 (2006): 17–47.

Guérot, Ulrike. "4,7 Prozent Europa." *Kulturaustausch: Zeitschrift für internationale Perspektiven* 11 (2006): 72–4.

Guillory, John. "Canon, Syllabus, List: A Note on the Pedagogic Imagery." *Best American Essays*. Ed. Susan Sontag and Robert Atwan. New York: Ticknor & Fields, 1992. 158–85.

Gupta, Suman. *Globalization and Literature*. Cambridge: Polity, 2009.

Gyssels, Kathleen. "D'une littérature insulaire vers une 'world literature' (Chamoiseau/ Schwarz-Bart)." *Anales del Caribe* 19–20 (1999–2000): 239–60.

Hall, Stuart. "When was 'The Postcolonial'? Thinking at the Limit." *The Postcolonial Question: Common Skies, Divided Horizons*. Ed. Ian Chambers and Lidia Curti. London: Routledge, 1996. 242–60.

Haller, Dieter. "Das Lob der Mischung. Nationalismus und Ethnizität in Gibraltar." *Patchwork: Dimensionen mulitkultureller Gesellschaften. Geschichte, Problematik und Chancen*. Ed. Andreas Ackermann and Klaus E. Müller. Bielefeld: Transcript, 2002. 211–56.

Hamm, Horst. *Fremdgegangen-freigeschrieben. Eine Einführung in die deutschsprachige Gastarbeiterliteratur*. Würzburg: Königshausen & Neumann, 1988.

Häußermann, Hartmut, and Walter Siebel, eds. *New York: Strukturen einer Metropole*. Frankfurt: Suhrkamp, 1993.

Häußermann, Hartmut, Martin Kronauer, and Walter Siebel, eds. *An den Rändern der Städte. Armut und Ausgrenzung*. Frankfurt: Suhrkamp, 2004.

Hayot, Eric. *On Literary Worlds*. Oxford: Oxford UP, 2012.

Haywood, Louise M., and Louise O. Vasvári, eds. *A Companion to the* Libro de Buen Amor. Woodbridge: Tamesis, 2004.

Hazaël-Massieux, Marie-Christine, and Didier de Robillard, eds. *Contacts de langues, contacts de cultures, créolisation*. Paris: L'Harmattan, 1997.

Heitmeyer, Wilhelm, Rainer Dollase, and Otto Backes, eds. *Die Krise der Städte. Analysen zu den Folgen desintegrativer Stadtentwicklung für das ethnisch-kulturelle Zusammenleben*. Frankfurt: Suhrkamp, 1998.

Helbig, Jörg. *Intertextualität und Markierung. Untersuchungen zur Systematik und Funktion der Signalisierung von Intertextualität*. Heidelberg: Winter, 1996.

Herlinghaus, Hermann. Alejo Carpentier. *Persönliche Geschichte eines literarischen Moderneprojekts*. München: text + kritik, 1991.

Herlinghaus, Hermann, and Utz Riese, eds. *Heterotopien der Identität. Literatur in interamerikanischen Kontaktzonen.* Heidelberg: C. Winter, 1999.

Herrera, Juan Felipe. *Border-Crosser with a Lamborghini Dream.* Tucson: U of Arizona P, 1999.

Herrera, Juan Felipe. *Giraffe on Fire.* Tucson: U of Arizona P, 2001.

Herrera, Juan Felipe. *Lotería Cards and Fortune Poems: A Book of Lives.* San Francisco: City Light, 1999.

Herrera, Juan Felipe. *Love after the Riots.* Willimantic: Curbstone, 1996.

Herrera, Juan Felipe. *Mayan Drifter: Chicano Poet in the Lowlands of America.* Philadelphia: Temple UP, 1996.

Hmoudane, Mohamed. *French Dream.* Paris: La Différence, 2005.

Hoesel-Uhlig, Stefan. "Changing Fields: The directions of Goethe's *Weltliteratur*." *Debating World Literature.* Ed. Christopher Prendergast. London: Verso, 2004. 26–53.

Hohnsträter, Dirk. "Homi K. Bhabhas Semiotik der Zwischenräume. Eine überzeugende Konzeptualisierung interkultureller Konflikte?" *Arcadia: Internationale Zeitschrift für Literaturwissenschaft / International Journal of Literary Studies* 31.1-2 (1996): 62–68. <http://dx.doi.org/10.1515/arca.1996.31.1-2.62>.

Hooft Comajuncosas, Andreu van. "El ser o no ser de las literaturas periféricas del estado español. El acercamiento de los sistemas literarios vasco, gallego, catalán y castellano desde sus traducciones y su recepción (1990-1998)." *Minorisierte Literaturen und Identitätskonzepte in Spanien und Portugal. Sprache-Narrative Entwürfe-Texte.* Ed. Javier Gómez-Montero. Darmstadt: Wissenschaftliche Buchgesellschaft, 2001. 41–72.

Howard, Mary, ed. *Interkulturelle Konfigurationen. Zur deutschsprachigen Erzählliteratur von Autoren nichtdeutscher Herkunft.* München: Iudicium, 1997.

Ibsch, Elrud. "Die Interpretation und kein Ende. Oder: warum wir auch nach der Jahrtausendwende noch interpretieren." *Interpretation 2000. Positionen und Kontroversen.* Ed. Henk De Berg and Matthias Prangel. Heidelberg: C. Winter, 1999. 15–30.

Ikas, Karin. *Die zeitgenössische Chicana-Literatur. Eine interkulturelle Untersuchung.* Heidelberg: C. Winter, 1999.

Iser, Wolfgang. *The Act of Reading: A Theory of Aesthetic Response.* Baltimore: The Johns Hopkins UP, 1978.

Jackendoff, Ray. *Foundations of Language: Brain, Meaning, Grammar, Evolution.* Oxford: Oxford UP, 2002.

Juvan, Marko. *History and Poetics of Intertextuality.* Trans. Timothy Pogačar. West Lafayette: Purdue UP, 2008.

Kalogeras, Yiorgos, Eletheria Arapoglou, and Linda Manney, eds. *Transcultural Localisms: Responding to Ethnicity in a Globalized World.* Heidelberg: C. Winter, 2006.

Karakus, Mahmut. *Interkulturelle Konstellationen. Deutsch-türkische Begegnungen in deutschsprachigen Romanen der Gegenwart.* Würzburg: Königshausen & Neumann, 2006.

Keller, Gary D. "The Literary Strategems available to the Bilingual Chicano Writer." *The Identification and Analysis of Chicano Literature.* Ed. Francisco Jimenez. New York: Bilingual, 1979. 263–316.

Keller, Ursula, ed. *Perspektiven metropolitaner Kultur*. Frankfurt: Suhrkamp, 2000.

Kemper, Peter, and Ulrich Sonnenschein, eds. *Globalisierung im Alltag*. Frankfurt: Suhrkamp, 2002.

Khalil, Iman. "Orient-Okzident-Stereotype im Werk arabischer Autoren." *Interkulturelle Konfigurationen. Zur deutschsprachigen Erzählliteratur von Autoren nichtdeutscher Herkunft*. Ed. Mary Howard. München: iudicium, 1997. 77–94.

Klitgård, Ida, ed. *Literary Translation: World Literature or "Worlding" Literature?* København: Museum Tusculanum, 2006.

Kloepfer, Rolf. "Grundlagen des 'dialogischen Prinzips' in der Literatur." *Dialogizität*. Ed. Renate Lachmann. München: Fink, 1982. 85–106.

Kloepfer, Rolf. *Poetik und Linguistik. Semiotische Instrumente*. München: Fink, 1975.

Knauth, Alfons K. "Multilinguale Literatur." *Literatur und Vielsprachigkeit*. Ed. Monika Schmitz-Emans. Heidelberg: Synchron, 2004. 265–89.

Knauth, Alfons K. "Multilingualisme national et international dans le modernisme brésilien." *Multilinguale Literatur im 20. Jahrhundert*. Ed. Manfred Schmeling and Monika Schmitz-Emans. Würzburg: Königshausen & Neumann, 2002. 207–32.

Knauth, Alfons K. "Translation & Multilingual Literature as a New Field of Research in between Translation Studies and Comparative Literature." *Translation & Multilingual Literature / Traduction & Littérature Multilingue*. Ed. K. Alfons Knauth. Berlin: LIT, 2011.

Knauth, Alfons K. "Weltliteratur. Von der Mehrsprachigkeit zur Mischsprachigkeit." *Literatur und Vielsprachigkeit*. Ed. Monika Schmitz-Emans. Heidelberg: Synchron, 2004. 81–110.

Koch, Manfred. *Weimaraner Weltbewohner. Zur Genese von Goethes Begriff "Weltliteratur*. Tübingen: Niemeyer, 2002. <http://dx.doi.org/10.1515/9783110953503>.

Kom, Ambroise. *La Malédiction francophone. Défis culturels et condition postcoloniale en Afrique*. Hamburg: LIT, 2000.

Koschmal, Walter. "Ästhetischer und universeller Wert. National- und weltliterarische Funktion. Die slawischen Literaturen am Rande der Weltliteratur?" *Weltliteratur heute. Konzepte und Perspektiven*. Ed. Manfred Schmeling. Würzburg: Königshausen & Neumann, 1995. 101–22.

Koselleck, Reinhart. *Zeitschichten. Studien zur Historik*. Frankfurt: Suhrkamp, 2003.

Köstlin, Konrad. "Kulturen im Prozeß der Migration und die Kultur der Migration." *Interkulturelle Literatur in Deutschland. Ein Handbuch*. Ed. Carmine Chiellino. Stuttgart: Metzler, 2000. 365–86.

Kraidy, Marwan M. *Hybridity, or the Cultural Logic of Globalization*. Philadelphia: Temple UP, 2005.

Kristal, Efraín. "'Considering coldly . . .': A Response to Franco Moretti." *New Left Review* 15 (2002): 61–74.

Krosigk, Friedrich von, and Pierre Jadin. "Frankreich in der Karibik. Von der Revolution zur Integration." *Interamerikanische Beziehungen: Einfluß-Transfer-Interkulturalität*. Ed. Helmbrecht Breinig. Frankfurt: Vervuert, 1990. 37–50.

Krusche, Dietrich, ed. *Der gefundene Schatten. Chamisso-Reden 1985 bis 1993.* München: A1 Verlag, 1993.

Krysinski, Wladimir. "Poétiques de la bouche invisible. Polyglossie et codes discursifs de la modernité. Joyce, Haroldo do Campos, E. Pound, T.S. Eliot, H. Heissenbüttel et M. Roche." *Multilinguale Literatur im 20. Jahrhundert.* Ed. Manfred Schmeling and Monika Schmitz-Emans. Würzburg: Königshausen & Neumann, 2002. 39–50.

Krysinski, Wladimir. "Récit de valeurs. Les nouveaux actants de la 'Weltliteratur.'" *Weltliteratur heute. Konzepte und Perspektiven.* Ed. Manfred Schmeling. Würzburg: Königshausen & Neumann, 1995. 141–52.

Kuder, Manfred. "Die portugiesische Verwirklichung zwischen Europa, Brasilien, Afrika und Asien." *Lusophonie in Geschichte und Gegenwart.* Ed. Richard Baum and António Dinis. Bonn: Romanistischer, 2003. 27–38.

Kureishi, Hanif. *The Buddha of Suburbia.* London: Faber & Faber, 1999.

Kuruyazıcı, Nilüfer. "Emine Sevgi Özdamars *Das Leben ist eine Karawanserei* im Prozeß der interkulturellen Kommunikation." *Interkulturelle Konfigurationen. Zur deutschsprachigen Erzählliteratur von Autoren nichtdeutscher Herkunft.* Ed. Mary Howard. München: iudicium, 1997. 179–88.

Kushner, Eva. "Is Comparative Literature Ready for the Twenty-First Century?" *Comparative Literature Now: Theories and Practice / La Littérature comparée à l'heure actuelle. Théories et réalisations.* Ed. Steven Tötösy de Zepetnek, Milan V. Dimić, and Irene Sywenky. Paris: Honoré Champion, 1999. 129–39.

Lachmann, Renate, ed. *Dialogizität.* München: Fink, 1982.

Lachmann, Renate. *Gedächtnis und Literatur. Intertextualität in der russischen Moderne.* Frankfurt: Suhrkamp, 1990.

Lahens, Yanick. *Dans la maison du père.* Monaco: Le Serpent à Plumes, 2005.

Lahiri, Jhumpa. *Interpreter of Maladies: Stories.* London: Flamingo, 2000.

Lamping, Dieter. *Die Idee der Weltliteratur. Ein Konzept Goethes und seine Karriere.* Stuttgart: Kröner, 2010.

Lange, Victor. "Nationalliteratur und Weltliteratur." *Weltliteratur und Volksliteratur.* Ed. Albert Schaefer. München: Beck, 1972. 15–35.

Laranjeira, Pires. *Literaturas Africanas de expressão Portuguesa.* Lisboa: U Aberta, 1995.

Las Casas, Bartolomé de. *Brief Account of the Devastation of the Indies.* Trans. Nigel Griffin. New York: Penguin, 1992.

Lauer, Enrik. *Literarischer Monetarismus. Studien zur Homologie von Sinn und Geld bei Goethe, Goux, Sohn-Rethel, Simmel und Luhmann.* St. Inbert: Röhrig, 1994.

Lawall, Sarah, ed. *Reading World Literature: Theory, History, Practice.* Austin: U of Texas P, 1994.

Lazarus, Neil, ed. *The Cambridge Companion to Postcolonial Literary Studies.* Cambridge: Cambridge UP, 2004. <http://dx.doi.org/10.1017/CCOL0521826942>.

Lennon, Brian. *In Babel's Shadow: Multilingual Literatures, Monolingual States.* Minneapolis: U of Minnesota P, 2010.

Lenz, Günter H. "Cultural Hybridity and Diaspora in African American Literature and Criticism: Fictions of Postmodern Multiculturalism." *Kontaktzone Amerika.*

Literarische Verkehrsformen kultureller Übersetzung. Ed. Utz Riese. Heidelberg: C. Winter, 2000. 73–108.

Lepenies, Wolf. "Vorwärts mit der Aufklärung. Folge VII. Die Zukunft der Intellektuellen." *Der Spiegel* 9 (1993): 128–31.

Lisiak, Agata Anna. *Urban Cultures in (Post)Colonial Central Europe.* West Lafayette: Purdue UP, 2010.

López Parada, Esperanza. "Los textos nómadas y la migración de las lenguas." *Migración y literatura en el mundo hispánico.* Ed. Irene Andres-Suárez. Madrid: Verbum, 2004. 376–87.

López-Varela Azcárate, Asunción, and Steven Tötösy de Zepetnek. "Comparative Cultural Studies, éducation, nouveaux médias et l'interculturalisme." Etudes et sciences de la culture. Une résistance française? Ed. Anne Chalard-Fillaudeau. Special Issue of *Revue d'Etudes Culturelles* 5 (2010): 73–96.

Luhmann, Niklas. *Social Systems.* Trans. John Bednarz, Jr., and Dirk Baecker. Stanford: Stanford UP, 1995.

Lüsebrink, Hans-Jürgen. "Globalisation et résistances locales. Jalon d'une poétique interculturelle en Amérique Latine et dans les Caraïbes." *Literatur im Zeitalter der Globalisierung.* Ed. Manfred Schmeling, Monika Schmitz-Emans, and Kerst Walstra. Würzburg: Königshausen & Neumann, 2000. 221–38.

Lützeler, Paul Michael. "Von der Postmoderne zur Globalisierung. Zur Interrelation der Diskurse." *Räume der literarischen Postmoderne. Gender, Performativität, Globalisierung.* Ed. Paul Michael Lützeler. Tübingen: Stauffenburg, 2000. 1–21.

Lützeler, Paul Michael, ed. *Schreiben zwischen den Kulturen. Beiträge zur deutschsprachigen Gegenwartsliteratur.* München: dtv, 1996.

Lützeler, Paul Michael, and Stephan K. Schindler, eds. *Gegenwartsliteratur. Ein germanistisches Jahrbuch. A German Studies Yearbook.* Tübingen: Stauffenburg, 2003.

Mall, Ram Adhar. "Interkulturalität, Intertextualität und Globalisierung." *Literatur im Zeitalter der Globalisierung.* Ed. Manfred Schmeling, Monika Schmitz-Emans, and Kerst Walstra. Würzburg: Königshausen & Neumann, 2000. 49–66.

Mani, B. Venkat. "The Good Woman of Istanbul: Emine Sevgi Özdamar's *Die Brücke vom Goldenen Horn.*" *Gegenwartsliteratur. Ein germanistisches Jahrbuch.* (2003). Ed. Paul Michael Lützeler and Stephan K. Schindler. Tübingen: Stauffenburg 2, 2003. 29–58.

Martinet, André. *Grundzüge der Allgemeinen Sprachwissenschaft.* Stuttgart: Kohlhammer, 1971.

Marx, Karl, and Friedrich Engels. *Manifest der Kommunistischen Partei.* Stuttgart: Philipp Reclam jun., 2002.

Mattenklott, Gert. "Wie bewährt sich Goethes 'Weltliteratur." *Spuren, Signaturen, Spiegelungen. Zur Goethe-Rezeption in Europa.* Ed. Bernhard Beutler and Anke Bosse. Köln: Böhlau, 2000. 601–17.

Mayer, Hans. *Weltliteratur. Studien und Versuche.* Frankfurt: Suhrkamp, 1994.

McClennen, Sophia A. "Inter-American Studies or Imperial American Studies?" *Comparative American Studies: An International Journal* 3.4 (2005): 393–413. <http://dx.doi.org/10.1177/1477570005058954>.

McClennen, Sophia A., and Earl E. Fitz, eds. *Comparative Cultural Studies and Latin America.* West Lafayette: Purdue UP, 2004.

Meddeb, Abdelwahab. *Phantasia*. Paris: Seuil, 2003.

Melas, Natalie. *All the Difference in the World: Postcoloniality and the Ends of Comparison*. Stanford: Stanford UP, 2007.

Mennemeier, Franz Norbert, and Conrad Wiedemann, eds. *Deutsche Literatur in der Weltliteratur. Kulturnation statt politischer Nation?* Tübingen: Niemeyer, 1986.

Meter, Helmut. "Kosmopolitismus und Schematismus in der zeitgenössischen Erzählliteratur Italiens." *Literatur im Zeitalter der Globalisierung*. Ed. Manfred Schmeling, Monika Schmitz-Emans, and Kerst Walstra. Würzburg: Königshausen & Neumann, 2000. 271–84.

Meyer, Thomas. *Die Identität Europas*. Frankfurt: Suhrkamp, 2004.

Miller, Christopher L. "Lesen mit westlichen Augen. Frankophone Literatur und Anthropologie in Afrika." *Kultur als Text. Die anthropologische Wende in der Literaturwissenschaft*. Ed. Doris Bachmann-Medick. Frankfurt: Fischer, 1996. 229–61.

Miller, Joshua. *Accented America: The Cultural Politics of Multilingual Modernism*. Oxford: Oxford UP, 2011. <http://dx.doi.org/10.1093/acprof:o so/9780195336993.001.0001>.

Milroy, Lesley, and Pieter Muysken, eds. *One Speaker, Two Languages: Cross-Disciplinary Perspectives on Code-Switching*. Cambridge: Cambridge UP, 1995. <http://dx.doi.org/10.1017/CBO9780511620867>.

Milz, Sabine. "The Hybridities of Philip and Özdamar." *Perspectives on Identity, Migration, and Displacement*. Ed. Steven Tötösy de Zepetnek, I–Chun Wang, and Hsiao-Yu Sun. Kaohsiung: National Sun Yat-sen UP, 2011. 25–47.

Miyoshi, Masao. "A Borderless World? From Colonialism to Transnationalism and the Decline of the Nation-State." *Critical Inquiry* 19.4 (1993): 726–51. <http://dx.doi.org/10.1086/448695>.

Mommsen, Katharina von. *Goethe und der Islam*. Frankfurt am Main: Insel, 2001.

Mommsen, Katharina von. *"Orient und Okzident sind nicht mehr zu trennen." Goethe und die Weltkulturen*. Göttingen: Wallstein, 2012.

Montaigne, Michel de. *Essais. Livre I*. Paris: Garnier-Flammarion, 1969.

Moore-Gilbert, Bart. *Postcolonial Theory: ConTexts, Practices, Politics*. London: Verso, 1997.

Moretti, Franco. "Conjectures on World Literature." *New Left Review* 1 (2000): 55–68.

Moretti, Franco. *Graphs, Maps, Trees: Abstract Models for Literary History*. New York: Verso, 2007.

Moretti, Franco. "More Conjectures." *New Left Review* 20 (2003): 73–81.

Moura, Jean-Marc. "L'Imagologie littéraire. Tendances actuelles." *Perspectives comparatistes*. Ed. Jean Bessière and Daniel-Henri Pageaux. Paris: Honoré Champion, 1999. 181–92.

Moura, Jean-Marc. "Sur quelques apports et apories." *Littératures Postcoloniales et Francophonie*. Ed. Jean Bessière and Jean-Marc Moura. Paris: Honoré Champion, 2001. 149–67.

Mouralis, Bernard. "Des Comptoirs aux empires, des empires aux nations. Rapport au territoire et production littéraire africaine." *Littératures Postcoloniales et Francophonie*. Ed. Jean Bessière and Jean-Marc Moura. Paris: Honoré Champion, 2001. 11–26.

Mukherjee, Bharati. *The Middleman and Other Stories*. New York: Fawcett Crest, 1988.

Molina, Muñoz, Antonio. *Carlota Fainberg*. Madrid: Suma de Letras, 2002.

Mura-Brunel, Aline. "Le Temps des 'oeuvres migrantes.' Le Modèle et le genre, mémoire du littéraire." *Problématique des genres, problème du roman*. Ed. Jean Bessière and Gilles Philippe. Paris: Honoré Champion, 1999. 125–40.

Myers-Scotton, Carol. *Duelling Languages: Grammatical Structure in Codeswitching*. Oxford: Oxford UP, 1997.

Naipaul, V. S. *A House for Mr Biswas*. London: Russell, 1964.

Naoum, Jusuf. *Die Kaffeehausgeschichten des Abu al Abed*. München: dtv, 1993.

Nassehi, Armin. *Der soziologische Diskurs der Moderne*. Frankfurt: Suhrkamp, 2006.

Nassehi, Armin. *Geschlossenheit und Offenheit. Studien zur Theorie der modernen Gesellschaft*. Frankfurt: Suhrkamp, 2003.

Nell, Werner. *Reflexionen und Konstruktionen des Fremden in der europäischen Literatur. Literarische und sozialwissenschaftliche Studien zu einer interkulturellen Hermeneutik*. St. Augustin: Michael Itschert Gardez, 2001.

Nethersole, Reingard. "Globalismus und Postmoderne. Leslie Fiedler aus heutiger Sicht." *Räume der literarischen Postmoderne. Gender, Performativität, Globalisierung*. Ed. Paul Michael Lützeler. Tübingen: Stauffenburg, 2000. 49–70.

Nettleford, Rex. "Evolving Paradoxes of Caribbean Culture in the Nineties." *Anales del Caribe* 19–20 (1999–2000): 201–20.

Neumann-Braun, Klaus, and Birgit Richard, eds. *Coolhunters. Jugendkulturen zwischen Medien und Markt*. Frankfurt: Suhrkamp, 2005.

Nicklas, Pascal. "Komparatistik als Kulturwissenschaft?" *Komparatistik: Jahrbuch der Deutschen Gesellschaft für Allgemeine und Vergleichende Literaturwissenschaft* (2004–2005): 35–46.

Oliveira Marques, A. H. de. *Breve História de Portugal*. Lisboa: Presença, 1996.

Oliver, José F. A. *Auf-Bruch*. Berlin: Das Arabische Buch, 1997.

Oliver, José F. A. *Austernfischer marinero Vogelfrau*. Berlin: Das Arabische Buch, 1997.

Oliver, José F. A. *Duende. Meine Ballade in drei Versionen*. Gutach: Drey, 1997.

Oliver, José F. A. *Fernlautmetz: Gedichte*. Frankfurt: Suhrkamp, 2000.

Oliver, José F. A. *Gastling*. Berlin: Das Arabische Buch, 1993.

Oliver, José F. A. *HEIMATT und andere FOSSILE TRÄUME*. Berlin: Das Arabische Buch, 1993.

Oliver, José F. A. *Nachtrandspuren*. Frankfurt: Suhrkamp, 2002.

Oliver, José F. A. *Vater unser in Lima*. Tübingen: Heliopolis, 1991.

Oliver, José F. A. *Weil ich dieses Land liebe*. Berlin: Das Arabische Buch, 1991.

Ondaatje, Michael. *Anil's Ghost*. New York: Knopf, 2000.

Ondaatje, Michael. *The English Patient*. Toronto: McClelland & Stewart, 1992.

Ong, Aihwa. *Flexible Citizenship: The Cultural Logics of Transnationality*. Durham: Duke UP, 1999.

Orsini, Francesca. "India in the Mirror of World Fiction." *New Left Review* 13 (2002): 75–88.

Özakin, Aysel. *Die blaue Maske*. Frankfurt: Luchterhand, 1989.

Özdamar, Emine Sevgi. *The Bridge of the Golden Horn*. Trans. Martin Chalmers. London: Serpent's Tail, 2007.

Özdamar, Emine Sevgi. *Der Hof im Spiegel*. Köln: Kiepenheuer & Witsch, 2001.

Özdamar, Emine Sevgi. *Mutterzunge. Erzählungen*. Köln: Kiepenheuer & Witsch, 2002.

Özdamar, Emine Sevgi. *Seltsame Sterne starren zur Erde*. Köln: Kiepenheuer & Witsch, 2004.

Parkinson Zamora, Lois. "Comparative Literature in an Age of 'Globalization.'" *CLCWeb: Comparative Literature and Culture* 4.3 (2002): <http://docs.lib.purdue.edu/clcweb/vol4/iss3/1/>.

Pazarkaya, Yüksel. *Odyssee ohne Ankunft. Dresdner Chamisso-Poetikvorlesungen 2000*. Dresden: Thelem, 2004.

Peñalva Vélez, María Luisa. "La imagen del inmigrante. El 'otro' en el discurso de la prensa." *Migración y literatura en el mundo hispánico*. Ed. Irene Andres-Suárez. Madrid: Verbum, 2004. 131–53.

Pèrez-Torres, Rafael. *Movements in Chicano Poetry: Against Myths, Against Margins*. Cambridge: Cambridge UP, 1995. <http://dx.doi.org/10.1017/CBO9780511527166>.

Pinxten, Rik. "Comparative Cultural Studies and Cultural Anthropology." *Companion to Comparative Literature, World Literatures, and Comparative Cultural Studies*. Ed. Steven Tötösy de Zepetnek and Tutun Mukherjee. New Delhi: Cambridge UP India, 2013.

Pivato, Joseph, Steven Tötösy de Zepetnek, and Milan V. Dimić, eds. *Literatures of Lesser Diffusion / Les Littératures de moindre diffusion*. Edmonton: Research Institute for Comparative Literature, U of Alberta, 1990.

Pizer, John. *The Idea of World Literature: History and Pedagogical Practice*. Baton Rouge: Loisiana State UP, 2006.

Poblete, Juan, ed. "Los Latino Americanos en una perspectiva global-hemisférica." *Iberoamericana* 17 (2005): 1–200.

Portillo Trambley, Estela. *Trini*. Binghamton: Bilingual, 1986.

Pozuelo, Yvancos, José María, and María Aradra Sánchez Rosa. *Teoría del canon y literatura española*. Madrid: Cátedra, 2000.

Pratt, Mary Louise. *Imperial Eye: Travel Writing and Transculturation*. London: Routledge, 1994.

Prawer, S. S. *Karl Marx and World Literature. 1976*. London: Verso, 2011.

Prendergast, Christopher, ed. *Debating World Literature*. London: Verso, 2004.

Quayson, Ato, and David Theo Goldberg. "Scale and Sensibility." *Relocating Postcolonialism*. Ed. Ato Quayson and David Theo Goldberg. Oxford: Blackwell, 2002. xi–xxi.

Rakusa, Ilma. *Love after love*. Frankfurt: Suhrkamp, 2001.

Rankin, Walter. "Mapping the Other in Eliot and Özdamar." *Mapping the World, Culture, and Border-crossing*. Ed. Steven Tötösy de Zepetnek and I–Chun Wang. Kaohsiung: National Sun Yat-sen UP, 2011. 113–26.

Reichardt, Ulfried. *Globalisierung. Literaturen und Kulturen des Globalen*. Berlin: Akademie, 2010. <http://dx.doi.org/10.1524/9783050052878>.

Rickheit, Gert. "Wer ist bilingual?" *Sprache und Multikulturalität*. Ed. Eleni Butulussi, Evangelia Karagiannidou, and Katerina Zachu. Thessaloniki: University Studio, 2005. 323–32.

Riese, Utz. "Kulturelle Übersetzung und interamerikanische Kontaktzonen. An Beispielen aus der autobiographischen Literatur der Chicanos." *Heterotopien der Identität. Literatur in interamerikanischen Kontaktzonen*. Ed. Hermann Herlinghaus and Utz Riese. Heidelberg: C. Winter, 1999. 99–149.

Riese, Utz. "Zonen kultureller Übersetzung in Amerika. Emergenz / Emanzipation / Chicano-Literatur." *Kontaktzone Amerika. Literarische Verkehrsformen kultureller Übersetzung*. Ed. Utz Riese. Heidelberg: C. Winter, 2000. 233–83.

Robillard, Didier de, and Michel Beniamino, eds. *Le Français dans l'espace francophone*. Paris: Honoré Champion, 1993.

Rodríguez Richart, José. "Literatura española y emigración. Nuevas aportaciones a su estudio." *Migración y literatura en el mundo hispánico*. Ed. Irene Andres-Suárez. Madrid: Verbum, 2004. 45–68.

Rosendahl Thomsen, Mads. *Mapping World Literature: International Canonization and Transnational Literatures*. London: Continuum, 2008.

Ross, Kristin. "The World Literature and Cultural Studies Program." *Critical Inquiry* 19.4 (1993): 666–76. <http://dx.doi.org/10.1086/448692>.

Rothe, Arnold. *Der literarische Titel. Funktionen, Formen, Geschichte*. Frankfurt: Vittorio Klostermann, 1986.

Rüdiger, Horst. *'Literatur' und 'Weltliteratur' in der modernen Komparatistik."* *Weltliteratur und Volksliteratur*. Ed. Albert Schaefer. München: Beck, 1972. 36–54.

Rudin, Ernst. *Tender Accents of Sound: Spanish in the Chicano Novel in English*. Tempe: Bilingual, 1996.

Ruiz, Ana. "Literatur der spanischen Minderheit." *Interkulturelle Literatur in Deutschland. Ein Handbuch*. Ed. Carmine Chiellino. Stuttgart: Metzler, 2000. 84–95.

Ruiz, Ana. "Literatura intercultural frente a canon nacional en Alemania. Pautas para la resolución de un conflicto." *Revista de Filología Alemana* 11 (2003): 27–48.

Rushdie, Salman. *East, West*. Stuttgart: Reclam, 2002.

Rushdie, Salman. *Imaginary Homelands: Essays and Criticism*. London: Penguin, 1991.

Rushdie, Salman. *The Satanic Verses*. London: Vintage, 2006.

Rushdie, Salman. "Yorick." *East, West*. By Salman Rushdie. Stuttgart: Reclam, 2002. 67–95.

Sassen, Saskia. *Migranten, Siedler, Flüchtlinge. Von der Massenauswanderung zur Festung Europa*. Frankfurt: Fischer, 2000.

Saul, John Ralston. *The Collapse of Globalism and the Reinvention of the World*. London: Atlantic Books, 2005.

Saussy, Haun, ed. *Comparative Literature in an Age of Globalisation*. Baltimore: John Hopkins UP, 2006.

Schaefer, Albert, ed. *Weltliteratur und Volksliteratur*. München: Beck, 1972.

Schami, Rafik. *Die Sehnsucht der Schwalbe*. München: Carl Hanser, 2000.

Schami, Rafik. *Die Sehnsucht fährt schwarz. Geschichten aus der Fremde*. München: dtv, 1988.

Scherpe, Klaus R. "Grenzgänge zwischen den Disziplinen. Ethnographie und Literaturwissenschaft." *Atta Troll tanzt noch. Selbstbesichtigungen der literaturwissenschaftlichen Germanistik im 20. Jahrhundert.* Ed. Petra Boden and Holger Dainat. Berlin: Akademie, 1997. 297–315.

Schlieben-Lange, Brigitte. "Kulturkonflikte in Texten." *Zeitschrift für Literaturwissenschaft und Linguistik* 97 (1995): 1–21.

Schmeling, Manfred. "Ist Weltliteratur wünschenswert? Fortschritt und Stillstand im modernen Kulturbewußtsein." *Weltliteratur heute. Konzepte und Perspektiven.* Ed. Manfred Schmeling. Würzburg: Königshausen & Neumann, 1995. 153–78.

Schmeling, Manfred. "Interpretation und Kulturvergleich. Überlegungen zu einer komparatistischen Hermeneutik." *Interpretation 2000. Positionen und Kontroversen.* Ed. Henk De Berg and Matthias Prangel. Heidelberg: C. Winter, 1999. 201–14.

Schmeling, Manfred. "Literarischer Vergleich und interkulturelle Hermeneutik. Die literarischen Avantgarden als komparatistisches Forschungsparadigma." *Vergleichende Wissenschaften. Interdisziplinarität und Interkulturalität in den Komparatistiken.* Ed. Peter V. Zima. Tübingen: Gunter Narr, 2000. 187–200.

Schmeling, Manfred. "Multilingualität und Interkulturalität im Gegenwartsroman." *Literatur und Vielsprachigkeit.* Ed. Monika Schmitz-Emans. Heidelberg: Synchron, 2004. 221–36.

Schmeling, Manfred, ed. *Weltliteratur heute. Konzepte und Perspektiven.* Würzburg: Königshausen & Neumann, 1995.

Schmeling, Manfred, and Monika Schmitz-Emans, eds. *Multilinguale Literatur im 20. Jahrhundert.* Würzburg: Königshausen & Neumann, 2002.

Schmeling, Manfred, Monika Schmitz-Emans, and Kerst Walstra, eds. *Literatur im Zeitalter der Globalisierung.* Würzburg: Königshausen & Neumann, 2000.

Schmidt, Siegfried J. *Foundations for the Empirical Study of Literature: The Components of a Basic Theory.* Trans. Robert de Beaugrande. Hamburg: Buske, 1982.

Schmidt, Siegfried J. "Literary Studies from Hermeneutics to Media Culture Studies." *CLCWeb: Comparative Literature and Culture* 12.1 (2010): <http://docs.lib.purdue.edu/clcweb/vol12/iss1/1>.

Schmitt, Rüdiger. "Grußwort." *Weltliteratur heute. Konzepte und Perspektiven.* Ed. Manfred Schmeling. Würzburg: Königshausen & Neumann, 1995. 1–4.

Schmitz-Emans, Monika. *Die Sprache der modernen Dichtung.* München: Fink, 1997.

Schmitz-Emans, Monika. "Globalisierung im Spiegel literarischer Reaktionen und Prozesse." *Literatur im Zeitalter der Globalisierung.* Ed. Manfred Schmeling, Monika Schmitz-Emans, and Kerst Walstra. Würzburg: Königshausen & Neumann, 2000. 285–316.

Schmitz-Emans, Monika, ed. *Literatur und Vielsprachigkeit.* Heidelberg: Synchron, 2004.

Schönberger, Gerhard. *Mosambikanische Literatur portugiesischer Sprache. Entstehung und Probleme einer Nationalliteratur.* Frankfurt: Domus, 2002.

Schrimpf, Hans Joachim. *Goethes Begriff der Weltliteratur. Essay.* Stuttgart: Metzler, 1968.

Schroer, Markus. *Räume, Orte, Grenzen. Auf dem Weg zu einer Soziologie des Raumes.* Frankfurt: Suhrkamp, 2006.

Schulte, Bernd. *Die Dynamik des Interkulturellen in den postkolonialen Literaturen englischer Sprache.* Heidelberg: C. Winter, 1993.

Schüttpelz, Erhard. "Weltliteratur in der Perspektive einer Longue Durée I. Die fünf Zeitschichten der Globalisierung." *Wider den Kulturenzwang. Migration, Kulturalisierung und Weltliteratur.* Ed. Özkan Ezli, Dorothee Kimmich, and Annette Werberger. Bielfeld: transcript, 2009. 339–60.

Schwab, Gabriele. "Restriktion und Mobilität. Zur Dynamik des literarischen Kulturkontakts." *Interkulturalität. Zwischen Inszenierung und Archiv.* Ed. Stefan Rieger, Schamma Schahadat, and Manfred Weinberg. Tübingen: Narr, 1999. 47–64.

Schwarz, Henry, and Sangeeta Ray. *Blackwell Companion to Postcolonial Studies.* Oxford: Blackwell, 2000.

Seeba, Hinrich C. "Nationalliteratur. Zur Ästhetisierung der politischen Funktion von Geschichtsschreibung." *Deutsche Literatur in der Weltliteratur. Kulturnation statt politischer Nation?* Ed. Franz Norbert Mennemeier and Conrad Wiedemann. Tübingen: Niemeyer, 1986. 197–207.

Selvadurai, Shyam. *Cinnamon Gardens.* New York: Hyperion, 1999.

Senís Fernández, Juan. "Un hispanista español en Estados Unidos (adapción, contraste, teoría literaria, lenguaje y corrección política en Carlota Fainberg de Antonio Muñoz Molina." *Migración y literatura en el mundo hispánico.* Ed. Irene Andres-Suárez. Madrid: Verbum, 2004. 101–18.

Seyhan, Azade. *Writing Outside the Nation.* Princeton: Princeton UP, 2001.

Siebel, Walter, ed. *Die europäische Stadt.* Frankfurt: Suhrkamp, 2004.

Simonsen, Karen-Margarethe, and Jakob Stougaard-Nieslen, eds. *World Literature, World Culture. History, Theory, Analysis.* Aarhus: Aarhus UP, 2008.

Sloterdijk, Peter. *Im Weltinnenraum des Kapitals. Für eine philosophische Theorie der Globalisierung.* Frankfurt: Suhrkamp, 2005.

Şölçün, Sargut. "Literatur der türkischen Minderheit." *Interkulturelle Literatur in Deutschland. Ein Handbuch.* Ed. Carmine Chiellino. Stuttgart: Metzler, 2000. 135–52.

Soler-Espiauba, Dolores. "De los campos de Níjar a los invernaderos de El Ejido: Rastreo del fenómeno migratorio de los últimos cuarenta años en la narrativa española contemporánea." *Migración y literatura en el mundo hispánico.* Ed. Irene Andres-Suárez. Madrid: Verbum, 2004. 193–210.

Sollors, Werner. "Cooperation between English and Foreign Languages in the Area of Multilingual Literature." *PMLA: Publications of the Modern Language Association of America* 117.5 (2002): 1287–94. <http://dx.doi.org/10.1632/003081202X61205>.

Spitta, Silvia. *Between Two Waters: Narratives of Transculturation in Latin America.* Houston: Rice UP, 1995.

Steiner, George. *After Babel. Oxford.* Oxford: Oxford UP, 1998.

Steinmetz, Horst. "Globalisierung und Literatur(geschichte)." *Literatur im Zeitalter der Globalisierung.* Ed. Manfred Schmeling, Monika Schmitz-Emans, and Kerst Walstra. Würzburg: Königshausen & Neumann, 2000. 189–201.

Strich, Fritz. *Goethe und die Weltliteratur.* Bern: Francke, 1957.

Strutz, Johann. "Komparatistik als Theorie und Methodologie des Kulturvergleichs. Zur Interkulturalität im Alpen-Adria-Raum." *Vergleichende Wissenschaften.*

Interdisziplinarität und Interkulturalität in den Komparatistiken. Ed. Peter V. Zima. Tübingen: Gunter Narr, 2000. 201–21.

Strutz, Johann, and Peter V. Zima, eds. *Literarische Polyphonie. Übersetzung und Mehrsprachigkeit in der Literatur.* Tübingen: Narr, 1996.

Sturm-Trigonakis, Elke. *Barcelona in der Literatur (1944–1988). Eine Studie zum Stadtroman unter besonderer Berücksichtigung urbaner Räume.* Kassel: Reichenberger, 1994.

Sturm-Trigonakis, Elke. *Global playing in der Literatur. Ein Versuch über die Neue Weltliteratur.* Würzburg: Königshausen & Neumann, 2007.

Sturm-Trigonakis, Elke. "Großstädtische Identitäten im Kriminalroman. Barcelona bei Manuel Vázquez Montalbán und Athen bei Petros Markaris." *Identitat, literatura i llengua.* Ed. Pilar Arnau i Segarra. Montserrat: L'Abadia de Montserrat, 2006. 191–219.

Sturm-Trigonakis, Elke. "Pikareskes Arbeiten? Hari Kunzrus *Transmission* (2004) und Aravind Adigas *The White Tiger* (2008) als Narrative von globalisiertem 'In-decent work.'" *Omnia vincit labor? Narrative der Arbeit—Arbeitskulturen in medialer Reflexion.* Ed. Torsten Erdbrügger, Ilse Nagelschmidt, and Inga Probst. Berlin: Frank & Timme, 2013. 339-56.

Sturm-Trigonakis, Elke. "True Cosmopolitanism or Skilled Migration? Two Dimensions of Globalized Life in *Carlota Fainberg* (2001) by Antonio Muñoz Molina." *Comparatio* (2013): 197–210.

Szegedy-Maszák, Mihály. "Bilingualism und Literary Modernity." *Multilinguale Literatur im 20. Jahrhundert.* Ed. Manfred Schmeling and Monika Schmitz-Emans. Würzburg: Königshausen & Neumann, 2002. 97–104.

Tapscott, Don. *Grown Up Digital: How the Net Generation is Changing Your World.* New York: McGraw Hill, 2009.

Tawada, Yoko. *Das Bad.* Tübingen: Konkursbuchverlag, 1993.

Tawada, Yoko. *Überseezungen.* Tübingen: Konkursbuchverlag, 2002.

Tawada, Yoko. *Verwandlungen. Tübinger Poetik-Vorlesungen.* Tübingen: Konkursbuchverlag, 2001.

Tawada, Yoko. *Where Europe Begins.* Trans. Susan Bernofsky. New York: New Directions, 2002.

Tekinay, Alev. "In drei Sprachen leben." *Denn du tanzt auf einem Seil. Positionen deutschsprachiger MigrantInnenliteratur.* Ed. Sabine Fischer and Moray McGowan. Tübingen: Stauffenburg, 1997. 27–34.

Tétu, Michel. *La Francophonie. Histoire-problématique-perspectives.* Paris: Hachette, 1988.

Tharoor, Shashi. *Riot.* New York: Arcade, 2001.

Todorov, Tzvetan. *The Conquest of America: The Question of the Other.* 1982. Trans. Richard Howard. Norman: U of Oklahoma P, 1984.

Tomiche, Anne. "Comparative Literature in French." *Companion to Comparative Literature, World Literatures, and Comparative Cultural Studies.* Ed. Steven Tötösy de Zepetnek and Tutun Mukherjee. New Delhi: Cambridge UP India, 2013.

Toro, Fernando de. *New Intersections: Essays on Culture and Literature in the Post-Modern and Post-Colonial Condition.* Madrid: Iberoamericana, 2003.

Tötösy de Zepetnek, Steven. *Comparative Literature: Theory, Method, Application.* Amsterdam: Rodopi, 1998.

Tötösy de Zepetnek, Steven. "Early German-Canadian Ethnic Minority Writing." *Canadian Ethnic Studies / Études ethniques au Canada* 27.1 (1995): 99–122.

Tötösy de Zepetnek, Steven. "Interculturalism and Europe." *Pädaktuell.*" *Fachzeitschrift der Pädagogischen Akademie der Diözese Linz* 1 (2006): 4–6.

Tötösy de Zepetnek, Steven. "Literary Theory, Ethnic Minority Writing, and the Systemic Approach." *Ethnic Minority Writing and Literary Theory.* Ed. Joseph Pivato. Special Issue of *Canadian Ethnic Studies / Études ethniques au Canada* 28.3 (1996): 100–06.

Tötösy de Zepetnek, Steven. "Migration, Diaspora, and Ethnic Minority Writing." *Perspectives on Identity, Migration, and Displacement.* Ed. Steven Tötösy de Zepetnek, I–Chun Wang, and Hsiao-Yu Sun. Kaohsiung: National Sun Yat-sen UP, 2010. 86–97.

Tötösy de Zepetnek, Steven. "Multilingual Bibliography of Books in Comparative Literature, World Literature, and Comparative Cultural Studies." *Companion to Comparative Literature, World Literatures, and Comparative Cultural Studies.* Ed. Steven Tötösy de Zepetnek and Tutun Mukherjee. New Delhi: Cambridge UP India, 2013.

Tötösy de Zepetnek, Steven. "The New Humanities: The Intercultural, the Comparative, and the Interdisciplinary." *Global Society* 1.2 (2007): 45–68. <http://dx.doi.org/10.2979/GSO.2007.1.2.45>.

Tötösy de Zepetnek, Steven. "Post-Colonialities: The 'Other,' the System, and a Personal Perspective, or, This (Too) is Comparative Literature." *Postcolonial Literatures: Theory and Practice / Les Littératures post-coloniales. Théories et réalisations.* Ed. Steven Tötösy de Zepetnek and Sneja Gunew. Thematic Issue of *Canadian Review of Comparative Literature / Revue Canadienne de Littérature Comparée* 22.3–4 (1995): 399–407.

Tötösy de Zepetnek, Steven, ed. *Comparative Cultural Studies and Michael Ondaatje's Work.* West Lafayette: Purdue UP, 2005.

Tötösy de Zepetnek, Steven, ed. *Comparative Literature and Comparative Cultural Studies.* West Lafayette: Purdue UP, 2003.

Tötösy de Zepetnek, Steven, and Asunción López-Varela Azcárate. "Education, Interculturalism, and Mapping a New Europe." *Mapping the World, Culture, and Border-crossing.* Ed. Steven Tötösy de Zepetnek and I–Chun Wang. Kaohsiung: National Sun Yat-sen UP, 2011. 38–49.

Tötösy de Zepetnek, Steven and Louise O. Vasvári. "Comparative Literature, World Literature, and Comparative Cultural Studies." *Companion to Comparative Literature, World Literatures, and Comparative Cultural Studies.* Ed. Steven Tötösy de Zepetnek, and Tutun Mukherjee. New Delhi: Cambridge UP India, 2013.

Turk, Horst. "Kulturkonflikte im Spiegel der Literatur?" *Arcadia: Internationale Zeitschrift für Literaturwissenschaft / International Journal of Literary Studies* 31.1-2 (1996): 4–26. <http://dx.doi.org/10.1515/arca.1996.31.1-2.4>.

Turrini, Peter. *Ich liebe dieses Land. Stück und Materialien.* Frankfurt: Suhrkamp, 2001.

Uribe, Antonio. "Emigración y retorno en la narrativa de Donato Ndongo-Bidyogo y de Inongo-vi-Makomé." *Migración y literatura en el mundo hispánico*. Ed. Irene Andres-Suárez. Madrid:Verbum, 2004. 119–30.

Van Peer, Willie, Frank Hakemulder, and Sonia Zyngier. *Scientific Methods for the Humanities*. Amsterdam: John Benjamins, 2012.

Vergès, Françoise. "Post-Scriptum." *Relocating Postcolonialism*. Ed. Ato Quayson and David Theo Goldberg. Oxford: Blackwell, 2002. 349–58.

Vieira, Patrícia I., ed. *Politics and Identity in Lusophone Literature and Film*. Thematic Issue of *CLCWeb: Comparative Literature and Culture* 11.3 (2009): <http://docs.lib.purdue.edu/clcweb/vol11/iss3/>.

Vilariño, Picos, María Teresa, and Anxo Abuín González eds. *New Trends in Iberian Galician Comparative Literature*. Special Issue of *CLCWeb: Comparative Literature and Culture* 13.5 (2011): <http://docs.lib.purdue.edu/clcweb/vol13/iss5/>.

Villanueva, Darío. "Possibilities and Limits of Comparative Literature Today." *Companion to Comparative Literaure, World Literatures, and Comparative Cultural Studies*. Ed. Steven Tötösy de Zepetnek and Tutun Mukherjee. New Delhi: Cambridge UP India, 2013.

Virk, Tomo. "Comparative Literature versus Comparative Cultural Studies." *CLCWeb: Comparative Literature and Culture* 5.4 (2003): <http://docs.lib.purdue.edu/clcweb/vol5/iss4/6>.

Wägenbaur, Thomas. "Hybride Hybridität. Der Kulturkonflikt im Text der Kulturtheorie." *Arcadia: Internationale Zeitschrift für Literaturwissenschaft / International Journal of Literary Studies* 31.1-2 (1996): 27–38. <http://dx.doi.org/10.1515/arca.1996.31.1-2.27>.

Wägenbaur, Thomas. "Kulturelle Identität oder Hybridität? Aysel Özakins *Die blaue Maske* und das Projekt interkultureller Dynamik." *Zeitschrift für Literaturwissenschaft und Linguistik* 97 (1995): 22–47.

Walcott, Derek. *Mittsommer/Midsummer*. München: Carl Hanser, 2001.

Walcott, Derek. *Tiepolo's Hound*. London: Faber & Faber, 2000.

Waldenfels, Bernhard. *Grundmotive einer Phänomenologie des Fremden*. Frankfurt: Suhrkamp, 2006.

Wallerstein, Immanuel, ed. *The Modern World System in the "Longue Durée."* London: Paradigm, 2004.

Walser, Martin. *Der Augenblick der Liebe*. Reinbek bei Hamburg: Rowohlt, 2006.

Walstra, Kerst. "Eine Worthülse der Literaturdebatte? Kritische Anmerkungen zum Begriff Weltliteratur." *Weltliteratur heute. Konzepte und Perspektiven*. Ed. Manfred Schmeling. Würzburg: Königshausen & Neumann, 179–207.

Warning, Rainer, ed. *Rezeptionsästhetik. Theorie und Praxis*. München: Fink, 1994.

Weagel, Deborah. *Women and Contemporary World Literature: Power, Fragmentation, and Metaphor*. Bern: Peter Lang, 2009.

Weinreich, Uriel. *Languages in Contact: Problems and Findings*. The Hague: Mouton, 1974.

Weinrich, Harald. "Vorwort." *In zwei Sprachen leben. Berichte, Erzählungen, Gedichte von Ausländern*. Ed. Irmgard Ackermann. München: dtv, 1992. 9–11.

Welz, Gisela. "Die soziale Organisation kultureller Differenz. Zur Kritik des Ethnosbegriffes in der anglo-amerikanischen Kulturanthropolgie." *Studien zur Entwicklung des kollektiven Bewusstseins in der Neuzeit*. Ed. Helmut Berding. Frankfurt: Suhrkamp, 1996. 66–81.

Wertheimer, Jürgen. "Editorial." *Arcadia: Internationale Zeitschrift für Literaturwissenschaft / International Journal of Literary Studies* 31.1-2 (1996): iii–iv. <http://dx.doi.org/10.1515/arca.1996.31.1-2.III>.

Wertheimer, Jürgen. "Jürgen Wertheimer über Yoko Tawada." *Verwandlungen. Tübinger Poetik-Vorlesungen*. By Yoko Tawada. Tübingen: Konkursbuchverlag, 2001. 61–62.

Wierlacher, Alois. "Interkulturalität. Zur Konzeptualisierung eines Leitbegriffs interkultureller Literaturwissenschaft." *Interpretation 2000. Positionen und Kontroversen*. Ed. Henk De Berg and Matthias Prangel. Heidelberg: C. Winter, 1999. 155–82.

Willke, Helmut. *Atopia. Studien zur atopischen Gesellschaft*. Frankfurt: Suhrkamp, 2001.

Willke, Helmut. *Dystopia. Studien zur Krisis des Wissens in der modernen Gesellschaft*. Frankfurt: Suhrkamp, 2002.

Willke, Helmut. *Heterotopia. Studien zur Krisis der Ordnung moderner Gesellschaften*. Frankfurt: Suhrkamp, 2003.

Willke, Helmut. *Systemtheorie*. 3 vols. Stuttgart: Lucius & Lucius, 2001.

Yeşilada, Karin. "Die geschundene Suleika. Das Eigenbild der Türkin in der deutschsprachigen Literatur türkischer Autorinnen." *Interkulturelle Konfigurationen. Zur deutschsprachigen Erzählliteratur von Autoren nichtdeutscher Herkunft*. Ed. Mary Howard. München: iudicium, 1997. 95–114.

Yildiz, Yasemin. *Beyond the Mother Tongue: The Postmonolingual Condition*. New York: Fordham UP, 2011. <http://dx.doi.org/10.5422/fordham/9780823241309.001.0001>.

Zaimoglu, Feridun. *Abschaum. Die wahre Geschichte des Ertan Ongun*. Hamburg: Rotbuch, 2003.

Zaimoglu, Feridun. *Kanak Sprak. 24 Mißtöne vom Rande der Gesellschaft*. Hamburg: Rotbuch, 2004.

Zimmermann, Klaus, ed. *Lenguas criollas de base lexical española y portuguesa*. Frankfurt: Vervuert, 1999.

Zybok, Oliver. "Aussichtslose Unabhängigkeiten. Kein Ende des Jugendwahns!" *Coolhunters. Jugendkulturen zwischen Medien und Markt*. Ed. Klaus Neumann-Braun and Birgit Richard. Frankfurt: Suhrkamp, 2005. 207–21.

Index